Democracy, Ethnic Diversity, and Security in Post-Communist Europe

Democracy, Ethnic Diversity, and Security in Post-Communist Europe

Anita Inder Singh

PRAEGER

Westport, Connecticut
London

DEC 14 2002

Library of Congress Cataloging-in-Publication Data

Inder Singh, Anita.
　　Democracy, ethnic diversity, and security in post-communist Europe / Anita Inder Singh.
　　p. cm.
　　Includes bibliographical references (p.   ) and index.
　　ISBN 0–275–97258–5 (alk. paper)
　　1. Comparative government.   2. Ethnic relations—Political aspects.   3. Democratization.
　　4. Post-communism—Europe, Eastern.   5. Post-communism—Former Soviet republics.   I. Title.
　　JF51.I53   2001
　　320.54'0947—dc21　　　00–052426

British Library Cataloguing in Publication Data is available.

Copyright © 2001 by Anita Inder Singh

All rights reserved. No portion of this book may be
reproduced, by any process or technique, without
the express written consent of the publisher.

Library of Congress Catalog Card Number: 00–052426
ISBN: 0–275–97258–5

First published in 2001

Praeger Publishers, 88 Post Road West, Westport, CT 06881
An imprint of Greenwood Publishing Group, Inc.
www.praeger.com

Printed in the United States of America

The paper used in this book complies with the
Permanent Paper Standard issued by the National
Information Standards Organization (Z39.48–1984).

10 9 8 7 6 5 4 3 2 1

For Anders Åslund

It is always when the world is undergoing a metamorphosis, when certainties are collapsing, when the lines are becoming blurred, that there is greatest recourse to fundamental reference points. . . .

> Boutros Boutros-Ghali, former Secretary-General of the United Nations, to the World Conference on Human Rights, Vienna, 14 June 1993, cited in *The United Nations and Human Rights* (New York: United Nations, 1995), p. 442.

Contents

Acknowledgments   xi

Abbreviations   xiii

Introduction   xv

1   Democracy, Ethnic Diversity and Post–Cold War Security: The Practical and Conceptual Dilemmas   1

2   Managing Ethnic Diversity Through Political Structures and Ideologies: The Experiences of the Soviet Union, India, Spain and Sri Lanka   27

3   Self-Determination, Democracy, Minorities and Sovereignty: The Issues Raised by the Collapse of Yugoslavia and the USSR   51

4   Reconciling the International and Domestic Dimensions of Democracy   69

5   On the Absence of War in the Former Communist Bloc: Magyar and Russian Minorities in Countries Neighboring Hungary and Russia   97

Conclusions   131

Selected Bibliography 147

Index 175

Acknowledgments

First and foremost I wish to thank the Leverhulme Trust for awarding me, through Professor James Mayall, a grant to take up a Research Fellowship in the Department of International Relations at the London School of Economics and Political Science (LSE). At the LSE Gus Stewart and his colleagues in the Research and Contracts Office helped on more than one occasion; Christopher Coker offered moral support.

Włodimierz Brus encouraged the book before it was even an idea and urged me to embark on an intellectual adventure. Dietrich Rueschmeyer invited me to present my first thoughts on the subject at a seminar hosted jointly by the Center for the study of Comparative Development and the Center for Foreign Relations at Brown University. I am grateful to Dominic Lieven for giving me the opportunity to try out an early version of chapter 5 at the seminar on post-communist politics at the European Institute at the LSE. Marc Plattner offered me a most hospitable environment as Visiting Fellow at the International Forum for Democratic Studies, National Endowment for Democracy, in Washington, D.C. Always patient and prompt, Art Kaufman answered endless queries by e-mail. Charles King, Elizabeth Chesman, George Schöpflin and Vanita Singh Mukerji read and commented on parts of the manuscript. Helpful information was provided by Dace Treija of the Embassy of Latvia and Tamás Magda of the Embassy of Hungary in London. Björn Lyrvall was generous with good advice and spicy lunches. Good librarians are indispensable: I particularly wish to thank Nerys Webster and Ken Gibbons at the LSE and Susan Franks at the Royal Institute of International Affairs in London. Patricia Mowbray brought good style and good art into my life. Last but not least, it has always been fun to discuss the world with Janine Finck.

Abbreviations

ASSR	Autonomous Soviet Socialist Republic
BBC/*SWB*	British Broadcasting Corporation/*Selected World Broadcasts*
BJP	Bharatiya Janata Party
CE	Council of Europe
CIS	Commonwealth of Independent States
CPSU	Communist Party of the Soviet Union
CSCE	Conference on Security and Cooperation in Europe
Doc/doc.	document
EC	European Community
EU	European Union
FBIS	Foreign Broadcasting Information Service
FLN	*Front Libération National*
HCNM	OSCE High Commissioner on National Minorities
IFOR	Implementation Force, Bosnia
ILM	International Legal Materials
KLA	Kosovo Liberation Army
NATO	North Atlantic Treaty Organisation
ODIHR	Office for Democratic Institutions and Human Rights
OSCE	Organization for Security and Cooperation in Europe
PACE	Parliamentary Assembly of the Council of Europe
RFE/RL	Radio Free Europe/Radio Liberty

RSFSR	Russian Soviet Federative Socialist Republic
UN	United Nations
UNESCO	United Nations Educational, Scientific and Cultural Organization
UNGA	United Nations General Assembly
UNHR	*The United Nations and Human Rights* (New York 1995).
UNPROFOR	United Nations Protection Force
UNSC	United Nations Security Council

Introduction

DEMOCRACY AND ETHNIC DIVERSITY:
A POST–COLD WAR INTERNATIONAL PRIORITY

In the early nineties international organizations including the United Nations (UN), the Organization for Security and Cooperation in Europe (OSCE) and the Council of Europe (CE) broke new ground by suggesting that states should accommodate their ethnically mixed populations through democratic rule. This advice, implicit in international instruments since 1990, questions some conventional thinking. The recommendation that ethnic diversity should be managed through democratic political structures does not assume that ethnic conflict is caused by ancient hatreds or that nationalism inevitably leads to war and disorder. At the same time it does not rule out the possibility that ethnic division can lead to conflict, but raises the hope that conflict can be prevented. These are just two of the reasons why the international community has suggested that democratic governance, based on the rule of law and respect for human and minority rights, will alleviate ethnic tensions and promote domestic and international security.

Since 1990 the international advocacy of democracy has been inspired by events in the former Communist bloc, notably the fall of the Berlin Wall in 1989 and the collapse of Yugoslavia and the USSR in 1991. In part, the underlining of democracy was a reaction against authoritarianism[1] and, in the *Charter of Paris for a New Europe* (1990), member-states of the Conference on Security and Cooperation in Europe (CSCE) undertook to "build, consolidate and strengthen democracy as the only system of government of our nations."[2]

But any optimism about the triumph of democracy was tempered by concern over the outbreak of the wars that attended the crumbling of the former Yugoslavia and fears that much of Eastern Europe and the former Soviet Union was an ethnic tinderbox.

The view that democracy within states offers the best prospect for handling ethnic variety and creating a stable international order has been inspired to some extent by the realization that most international conflicts have domestic roots. Internal solutions are most likely to keep regional and international strife at bay. Authoritarian states such as the former Yugoslavia and Soviet Union signally had failed to do so: in fact their policies had fomented ethnic conflict. Could democracies succeed in containing or preventing ethnic wars where authoritarian states had failed? Also, in a world in which there is only one superpower, international policy-makers probably deduced that it would be easier to prevent conflicts than to find cures for them. At one level, then, the debate is essentially about the means by which stability can best be preserved within countries. The hope is that democracy and respect by governments for minority rights will maintain domestic peace, preserve the territorial integrity of states and enhance international security.

NATIONALISM IS NOT THE ONLY CAUSE OF WAR

The suggestion that the practice of democracy can forge ethnic harmony questions the perception of nationalism as a cause of war and disorder. Among the most eloquent proponents of this idea was Elie Kedourie. There were two strands in his argument. Kedourie argued that imperial withdrawal from the Middle East and Africa had caused conflict and disorder and that the culture of countries in these regions would more or less rule out their becoming democracies.[3] Do the views of the pessimists have universal validity? The disintegration of the former Yugoslavia and the Soviet Union raised analogous fears of ethnic turbulence in the former communist bloc, and almost a decade later it can well be asked whether these fears have proved to be justified.

Nationalism inspired the demand for independence and undoubtedly caused many wars in Asia, Africa and Europe. Most European states in the nineteenth century were forged by war. War was also the midwife of many newborn states in the twentieth century, including Ireland, India, Pakistan, Bangladesh, Algeria, Angola, Georgia, Croatia and Bosnia. But frequently new states were carved out by great powers. The borders of many of the new states that emerged from the detritus of empires in 1918 were drawn not by nationalists but by the victorious Allies.[4] They acted in the name of self-determination, but many of the boundaries etched by them contained large segments of minorities whose wishes were not ascertained.

Yet this is not the whole story. War is older than nationalism; indeed war is as old as history. Some regard war as the normal state of relations between men, as an inevitable feature of human existence. According to an estimate made in

Introduction   xvii

1986, in more than 3,400 years of recorded history there had been only 250 years of peace.[5] War is the principal means by which the balance of advantage among states has been adjusted from time to time. War has also been fought in the name of religion or ideology: for Marxist-Leninists war is a necessary, even legitimate means to spread the revolution of the proletariat throughout the world.[6]

NATIONALISM, WAR, SOVEREIGNTY AND INTERNATIONAL SECURITY

Moreover, the idea that the international order upheld by the great powers after 1945 was desirable because it kept peace in Europe for over half a century was not shared by the nationalists who wanted and attained independent states.[7] And while protagonists of the Yalta accord might say that it kept the peace for well-nigh fifty years, many East Europeans would question the justice of the "order" imposed by Yalta, for it meant their subjugation to the Soviet Union.

International society has never renounced the use of war. War has been its instrument along with diplomacy. But war is intended to achieve limited political ends, not to destroy states. This is why secessionist nationalisms, which can dismember states, are viewed by their critics as being subversive of the international order that is premised on the principle of the sovereignty of states. The principle of sovereignty means that international order is "based on property." Hence the significance of the principle of the territorial integrity of states, which cannot easily be surrendered. The use of force by nationalists to change international boundaries challenges the idea that states alone have a monopoly of force on their territory. International society has, in fact, no concept of armed struggle within states, except to overthrow colonial rule, and no criteria by which to judge the legitimacy of a national movement.[8]

NATIONALISM CAN HELP TO FORGE DEMOCRATIC CONSENSUS

War was considered an acceptable way of building states at least until 1945. Most European states were carved out though war; many went on to become democracies. After 1945 *democracy* was the *leitmotif* of the political leadership in countries as varied as India and (after 1978) Spain. It was the idea around which the *nation* was constructed.

In post–cold war Eastern Europe nationalism has worked in two ways. First, many East European countries have linked nationalism with democracy to distance themselves from their Communist past. Communist internationalism and foreign domination have been "the other" against which most East Europeans have sought to forge an identity. Second, nationalism has helped the leadership of many East European countries to mobilize their peoples in favor of democracy, an idea around which consensus is being crafted. Nationalism, in this way, has contributed to the cohesion of societies.[9] But where minorities are uncertain about their future or where states or political parties have indulged in or advocated exclusivist or assimilationist policies, nationalism has contributed to ethnic tension. In contrast to Britain or France, where the state was consolidated through war and conquest centuries before the process of nation-building began, democracy is the method—or is expected to be the method—by which state-nations will be consolidated in the past–cold war era. Is this expectation realistic? Or is it a case of the wish giving birth to the thought? To what extent can the international community influence states to resolve differences between ethnic groups through democratic norms with a view to preserving existing international borders? Are democracy and the principle of sovereignty set on a collision course? These are among the questions to be discussed in this book.

DEFINITIONS

Any attempt to study democracy and ethnic diversity in post-communist Europe comes head on against several contested and ambiguous concepts for which there are no universally agreed definitions, so it is necessary to explain how terms like "democracy," "ethnic diversity," "minorities," "nationalism" and "self-determination" will be used in this book. *Democracy* has not been defined in international law,[10] and I have used the terms "democratization" and "democracy" as defined by policy-makers in the United Nations, OSCE and the Council of Europe since 1990. From this we can assess the extent to which these organizations have been able to carry out their policies and to achieve their aims.

The concept of democracy was first placed on the formal agenda of the UN after the end of the cold war. The two main documents focusing on concepts of democracy and democratization are the *Vienna Declaration and Programme of Action* (1993) and the UN Secretary-General's report on the efforts made by the UN to promote and consolidate new or restored democracies (1995).[11] International policy-makers see democracy as a universal right,[12] but they are realistic about the chances of its being made strong and secure in countries which have long been under authoritarian rule and have fragile democratic traditions. In his report to the UN General Assembly in 1995, the former UN Secretary-General, Boutros Boutros-Ghali, explained that by democratization he meant

a process by which an authoritarian society becomes increasingly participatory through such mechanisms as periodic elections to representative bodies, the accountability of public officials, a transparent public administration, an independent judiciary and a free press. It is inherent in this concept that democratization does not necessarily lead immediately to a fully democratic society.... The pace at which democratization can proceed is inevitably dependent on a variety of political, economic, social and cultural factors some of which, in a given society, may not be susceptible to rapid change.[13]

Boutros-Ghali was not altogether sanguine about the likelihood of its success. Democratization would take root in a society "only if a number of conditions are met." These included the political will, both at the government level and in the community of citizens, to move toward a more democratic approach to government. Citizens must also be provided with the opportunity to participate in free and fair elections and to form political associations. Democracy, he believed, cannot be based on political structures alone, but requires a developed and articulate civil society as well as a political culture of participation and consultation.[14]

There is consensus among international officials in the UN, Council of Europe, OSCE and the European Union (EU) about what they mean by democracy, and international instruments after 1990 have stressed certain general principles of democracy. For instance, the CSCE *Charter of Paris* describes democratic government as being based on the will of the people, expressed regularly through free and fair elections. Democracy has as its foundation respect for human beings and the rule of law. Democracy is the best safeguard of freedom of expression, tolerance of all groups of society and equal opportunity for each person. It entails accountability to the electorate, the obligation of public authorities to comply with the law and the impartial administration of justice. No one is above the law, and minorities have the right freely to express, preserve and develop their identities without any discrimination and in full equality before the law. This understanding of democracy has inspired all post–cold war international instruments on minorities issues, including the UN *Declaration on the Rights of Persons Belonging to National or Ethnic, Religious and Linguistic Minorities* (1992)[15] and the Council of Europe *Framework Convention for the Protection of National Minorities* (1995)[16] Advice by international organizations including the UN, CE, and OSCE to governments on minorities problems is also based on these definitions.

The term "ethnic" is used in this book as a convenient shorthand for "national," "ethnic," "religious," "linguistic" and "cultural." The term "national diversity" would provoke endless argument about whether a group was a nation or a minority: it would also open the Pandora's box inherent in the old Soviet term "nationalities problem" and the former Yugoslav distinction between "nation" and "nationality." For instance, the Yugoslav constitution of 1974 gave the theoretical right of secession to "nations" like the Croats and Slovenes but not to "nationalities" like the Kosovar Albanians.

Ethnic diversity[17] refers to the fact that most states are multinational states, not *nation-states*, in the sense that ethnicity and territory are aligned. Communities are interspersed in such a way that no area could secede on the grounds that it is a nation-state without causing regional instability. The wars in Bosnia,

Croatia, Abkhazia and Nagorno-Karabakh illustrated this. It is precisely to prevent strife in multiethnic countries that the question whether democracies can manage ethnic variety has assumed significance in post–communist Europe and will remain a high priority for international statesmen well into the twenty-first century.

The term "minority," like democracy, has yet to be defined in international law. The OSCE High Commissioner on National Minorities (HCNM), Max van der Stoel,[18] summed up the difficulty of agreeing on what constitutes a minority when he said that "the existence of a minority is a question of fact not of definition."[19] International instruments including the *Copenhagen Document* (1990), the UN *Declaration of Minorities*, and the CE *Framework Convention for National Minorities* may have compounded the problem by suggesting that it is for individuals to decide whether they belong to a minority. In this book a minority is defined as an ethnic, religious, linguistic or national group which constitutes a numerical minority and has a nondominant position in a state. This definition does not cover refugees, gypsies, indigenous peoples, aliens and migrant workers. The UN *Declaration on Minorities* refers to national, ethnic and religious "minorities"; the CE *Framework Convention for National Minorities* and OSCE documents refer to "national minorities" rather than to multinational states or ethnically heterogeneous societies; all international instruments implicitly acknowledge the existence of multiethnic countries.[20]

What definition can convey adequately the meaning of terms like "nationalism" and "self-determination,"[21] which have been developed through the aspirations of intellectuals, political leaders and peoples over two centuries and have reflected men's basest motives and inspired their noblest acts? Every demand for a "nation" or "self-determination" has added to the plethora of meanings or interpretations of those terms.[22] In the spring of 1999, NATO's justification of its intervention in Kosovo on the grounds that it was upholding the values of democracy against those of the nation-state only compounded the related conceptual and practical problems arising from these concepts. It is easy to see why.

Nationalism[23] is usually, but not always, a demand for a sovereign state. The national idea holds that the world is divided into nations and that the nation is the proper basis for a sovereign state and the fount of sovereign authority. But not all nationalisms are secessionist. Some of the nationalisms discussed in this book—like those in Croatia, Slovenia, Estonia and Latvia—were secessionist.[24] Others—like those of Uzbeks and Kazakhs in the former Soviet Union or of Magyar minorities in Slovakia and Romania—sought accommodation within existing state frameworks.[25]

The nation-state[26] implies the congruence of territory and ethnicity. By assuming that ethnic communities are monolithic wholes and that intellectual and political differences within ethnic groups are inconsequential—or even that they cannot or should not exist—the idea of the nation-state goes against the grain of democracy. For democracy is premised first and foremost on the existence of intellectual and political choice within and between communities. Free and

Introduction

fair elections give all communities the opportunity to choose their rulers. Can these ideals be achieved? Already, in the summer of 1999, there was news of an exodus of Serbs—a minority in Kosovo—as Albanian refugees returned to their homes and extracted revenge for their sufferings at the hands of the Serbian army. Serbs in Kosovo could have little faith in NATO assurances of protection while their homes were destroyed by Albanians. Could the reversal of ethnic cleansing promised by NATO ultimately come to mean that the flight of Serbs would result in the establishment of an Albanian nation-state established under NATO auspices in Kosovo?[27]

Self-determination, based on the idea of popular sovereignty, is another contested and ambiguous term.[28] In the sense of being an expression of the will of the people, it appears synonymous with democracy, and that is how it often has been interpreted by the international community since the end of the First World War. It has variously referred to the right of people to choose their own government, the right of ethnic groups to call for changes in their country's borders in order to achieve sovereign states, a demand for autonomy without a call for secession and a call for union with other countries. "Self-determination" has been put to a variety of uses. It was employed first in the international context by Lenin in 1915–16 to imply freedom from imperial rule, but it was never intended to apply to the national groups of the former USSR or to suggest a democratic style of governance. In 1938 Hitler justified the annexation of the Sudetenland in the name of self-determination. For much of the twentieth century, self-determination was used with reference to peoples subjected to imperial rule in Europe, Asia and Africa, but it did not apply to resistance against foreign aggression such as the Soviet invasions of Czechoslovakia in 1968 and Afghanistan in 1979. Moreover, the international community did not intend that "self-determination" should be used to break up sovereign states and only recognized reluctantly breakaway states like Bangladesh in 1971. In 1989 self-determination implied for Germans the reunification of East and West Germany. Many in the West interpreted self-determination as the right of East European countries to escape Soviet domination but not the right of Soviet republics to leave the union.[29] In post–cold war Europe the recurrent problem in both the former Yugoslavia and Soviet Union has been to reconcile self-determination as a reflection of the will of the people with self-determination as a demand for secession which can undermine the sovereignty and territorial integrity of states. Self-determination remains a contested concept: this is probably a major reason why the international community cannot apply it with any consistency.

DEMOCRACY, ETHNIC DIVERSITY AND SECURITY IN POST-COMMUNIST EUROPE: THE QUESTIONS RAISED IN THIS BOOK

For purposes of publishing deadlines, note that all facts have been updated through December 2000. Also, to avoid confusion: "Yugoslavia" refers to the

Socialist Federal Republic of Yugoslavia until its breakup in 1991; "Serbia" refers to the post–1991 Federal Republic of Yugoslavia; and in chapter 5 I have used the terms "Magyars" or "Magyar minorities" and "Hungary" for the state of Hungary.

Chapter 1 asks why, after the end of the cold war, the international community advocated democracy as the best way to manage ethnic diversity. Events in Eastern Europe and the Commonwealth of Independent States (CIS) since 1989 have served as the immediate context for post–cold war international instruments on minorities issues, but there is also a wider significance. Chapter 1 analyzes the international community's recommendations for handling ethnically diverse populations through democracy. The OSCE High Commissioner on National Minorities, Max van der Stoel, has observed rightly that the grievances of minorities can, if left unaddressed or handled in the wrong way, "strike at the very heart of the existence of States."[30] Minorities have long been an issue in relations between states, but international attempts to solve minorities issues have frequently ended in failure. Post–cold war international recommendations have taken into account the reasons for the failure of the League of Nations to enforce the Minorities Treaties and the consequences of this failure on European security between the two world wars. Now, from a contemporary perspective, the international proposals reflect the hope that a post–cold war international order based on democratic norms can be built.

Chapter 2 assesses the extent to which ethnic diversity can be accommodated through political structures and ideologies—in particular through democracy. It compares the experiences of authoritarian states like the former Soviet Union with those of democracies like India, Sri Lanka and Spain. All became democracies after 1945; none had strong democratic traditions. A study of their mixed experiences may throw light on possible grounds for optimism about the chances of ethnic variety being reconciled through democratic institutions in East European countries which also have weak democratic traditions.

Chapter 3 discusses the implications of "self-determination," "democracy" and the tension between the bedrock principle of the sovereignty of states and their international obligations, with particular reference to the recognition of new states in Eastern Europe and the CIS between 1991 and 1992. In recognizing the successor states to the former Yugoslavia and USSR, was the international community guided by concern for building democracy?

Chapter 4 asks whether the international and domestic dimensions of democratization can be reconciled with reference to the mechanisms created by the OSCE and Council of Europe to promote the implementation of minority rights through democratic principles in post-communist countries. Elections are a necessary prerequisite for democracy: to what extent do elections augur the forging of ethnic harmony in the former Yugoslavia and USSR? And to what extent can the international community promote democracy, safeguard minority rights and reconcile the competing claims of self-determination, democracy, sovereignty and the territorial unity of states? With reference to the wars in Chechnya and Kosovo, chapter 4 will show why Chechen separatists failed to win international support for their secessionist claims despite massive human rights abuses by the Russian army in 1994–95 and 1999, why the demand of Kosovar Albanians for sovereign statehood were ignored by international officials in 1991 and 1995, and how and why in 1999 the international community hoped that democratic political arrangements in Kosovo would reconcile the Albanian call for self-determination with the territorial integrity of Serbia.

The wars that attended the breakup of the former Yugoslavia and Soviet Union raised fears that nationalism would lead to a complete breakdown of the international system. Even as international officials asserted that democracy within states could be the basis of a new world order, there were warnings that the culture of former communist bloc countries, their weak liberal traditions and the existence of ethnic divisions in many of them would render democracy a nonstarter. Has nationalism inevitably provoked war and overturned democracy in post-communist countries?

Chapter 5 will discuss whether the absence of war between Hungary, Russia and their neighbors can be explained by the domestic policies of governments toward their Magyar or Russian minorities or by their international relations. And to what extent does democratization account for the absence of war?

NOTES

1. In his address to the World Conference on Human Rights at Vienna in June 1993, Boutros Boutros-Ghali, then Secretary-General of the UN said, "the Berlin Wall had fallen, carrying away with it a certain vision of the world, and thereby opening up new perspectives. It was in the name of freedom, democracy and human rights that entire peoples were speaking out." *The United Nations and Human Rights* (New York: United Nations, 1995), referred to hereafter as *UNHR*, pp. 441–42.

2. *Charter of Paris for a New Europe*, November 1990. In 1973 the series of conferences that came to be known as the Conference on Security and Cooperation in Europe (CSCE) opened. Following the end of the cold war the increased activities of the CSCE underlined the need to institutionalize it and establish a permanent administrative structure, and in January 1995 the CSCE was renamed the Organization for Security and Cooperation in Europe (OSCE).

3. Elie Kedourie, "A New International Disorder," in Hedley Bull and Adam Watson, eds., *The Expansion of International Society* (Oxford: Clarendon Press, 1984), pp. 347–55 and Elie Kedourie, *Nationalism*, 3rd ed. (London: Hutchinson, 1960). See also the issue of the *New Statesman and Society*, 19 June 1992, which was headlined, "Eurogeddon? The Coming Conflagration in East-Central Europe."

4. For a recent account of the involvement of the great powers in the Balkans see Misha Glenny, *The Balkans 1804–1999: Nationalism, War and the Great Powers* (London: Granta Books, 1999).

5. Independent Commission on International Humanitarian Issues, *Modern Wars: The Humanitarian Challenge: A Report for the Independent Commission on International Humanitarian Issues* (London: Zed, 1986), p. 24.

6. V. I. Lenin, *Collected Works*, vol. 21, cited in Bernard Semmel, *Marxism and the Science of War* (Oxford: Oxford University Press, 1981), pp. 164–67.

7. The laws of war were framed by great powers and applied to wars between themselves. They did not apply to wars of colonization, which were regarded by great powers as "civilizing wars." Also in international law, conquest of territory at a time when the use of force to acquire territory was not illegal conferred good title on the territory. But in 1954 the *Front Libération National* (FLN) claimed that it belatedly was repelling the French invasion of Algeria in 1830. In 1961 India justified its liberation of Goa from Portugal on the grounds that Portugal had committed aggression in 1510. Heather Wilson, *International Law and the Use of Force by National Liberation Movements* (Oxford: Clarendon Press, 1988). See also Sharon Korman, *The Right of Conquest: The Forcible Annexation of Territory in International Law and Practice* (Oxford: Clarendon Press, 1996).

8. James Mayall, *Nationalism and International Society* (Cambridge: Cambridge University Press, 1990), pp. 23, 28–32, and Hedley Bull, *The Anarchical Society: A Study of Order in World Politics*, 2nd ed. (Basingstoke: Macmillan, 1995), pp. 178–93.

9. Pál Dunay, "Nationalism and Ethnic Conflicts in Eastern Europe: Imposed, Induced or (Simply) Reemerged?" in István Pogany, ed., *Human Rights in Eastern Europe* (Aldershot: Edward Elgar, 1995), p. 44. In the case of the former Soviet Union, Roman Szporluk observes that "the remarkably peaceful—by contemporary world standards—transition from the Soviet Union to the independent states of Russia, Ukraine, Belarus . . . was carried out in the name of nationalism. Nationalism represents an element of continuity." See Roman Szporluk, "Nationalism after Communism," *Nations and Nationalism*, vol. 4, part 3 (July 1998), p. 318.

10. James Crawford, *Democracy in International Law* (Cambridge: Cambridge University Press, 1993).

11. *UNHR*, especially p. 450. See also United Nations General Assembly, 50th session, *Support by the United Nations System of the Efforts of Governments to Promote and Consolidate New or Restored Democracies. Report of the Secretary-General*, referred to hereafter as UNGA doc. A/50/332, 7 August 1995.

12. Boutros-Ghali's address to the Vienna Conference on Human Rights, *UNHR*, p. 442, and United Nations Commission on Human Rights, resolution on the Promotion of Democracy, E/CN.4/RES/1999/57, 27 April 1999.

13. UNGA doc. A/50/332, 7 August 1995.

14. Ibid.

15. Referred to hereafter as UN *Declaration on Minorities*.

16. Referred to hereafter as the CE *Framework Convention for National Minorities*. 34.I.L.M.351 (1995+).

17. Walker Connor used this term in "Nation-Building or Nation-Destroying?" in his *Ethno-Nationalism: The Quest for Understanding* (Princeton: Princeton University Press, 1994), p. 30. I have used this term in my "Democracy and Ethnic Diversity: A New International Priority?" *The World Today*, vol. 52, no. 1 (January 1996): 20–22.

18. Since January 1993 the first OSCE High Commissioner on National Minorities, referred to hereafter as HCNM.

19. HCNM's address to CSCE Human Dimension Seminar, "Case Studies on National Minority Issues: Positive Results," Warsaw, 23 May 1993, referred to hereafter as HCNM, Warsaw address, 23 May 1993.

20. Some of the works on minorities that I have found useful include Inis Claude,

National Minorities: An International Problem (Cambridge, Mass.: Harvard University Press, 1953); J. La Ponce, *The Protection of Minorities* (Berkeley and Los Angeles: University of California Press, 1960); Francesco Capotorti, *Study of the Rights of Persons Belonging to Ethnic, Religious and Linguistic Minorities* (New York: United Nations, 1991). Jennifer Jackson Preece uses the term "national minority" to highlight the connection between minorities and the concepts of nation and nationalism. A minority, like a nation, may have a culture, a system of ideas and values. Minorities are "ethnonations who have failed to secure sovereign states. They exist within the boundaries of another nation's state." *National Minorities and the European Nation-States System* (Oxford: Clarendon Press, 1999), pp. 28–29.

21. For a recent discussion see James Mayall, "Sovereignty, Nationalism and Self-Determination," *Political Studies*, vol. 47, no. 3 (September 1999): especially pp. 476–84.

22. Connor, "A Nation Is a Nation, Is a State, Is an Ethnic Group, Is a . . . ," pp. 89–117.

23. On a subject on which the reading list seemingly is endless see Ernest Gellner, *Nations and Nationalism* (Oxford: Blackwell, 1983); Eric Hobsbawm, *Nations and Nationalism since 1780: Programme, Myth, Reality* (Cambridge: Cambridge University Press, 1990); and Anthony D. Smith *National Identity* (London: Penguin Books, 1991). James G. Kellas, *The Politics of Nationalism and Ethnicity* (Basingstoke: Macmillan, 1991), has a useful bibliography.

24. See chapter 3.

25. See chapters 4 and 5.

26. On the concept of the nation-state see, among others, Alfred Cobban, *The Nation-State and National Self-Determination* (London: Collins, 1944); F. H. Hinsley, *Nationalism and the International System* (London: Hodder and Stoughton, 1973); Smith, *National Identity*.

27. A fear expressed by Emma Bonino, EU Commissioner for Humanitarian Affairs, "EU official urges action to prevent a total Serb exodus from Kosovo," *International Herald Tribune*, 25 June 1999.

28. Among the works on self-determination that I have found most stimulating are Dov Ronen, *The Quest for Self-Determination* (New Haven: Yale University Press, 1979); Morton H. Halperin and David Scheffer with Patricia Small, *Self-Determination in the New World Order* (Washington, D.C.: Carnegie Endowment for International Peace, 1992); James Mayall, "Sovereignty and Self-Determination in the New Europe," in Hugh Miall, ed., *Minority Rights in Europe: Prospects for a Transnational Regime* (London: Royal Institute of International Affairs, 1994), pp. 7–13; Antonio Cassese, *Self-Determination of Peoples: A Legal Appraisal* (Cambridge: Cambridge University Press, 1995); Thomas Musgrave, *Self-Determination and National Minorities* (Oxford: Oxford University Press, 1997); and Benyamin Neuberger, "National Self-Determination: Dilemmas of a Concept," *Nations and Nationalism*, vol. 1, part 3 (November 1995): 297–325.

29. Misha Glenny, *The Fall of Yugoslavia: The Third Balkan War* (London: Penguin Books, 1992).

30. *Report of Mr Max van der Stoel, OSCE High Commissioner on National Minorities, 12 November 1997*, to the OSCE Implementation Meeting on Human Dimension Issues, Warsaw, 12–28 November 1997.

Chapter 1
Democracy, Ethnic Diversity and Post–Cold War Security: The Practical and Conceptual Dilemmas

> ... [N]ational minorities form an integral part of the society of the States in which they live and ... are a factor of enrichment of each respective State and society ... [Q]uestions relating to national minorities can only be satisfactorily resolved in a democratic political framework ...
> CSCE *Geneva Report*, 1991[1]

> ... [T]he notion that the state can only serve the interests of one ethnic or cultural group is antiquated.[2]
> Max van der Stoel, 23 May 1993

THE REALITY OF THE MULTIETHNIC STATE

Democracy and Ethnic Diversity: The Hopes of the International Community

The idea that political structures can accommodate ethnic variety is not new.[3] Many a ruler—authoritarian or democratic—has fashioned political arrangements to take the sting out of nationalisms. For example, the political structures of the Soviet Union and India were explicitly intended to manage their ethnic diversity—one through the dictatorship of the proletariat, the other through parliamentary democracy.[4] But it is in the last decade of the twentieth century that international and regional European organizations—especially the UN, the OSCE and the Council of Europe—gave priority to the forging of stability through democracy in ethnically mixed countries. Their recommendations were inspired by a coincidence of unprecedented events since the mid-1980s in Eastern Europe and the former Soviet Union. The collapse of the Soviet Union did away with any idea that it had made good its claim to have "solved" its "nationalities problems" or that communism could compete successfully with democracy in conferring legitimacy on rulers.[5] And the end of the cold war swept away the certainties that had made up the weft and warp of the cold war *mentalité*. There were no new real or imagined truths that could easily replace them. Boutros Boutros-Ghali, the former UN Secretary-General, saw the world entering a new period in history and searching for a new identity.[6] For him and other policy-makers in the West, Eastern Europe and the CIS,[7] freedom, democracy and human rights were the fundamental reference points that would form the basis of a new international order.

Moreover, the outbreak of the wars that attended the breakups of Yugoslavia and the Soviet Union in Bosnia, Croatia, Georgia and Azerbaijan recalled the worst of conflict between national groups in Europe before 1945: attempts to change state frontiers by force of arms; mass migrations, brought on by discrimination against minorities and by war; and that most bigoted of nationalisms, encapsulated in the 1990s phrase, "ethnic cleansing."

Yet, as the war in Bosnia made clear, even the most determined ethnic cleansing does not necessarily result in "ethnically pure" states. Moreover, ethnic strife appeared to pose one of the greatest challenges to international security in the post–cold war era. The incongruence of most cultural and political frontiers in Europe and Asia and the dispersal of ethnic groups across different states raised the spectre of quarrels within multiethnic countries spilling over into neighboring countries.

In the 1990s the stability—even the survival—of many states was put at risk by domestic quarrels and challenges.[8] Most of these armed conflicts were caused by the wish of ethnic groups in multiethnic countries to attain independent states or to match territorial and ethnic borders. This desire presented the international community with a dilemma. On the one hand, a desire for a separate state may be understandable if an ethnic group perceives itself to be the victim of discrimination. On the other hand, partitions or secessions creating nation-states have not necessarily resulted in countries with homogeneous populations or contributed to regional peace. The discord between Catholics and Protestants in Northern Ireland, a legacy of the partition of Ireland, readily comes to mind. And Pakistan, which in 1947 was created as a homeland for Muslims in South Asia, today has a smaller Muslim population than India, which identifies itself as a secular state.

If the multinational state seems destined continually to face the challenges of discontent and secession, the nation-state has seldom been achieved. Attempts by the world's 2,000-odd nations to achieve independence would lead to a complete breakdown of the international system. The question is whether all these contradictory realities can be reconciled, especially in a world with no omnipotent superpowers.

Here, then, is the immediate background to the proposals made by international organizations and the reason why, since the end of the cold war, international policy-makers have focused attention on the question of whether ethnic diversity can be accommodated through political structures and ideologies.[9] The UN, OSCE and CE have advocated the management of ethnic variety through democratic governance, the rule of law and human rights, hoping that fair treatment for minorities through democratic institutions will protect them from any action aimed at assimilation and prevent ethnic conflict. The CSCE *Copenhagen Document* and *Charter of Paris*, the UN *Declaration on Minorities* and the CE *Framework Convention for National Minorities* all recommend giving minorities the right to establish and maintain their own educational, cultural and religious institutions, which can seek voluntary financial aid as well as public assistance. Minorities should be allowed to practice their religions and conduct religious activities in their mother tongues. The CSCE *Copenhagen Document* recommends that governments protect the identities of minorities and create conditions for the promotion of those identities after consultation with minority organizations. Governments should be guided by the principles of equality and nondiscrimination with respect to all ethnic groups in order to prevent calls for secession and preserve existing state boundaries. The CE *Framework Convention for National Minorities* dissuades states from carrying out assimilationist and discriminatory policies.[10] All these international instruments assume that equitable treatment for minorities will maintain domestic equilibrium and international stability and call on states to cooperate on minorities issues.[11]

Breaking New Ground: Democracy and the Prevention of Ethnic Conflict

These international instruments break new ground in three ways. First, the idea that minorities can best be protected in a democracy based on the rule of law with an independent judiciary is a reaction against strong-arm methods to manage ethnic diversity. The CSCE *Copenhagen Document* "clearly and unequivocally" condemned "totalitarianism" as well as discrimination against and persecution of minorities.[12] The UN *Declaration on Minorities* underlines "a democratic framework" and the rule of law and calls for the "constant promotion and realization" of minority rights. The CE Framework Convention affirms that "a pluralist and genuinely democratic society *should* not only respect the ethnic, cultural, linguistic and religious identity of each person belonging to a national minority, but should also create appropriate conditions enabling them to express, preserve and develop this identity."[13]

Mindful of the part played by minority grievances in sparking two world wars as well as the armed conflicts accompanying the disintegration of the former Yugoslavia and USSR, the CE *Framework Convention for National Minorities* observes that the protection of minorities is essential for democracy and peace in Europe. It is in a pluralist and genuinely democratic society that the social and cultural identity of individuals will be respected, thus enabling minorities to preserve their identities. Minorities are then less likely to demand separate statehood, and the chances of preserving existing frontiers of countries are greater. The international recommendations envisage the sovereign state as the cornerstone of international architecture and reflect the desire of international officials that the territorial integrity of states be maintained. Democracy, then, is both a means to an end and an end in itself.

The Incompatibility of Democracy and the Nation-state

Second, the underlining of the need for domestic policies to assuage the fears of minorities tacitly acknowledges the limits of any international intervention in maintaining domestic and regional stability, while reflecting the hope that it may be easier to avert ethnic conflict than to end it. This assumption is reasonable. The conflicts in the former Yugoslavia and Soviet Union had domestic roots, and it follows that internal solutions to ethnic quarrels will enhance regional security. In this century most international attempts to ease ethnic tensions have underlined the recognition of ethnic diversity by states as well as the obligations of states and minorities toward one another.

However, any debate on domestic prevention of conflict, minority rights or self-determination has come up against the concept of the nation-state. The conventional idea of "nation," implying the fusion of state with one national group, is a procrustean bed. The historical record establishes that in countries with ethnically mixed populations attempts by a state to compel all its members to identify with the ruling nation have triggered war, violations of human rights, genocide and mass migrations. An exclusivist definition of the nation spells exclusion of minorities; it is particularistic rather than pluralistic and is usually a recipe for ethnic battles.

The armed conflicts in Georgia, Bosnia, Serbia and Croatia have shown that breakaway groups or states which subscribe to exclusivist concepts of "nation" are likely to become embroiled in war with other ethnic groups living on the same territory and, therefore, to have difficulty in establishing control over the territory they claim. Diplomatic recognition by the international community of the claims to statehood by seceding communities which have not won the support of minorities on their territories can contribute to an escalation of ethnic hostilities.

Third, the slant against assimilation[14] and the advocacy of respect for the rights of minorities have been inspired by awareness that grievances of minorities have almost always contributed to ethnic tension.[15] Most states have ethnically interspersed populations, and assimilationist or discriminatory policies have frequently provoked ethnic unrest and interstate conflict. It is therefore not surprising that international statesmen have, from time to time, suggested ways of improving the relationship between states and minorities. The Minorities

Treaties signed between the League of Nations and new states emerging from the wreckage of empires in 1918 stressed freedom from racial, religious or linguistic discrimination, the right to citizenship and the right to establish religious, social and educational institutions. Thus the League of Nations hoped, simultaneously, to shield minorities from discrimination or zealous assimilationist policies, to counter pressures for separate statehood by minorities and to preserve regional peace.[16] However, the implementation of these rights was not linked to democracy, and the general expectation was that minorities would assimilate eventually. By linking safeguards for minority rights to democratic practices and institutions, post–cold war international instruments diverge sharply from the Minorities Treaties.

The idea, then, of creating political institutions in a system based on the rule of law, through which different ethnic groups can articulate their interests and identities, challenges the concept of the nation-state. Simultaneously, it also questions the idea that modernization by strong states would see the disappearance of ethnic identities and the blossoming of more homogeneous countries.[17] Post–cold war international instruments take for granted the reality of ethnically mixed groups and multiple identities. Pluralistic[18] solutions to safeguard minorities have been linked to democracy because that is the only system of governance that allows diverse identities and interests to be expressed. It implies a pluralist conception of the nation-state, a "pluralist nation" or a "multinational democracy."[19]

A state that is able to build consensus is more likely to sustain communal harmony and political stability. Consensus can only emerge from the practice and institutions of democracy. This reality alone makes it desirable to work for democracy as a method of managing ethnic diversity. Democracy is the only known political system which assumes a diversity of political ideas, power centers, and the separation of state from civil society; it is a political arrangement for the articulation, expression and mediation of differences; it assumes the existence of conflict rather than a Utopian end to all conflict.

Conflict and consensus are characteristics of democracy. Ethnic divisions are only one of many kinds of division that can exist in a society, and if institutions do not exist to reconcile differences between political parties, social groups, the individual and the state, they are unlikely to exist to reconcile differences between ethnic groups.

The recognition of political and intellectual diversity both within groups and between ethnic groups is vital. Ethnic nations are not intellectual or social monoliths, and there can be tension between the claims of a group and the rights of individuals who belong to a particular community but who distance themselves from the politics of its leaders. Whether cultural variety enriches a society or kindles strife depends on the way it is handled. Post–cold war international instruments accept cultural diversity as a *fait accompli*, requiring the opportunity to be represented and articulated through democratic political institutions. For instance, the CE *Charter for Regional or Minority Languages* (1992) affirms that the protection of regional languages will contribute to the maintenance and development of Europe's cultural wealth and traditions.[20]

Ethnic Conflict Is Avoidable

Ethnic identities and demands and the degree and intensity of ethnic conflict vary with changing political, social and economic conditions. Moreover, ethnic and political schisms do not necessarily coincide, and, frequently, the ethnic nation is politically divisible. In the former USSR Russians dominated the Communist Party and Soviet government, yet between 1990 and 1991 it was the Russian government under Boris Yeltsin which disengaged "Russia" from the Soviet state. In Canada and Spain, Quebecois and Basque separatists have failed repeatedly to get majority support for their respective causes, and Quebecois nationalists disagree on even so fundamental an issue as Quebec's relationship with Canada.

Paradoxes abound. Nationalism is usually a demand for a sovereign state, but it has rarely been the initial demand of nationalists. And not all nationalisms have been secessionist. In the nineteenth century some Czech nationalists thought their nationhood could be realized within the Habsburg empire, while the Indian National Congress, founded in 1885, did not demand independence until 1920 or the complete severance of all ties with the British Crown until 1930. Moreover, a cursory look at the uneven nature of the nationalisms in the USSR in the 1980s reveals that most of them were not secessionist.[21] Why a nationalist movement turns secessionist may be explained by factors as varied as the circumstances of time and place under which it has arisen, the character of its following and leadership and also the nature of the state that it challenges. A nationalist movement is shaped by the political environment in which it emerges, and the state plays a significant role in establishing the social, political and cultural rules or values within which different political parties and communities exist and operate.

The state's ability to intervene can offset forces as dissimilar as tradition or the market in ways that may exacerbate or diminish ethnic tensions. States usually wish to preserve their territorial integrity, but their political tactics may sometimes foster secession. In this sense, demands for secession—reflecting the inability or unwillingness to find a common meeting ground—may be equally the outcome of the designs of nationalists and policies of state.

The idea that democratic governance can facilitate ethnic rapprochement[22] will not necessarily be greeted with universal enthusiasm. Skeptics will contend that ethnic divisions have overturned democracy in many countries: The strife between Hutus and Tutsis in Rwanda, between Georgians and Abkhaz in Georgia and between Serbs and Albanians in Kosovo may suggest that in ethnically divided societies democratization will remain a pipe dream. However, the extent to which ethnic schisms contribute to the unraveling of democracy is debatable,[23] not least because democracy appears to be taking off—albeit in fits and starts—in many post–communist countries.[24] It is unlikely that such schisms alone retard democratization, and the part played by them should be seen in relation to other possible factors ranging from socioeconomic inequalities, tradition or corruption to external intervention. Moreover, democracy has not made much headway, or has broken down, in many countries in Latin America, Eastern Asia and the Middle East which have not been riven by ethnic fault-lines. But if democracy really cannot alleviate ethnic tensions, the only alternative is the authoritarian one. What does the record of authoritarian states show?

THE RECORD OF AUTHORITARIAN STATES

Divide and Rule: The Consequences of Authoritarian Statecraft

The splintering of Yugoslavia and the Soviet Union has called into question a common assumption that authoritarian states, whether of the imperial or non-imperial variety, could keep the ethnic genie in the bottle. This line of thought is of distinguished vintage. In 1861 John Stuart Mill wrote that "free institutions were impossible in a country made up of different nationalities."[25] Lord Acton regarded nationalism as incompatible with liberty and observed that the "combination of different nations in one state is as necessary a condition of civilised life as the combination of men and women in society." But Acton went on to praise empires like those of Great Britain and Austria, which in his view "included distinct nationalities without oppressing them," and he believed "that [i]nferior races are raised by living in political union with races intellectually superior."[26] Such observations are controversial, if only because nationalism has contributed to the disintegration of empires and because imperial rulers were frequently unable to reconcile differences between ethnic communities or win the support of the "nations" they governed. Nonetheless, the notion of ethnic harmony under empires endures, and the question is, why?

One possible reason is that in the post–cold war context the spotlight often falls on experiments in democratization that have resulted in the coming to power of intolerant nationalists, including Slobodan Milošević, Franjo Tudjman and Zviad Gamsakhurdia. In the 1990s expectations of "instant democracy" rode high: Ernest Gellner wrote that *"instant* pluralism and compromise—is unpredictable and constitutes *the* issue of the time."[27] Reports of ethnic strife foster nostalgia for the imagined certainties of the past or pessimism about the future. The machinations of Balkan autocrats are reported in the Western media, while past empires appear as havens of stability, but few ask how this stability was achieved. It was seldom achieved without war.[28] However, in the nineteenth century international society, acting on the principle of *cuius regio eius religio* (the sovereignty of states), did not pass judgment on the domestic conduct of rulers, the use of force to consolidate the state or the morality of territorial expansion. The unprecedented expectation of the nineties was that post-communist states should make themselves strong and secure through democratic practices and institutions. The wars that erupted in a minority of post–communist countries led some to conjure up visions of disorder caused by "chaos-prone" nationalism and democracy.

Much has been written about the failure of democracies to handle ethnic diversity. In contrast, the ability of authoritarian states, *as a category*, to overcome ethnic schisms has not been analyzed. More generally, the qualitative differences between authoritarian and democratic states in managing ethnic variety have not been discussed. There are many works on ethnic conflict and democracy, but it is hard to find one on ethnic divisions and autocracy.

Moreover, early literature on democratization did not deal with the problems of multinational democracies because ethnic divisions were not prominent in the countries dealt with.[29] It is only since the end of the cold war that some scholars have asked whether the logic of the nation and democracy can be reconciled.[30] There are relatively few accounts of democracies that achieved even a modicum of success[31] in coping with changing ethnic demands and interests and in defusing ethnic tensions. This intellectual vacuum tends to convey the impression that democracy simply cannot take off in multiethnic countries.

Scholarly debates on political structures and ethnic cleavages tend to focus on concepts of the multinational state, divided societies, federalism, autonomy and power-sharing.[32] In my view it is necessary to probe further. After all, federal political structures may not necessarily imply democracy, as was shown in Yugoslavia and the USSR. Unitary states like Britain and France are not dictatorships.[33] Power-sharing has often been recommended: indeed, some are inclined to think that no divided society can survive without it.[34] Others are less sanguine. At best power-sharing seems to work during periods of transition,[35] but it has often failed, partly because it has been too rigid. Where it has succeeded, as in Belgium, Switzerland and Italy, it is to some extent due to the existence of institutions for reconciliation and mediation. There is still little analysis of how these institutions have helped to alleviate conflict in democracies or how "civic nationalism" has transcended and co-existed with regional, linguistic or cultural identities in countries as diverse as Spain, India, Finland and Italy.[36]

Authoritarian States Cannot Forge Consensus

Consensus is essential for stability in a multiethnic state, and it can only be forged through democracy. It is all too apparent that authoritarian states—whether of the imperial or nonimperial variety—have failed to forge consensus because they have, almost without exception, followed the policy of divide and rule. Authoritarian rulers do not seek consensus, which in the long run is the best guarantee of the stability of a multinational state. Divide and rule tactics are, in my view, inherent in authoritarian statecraft. Force implies the suppression of conflict; it precludes reconciliation of differences through mediation and accommodation between nationalities. Authoritarian rulers have tended to pit national groups against one another to strengthen their own positions. There usually have been several strands to this policy, running parallel to, cutting across and contradicting one another. The policy of divide and rule has taken for granted that national division implies political division: thus it has assumed the potential or existence of nationalism as a political force. Authoritarian rulers have tolerated and even encouraged some measure of cultural diversity, partly out of necessity, partly because they thought they could turn it to their advantage, but this has implied neither acceptance of political or ideological differences nor a wish to build consensus.

Divide and rule by authoritarian states has never brought nationalities together: the divisions between the nationalities of the Habsburg and Romanov empires are easily remembered. And during this century, British withdrawals from formal and informal empire were attended by partition on no less than four occasions: in Ireland, India, Palestine and Cyprus. Divide and rule carries its own contradictions: it usually has failed to sustain the states that have practiced it, and its main legacy has been a backlog of hatred between communities in these states. The British divided Hindus and Muslims in India; the Belgians, Hutus and Tutsis in the Congo; and the Habsburgs, the Germans and Magyars from other nationalities in their empire. Political representation was given to the different nations not with a view to forging consensus—for that could have gone against imperial rulers—but to win them over to the imperial cause.

Divide and rule yielded fruit, though not necessarily the one sought by the rulers. The Abkhazian-Georgian and Armenian-Azeri conflicts can be traced back to Stalin's policy of exploiting divisions between Georgians and Abkhazians and Armenians and Azeris. In the Soviet Union and Yugoslavia another consequence of this same policy was that every republic perceived itself to be exploited by other. Almost every country emerging from the former Soviet Union and Yugoslavia in 1991 inherited a legacy of ethnic divisions.[37]

Allied to the strategy of divide and rule was a policy of identifying with one community. Much has been written about democracy failing because rulers have identified with an ethnic group or manipulated communal divisions to gain votes. The point is well taken, if only because such tactics have harmed democracy and aggravated communal tensions. But what is rarely brought out is that divide and rule by authoritarian rulers has often gone hand in hand with a policy of associating with one "nation." Here some comparisons between the Habsburg and Romanov empires may be illuminating. The Habsburgs identified with the Germans, who in 1910 were 23.9 percent of their empire. After the *Ausgleich* of 1867 the Magyars, who ran the Dual Monarchy in Austria-Hungary, comprised 20.2 percent of the population of the empire, while the Slavs accounted for 45 percent. An analogous policy was followed by communist states. For example, Nicolae Ceaușescu, when confronted with a series of economic failures in the seventies and eighties, exhorted Romanians to be "masters in their own home" and whipped up xenophobia against Romania's Magyar and Jewish minorities.[38] In Poland, where Poles comprised more than 98 percent of the population, the communists launched a virulent anti-Semitic campaign in the sixties, which in 1968 culminated in the expulsion of Jews from the country.[39]

In the First World War imperial regimes appealed to disaffected minorities in the empires of their antagonists to defeat them. A case has been made[40] that the Romanovs did not identify with nationalities but saw communities as loyal or disloyal. But this identification in itself points to the creation and recognition of ethnic categories. For the Romanovs the loyalists were Russians, while Germans, Poles, Tatars and Ukrainians were viewed as real or potential traitors.[41] That the nationalities question remained a festering sore under the Romanovs is illustrated by the fact that the Bolsheviks found it to be a far greater problem than anticipated. The political institutions of the Soviet Union were created partly with the intention of winning over the nationalities that had tried to break away as the Romanov empire disintegrated. It took the Bolsheviks four years—from 1918 to 1921—to absorb into the USSR, through a mixture of coercion, coaxing and cajolery, some of the nations which had seceded from the Romanov empire, including Ukraine, Georgia, Azerbaijan and Armenia.

Some stimulating comparisons between the nationalities policies of the Habsburg and Romanov empires and the Soviet Union have been made.[42] Michael Doyle takes the view that empires do not have a *Staatsidee* (idea of state) around which to unite their subjects.[43] The Soviet Union certainly had one in its communist ideology. Moreover, empires do not try to create citizens, but the Soviet Union, like most state-nations, did try to create citizens. Yet its history and that of Yugoslavia show that to build consensus it is not enough for a state to have a *Staatsidee*—even a cosmopolitan one—embracing all its diverse peoples. Only a democracy can accomplish that, but it is by no means a foregone conclusion.

The identification of many communist states with the preponderant nation did not secure their legitimacy. Political institutions in Romania, Bulgaria and Poland were all dominated by the ethnic majority: assimilationist and discriminatory policies were carried out against minorities by communist states, but the velvet revolutions in the eighties revealed that none had managed to win the support of the majority or to earn legitimacy.[44]

IMPLEMENTING DEMOCRATIC NORMS

Minorities and Self-determination in Relations between States

Neither the lack of realism inherent in the concept of the nation-state nor the failures of authoritarian states assure the success of democracy in handling ethnic diversity. The imprecise connection between "democracy" and "self-determination" goes some way to explain why. Whether associated with minorities or democracy, self-determination is an ambiguous concept; its enforcement has created rather than solved problems. The idea of self-determination, implying self-rule, can be traced back to the American War of Independence (1776) and the Declaration of the Rights of Man and the Citizen during the French Revolution (1789). Since the nineteenth century self-determination has inspired the creation of many new states. Defined as a human right by the International Covenants on Civil and Political Rights and on Economic, Cultural and Social Rights (1966), self-determination revolves around the problems of defining the political entities that may participate in international relations, the community within which human rights are to be protected and the individuals making up that community whose human rights are to be safeguarded. Self-determination is for peoples, and the question of defining "the people" has long plagued statesmen, largely because the territorial and ethnic boundaries of most states have been incongruent. Governments of countries with ethnically mixed populations have had to handle religious, ethnic or linguistic minorities. And minorities have frequently appropriated the term "self-determination" to articulate their political claims.

International officials have long been aware of the risk of discontented minorities being manipulated by foreign powers and destabilizing states, and many rulers have been concerned by the existence of significant irredenta outside the borders of their states. Since the sixteenth century minorities have been the subject of treaties between several European states, which have tried to assuage the fears of minorities by declaring their intent to allow minorities to practice their religions and preserve their cultures. These treaties included the Peace of Westphalia (1648), on which the present international society is based, the Vienna Congress settlement (1815) and the Treaty of Berlin (1878).[45]

After the First World War the victorious Allies drew new borders for Austria, Bulgaria, Hungary, Romania, Turkey, Czechoslovakia, Poland and Yugoslavia from the ruins of the Hohenzollern, Romanov and Ottoman empires. Between the two world wars one-third of the population of Europe was comprised of minorities. To shield minorities from any assimilationist zeal of these so-called "nation-states," the League of Nations signed Minorities Treaties with them. Special provision for minorities was also made by the authorities of Danzig, the Åland Islands, the Memel territory and Upper Silesia. Taken together these treaties represented the first concerted international effort to protect minorities. However, failure to enforce the treaties provided Nazi Germany with the pretext to invade Czechoslovakia in 1938, thus bringing the very concept of minority rights into disrepute. Minority grievances were also exploited by Nazi Germany to transfer southern Transylvania and southern Slovakia to Hungary in 1940 and to create the Slovak and Croat puppet states.

Consequently, after World War II, the international community played down the importance of minorities, and neither the *Charter of the United Nations* (1945) nor the *Universal Declaration of Human Rights* (1948) mentioned minority rights. There is no agreed definition of minorities. During the seventies African countries contended that it was one thing to talk of "minorities" in Europe, where political stability, forged over centuries, could be taken for granted, and another to apply the label "minorities" to Africa's myriad of tribes that could endanger the unity of newly independent states "torn by opposing social forces."[46] Some states, notably in Latin America, claimed that they did not have any minorities. Many works on nationalism ignore the subject, although the survival of multiethnic states can hinge on their ability to accommodate minorities.

At the heart of any "minorities problem" are a minority's rights to identity and existence. The *Convention on the Prevention and Punishment of the Crime of Genocide* (1948) attempts to protect both rights by defining genocide as "acts committed with intent to destroy, in whole or in part, a national, ethnical, racial or religious group"[47] and making it a crime under international law. The UN Charter does not specifically mention minority rights but Article 1(3) refers to the need for international cooperation "in promoting and encouraging respect for human rights and fundamental freedoms for all without distinction as to race, sex, language, or religion."[48] The *Convention Against Discrimination in Education* (1960) recognizes the rights of members belonging to national minorities to maintain schools and study in their own language.[49] These principles were reiterated in the *Convention on the Rights of the Child* (1989).[50] The *Declaration on Race and Racial Prejudice* (1978) affirmed that "education in its broadest sense" should enable individuals to respect the rights of all groups to their own cultural identities, "it being understood that it rests with each group to decide in complete freedom on the maintenance, and ... the adaptation or enrichment of the values which it regards as essential to its identity."[51] States that were parties to the *International Convention on the Elimination of All Forms of Racial Discrimination* (1965) undertook to do away with racial discrimination "in all its forms" and condemned propaganda and organizations based on theories of superiority of race, color or ethnicity.[52] Since 1966, Article 27 of the *International Covenant on Civil and Political Rights* has served as the international standard on minority rights. It states that minorities should "not be denied" the right to enjoy their own cultures, practice their religions or use their own languages. The principles of nondiscrimination and of equal and inalienable rights of all human beings are enunciated in the *Universal Declaration of Human Rights*,[53] the *International Covenant on Civil and Political Rights*,[54] the *International Covenant on Economic, Social and Cultural Rights* and the *European Convention for the Protection of Human Rights and Fundamental Freedoms* (1950).[55]

Although the international community put minorities issues on ice after the Second World War, minorities remained a source of friction within and between many countries in Europe, Asia and Africa, and many neighboring countries signed bilateral treaties in the hope of defusing domestic and interstate tension. The outcome of such treaties was mixed. An agreement between India and Pakistan in 1950 failed to resolve causes of dispute between them, notably in the case of Kashmir. And in the Middle East, it is hard to see an early alleviation of the problems of Kurd minorities, who are spread over several countries, including Turkey, Iran, Iraq and Syria. In Europe, however, Finland, Sweden,

Austria, Italy, Hungary, Slovakia and Romania, Ukraine and Russia have entered into bilateral treaties that have helped to ease tension over minorities.[56] More important, perhaps, these countries have not encouraged irredentism.

The search for ways to assuage minority grievances has provoked much debate about individual and group rights.[57] In Europe the contradiction between these concepts stirred up diplomatic rows between newly democratizing countries like Hungary, Slovakia and Romania. Hungary's "good-neighbor treaties" with Slovakia (1995) and Romania (1996) have eased some tensions, but Slovakia and Romania spurned Hungarian calls for safeguards for the cultural rights of Magyar minorities on the grounds that the emphasis on group rights was against international norms.[58] Controversies abound: what is the moral high ground between the right of a democracy to preserve its territorial integrity and the right of its illiberal minorities to self-determination and their attempts to achieve it by force of arms? Where does one draw the line between minority (or majority) rights and the institutionalization and perpetuation of ethnic division?[59] What is to be done when the very term "minority" appears offensive to a group like the Serbs in Croatia, who viewed themselves not as a minority but as peers of the Croat "nation"? The dilemma is not confined to Europe. It is analogous to the call made by the Muslim League in 1940 for a sovereign Muslim homeland on the Indian subcontinent on the grounds that there were literally two nations in British India which could not co-exist within a single state. At the intellectual level, liberal and Marxist theorists alike have stressed ethnic homogeneity and have been dismissive of minorities as historically inconsequential or simply a nuisance.[60] Wittingly or unwittingly echoing official Soviet claims, Western advocates of modernization thought that the USSR had solved its nationalities problems,[61] but its dismantling, like that of Yugoslavia, has shown the inability of political theorists of different ideological hues either to grasp the ethnic nettle or to wish it away.

International resolutions and conventions since 1990 have tried to grapple with these dilemmas. The Helsinki Accord of 1975 advocated equality before the law for minorities and anticipated that human rights and fundamental freedoms would "in this manner" protect their legitimate interests. Principles I and VI stressed the sovereignty of states; Principle VIII the right of people to self-determination in accordance with the UN Charter. In trying to reconcile individual and group rights, the *Copenhagen Document* and the CE *Framework Convention for National Minorities*[62] are clear that individuals have the right to decide whether they wish to belong to minority groups. Article 3(2) of the UN *Declaration on Minorities* states in somewhat circumlocutory manner that there should be no disadvantage "for any person belonging to a minority as the consequence of the exercise or non-exercise of the rights set forth in the present Declaration." It gives individuals the right to decide whether they want to be treated as a member of a minority group.[63] These are attempts to do away with the friction between individual and group rights.

Self-determination and Democracy: The Tyranny of the Majority Community?

The significance of "self-determination" for international society has, then, been many-sided. Self-determination has had diverse meanings. It has been an inspiration for nationalists seeking a sovereign state, a democratic idea and a human right. It has also been used to legitimize the creation of homogeneous states when it has caused interstate conflict as well as tensions between the principle of sovereignty and the international obligations of states on minorities, human rights and democracy.

Self-determination as a democratic idea has posed two major problems. First, the only way to legitimize it has been through plebiscites, referenda or elections, and second, in a multiethnic country voting can all too often result in victory for parties or leaders representing the majority community.

Not surprisingly international officials have found it hard to find a consistent approach in addressing the dilemmas posed by self-determination and democracy. State practice has mirrored the contradictions between ideal and reality. The idea of self-determination as self-rule has often raised the expectation that it would clear the path to democracy. The notion of self-determination as synonymous with democracy is linked with President Woodrow Wilson, for whom government had to be based on the consent of the governed. Seeking to fashion a new international architecture after the First World War, Wilson called for democratic elections to be conducted without violence under international law. He anticipated the realization of self-determination through plebiscites and referenda under international supervision.[64]

However, the gap between intentions and acts and between intended and unintended consequences of policies recurred. This was partly because, throughout history, the borders of most states have been carved out by conquest. Until the twentieth century plebiscites were the exception rather than the rule as a method of determining the wishes of the people on a territory annexed by a state. Britain did not conduct plebiscites to ascertain the wishes of the Scots, Welsh or Irish. Nor did the United States when it bought Louisiana in 1803 and Alaska in 1867 or when it annexed Texas, New Mexico and California.

Plebiscites were first held in territories conquered by France. They included Comtat-Venaissin and Avignon (1791) and Savoy, Mulhouse, Hainaut and Rhineland (1792). The plebiscites were an attempt to reconcile the professed renunciation of conquest by Revolutionary France with the wishes of the peoples living on annexed territories. Unable to reconcile the will of "the people" with territorial expansion, Revolutionary France simply stopped conducting plebiscites after 1795. At the Congress of Vienna (1815), which marked the defeat of Revolutionary France, the victorious powers gave short shrift to plebiscites and revised the political map of Europe by confirming the gains made by Russia, Austria, Prussia and Britain in war. However, the principle of popular sovereignty had taken hold in Europe, and the unification of Italy (1861) was sealed by a plebiscite based on universal manhood suffrage. International monitoring of elections was first carried out in Moldavia and Wallachia in 1857 by a European commission composed of representatives from Britain, France, Prussia, Turkey and Russia. Plebiscites in British and French colonies in Africa after World War II did not necessarily result in the creation of democracies.

The holding of free, fair and periodic elections to create representative government reflects the standard laid down in the *Universal Declaration of Human Rights* that "[t]he will of the people shall be the basis of the authority of government." This norm was reiterated in the *International Covenant on Civil and Political Rights*[65] and the *European Convention on Human Rights*.[66]

Democracy implies the rule of the majority and it is all too easy to slide over the distinction between an ethnic and a political majority. In some countries, such as Sri Lanka, Georgia or Croatia, the ethnic majority may indeed on occasion turn out to be the political majority. But in many countries the two are distinct. In Russia extreme nationalists led by Vladimir Zhirinovsky have never won a majority. In India Hindus form 82 percent of the population, but since 1997, Hindu nationalist parties have been able to form a government at the center only by coalescing with regional parties. In Spain the choice of electoral sequence helped to create a democratic state and to construct multiple and complex political identities.[67] And in many post-communist countries, including Russia, Ukraine and Hungary, ethnic and political identities are quite distinct.[68]

Denial by a state of equal rights to all ethnic groups goes against the grain of democracy and shows that exclusivist policies require a legal framework that is incompatible with democracy. Intrinsic to democracy are equal rights to participate in government, respect for freedom of association[69] and expression, and equality before the law. Such principles are also the underlying principles of human rights and, if put into practice, would give minorities the chance to see themselves as citizens rather than as members of an ethnic group. The rights of minorities and cultural rights have little meaning if they are not linked with human rights, and suppression of minority rights often accompanies violations of human rights.

Ethnically defined governments, by their very nature, discriminate against minorities and fail to provide safeguards for human rights, while authoritarian states show little concern for human rights. Democracy may not be sufficient to guarantee human and minority rights, yet they cannot be safeguarded without it. This paradox suggests why the issues of democratization, minorities and human rights have become important both within states and in relations between states. The emphasis on democracy, individual and minority rights has a wider international significance because the UN Charter lays down that the UN will promote universal respect for the observance of human rights and fundamental freedoms for all.

Self-determination, Democracy and Human Rights

The international preference for resolving ethnic problems through democratic institutions and respect for human rights has compounded many conceptual and practical problems. The emphasis on democracy and human rights implies outside scrutiny of the internal affairs of states and gratuitous advice about their political institutions. It thus comes into collision with the principle of sovereignty which anchored international society long before the emergence of nationalism.

During the French Revolution nationalism brought about the substitution of popular sovereignty for the traditional prescriptive principle of sovereignty. Since then nationalism has inspired the demand for sovereign states and legitimized them in the name of "the nation" or "the people."[70] But nationalism has left unchanged the traditional meaning of sovereignty, implying the unrestricted power of the state to do what it pleases within its own territory. Sovereignty, in this way has been concerned with the very existence of the state. So when nationalism calls for or leads to the breakup of existing states it challenges one of the most cherished axioms of international society: the maintenance of the territorial integrity of states.

It is only since 1945 that human rights have received international attention; indeed they have been an important concern of post–1945 international society. Shock at the barbarities of the Holocaust aroused international anxiety about the treatment of citizens by states. Human rights are enshrined in international conventions; they are universal moral rights to which every individual is entitled. Human rights became an issue in relations between states through the United Nations. The UN Charter[71] is the first international treaty to be based expressly on universal respect for human rights and fundamental freedoms. The *Universal Declaration of Human Rights* aspired to becoming "a common standard of achievement for all peoples and nations" and many of its provisions, and its supporting Covenants on Civil and Political Rights and on Economic, Social and Cultural Rights[72] are now established international norms. International conventions reflect and take into account the experiences and interests of several countries. The spirit and character of these conventions as a synthesis raise expectations that they will be widely respected. But there lies the rub. International society is based on the sovereignty of states, and human rights are intended to ensure that the "needs of the individuals who comprise those states are not ignored."[73]

Since 1945 minority rights have come under the rubric of human rights on the grounds that the protection of individual rights is the best way of safeguarding minority rights. There is much to be said for this: abuses of human and minority rights often go together, and many an ethnic conflict has been exacerbated by violations of human rights. Human and minority rights can only be granted and protected by states, and moral questions apart, failure—for whatever reason—to safeguard these rights can upset regional and international peace and interstate relations. This is why the international community seeks to keep an eye on the domestic character and policies of states. In other words, human rights have become a security issue. Human rights appear to do away with the distinction between the domestic domain and the international arena, but international conventions on human rights rest on the sovereignty of states, and outside scrutiny of the way in which states treat their citizens is usually resented and resisted by states as an infringement of their sovereignty.

The conflict between the need for, or justification of, international intervention to safeguard human and minority rights on the one side and the principle of noninterference in the domestic affairs of states on the other is likely to prevail in international affairs, not least because international conventions do not give minority rights precedence over the rights of states and individuals. Moreover, since 1945, the rights of states have ranked higher than human rights in international priorities.[74] Furthermore, international society reflects the interests of its member states, and it is seldom easy to separate political from humanitarian considerations, so the motives behind any international intervention are always open to question.[75] Yet, in the post–cold war world, that may not be the whole story, despite the apparent difficulty of persuading the governments of, for example, Serbia, Croatia, Turkey, Burma and China to comply with international standards on human rights. Some states, including Hungary,[76] have, out of inclination or geopolitical reality, actually sought the framing of international norms on minorities and human rights as a way of easing tensions with neighboring countries; others, like Estonia and Latvia,[77] have been amenable to international advice.

The idea of democracy and human rights as the basis of international society is of recent origin. Until the end of the cold war Western democracies did not refer to human rights in their foreign policies. Except for a brief period at the beginning of the Carter administration, the United States resisted the linking of human rights and foreign policy. An exception was made in the case of the CSCE, where such a connection served the obvious political purpose of embarrassing the USSR.

Whether democracy and human rights should be linked is a matter of some controversy, and the relationship between them is ambiguous.[78] Democracy refers to a country's system of governance, which its people have the right to choose. Human rights belong to all individuals, regardless of the political system prevailing in a country. Since 1990 UN and CSCE/OSCE declarations have connected both. During the cold war East European countries stressed economic and social rights, but these did not satisfy the desire of their peoples for political and civil rights. Post-communist East European governments have stressed political and civil rights, which can only be safeguarded through democracy. While democracy cannot guarantee human rights, they cannot be protected without it. The point was reaffirmed in the resolution of the UN Commission on Human Rights on 27 April 1999, which referred to "the indissoluble links between the principles enshrined in the *Universal Declaration of Human Rights* and the foundation of any democratic society," and recognized that "democracy, development and respect for all human rights and fundamental freedoms are interdependent and mutually reinforcing."[79]

Nowhere is the tension between democracy and human rights, on the one hand, and the interests of state, on the other, more evident than on the issues of minorities and self-determination. Since the First World War most states that have fractured have done so along ethnic lines. Most conflicts since 1945 have occurred within states, and many were fuelled by the discontent of minorities. The war in Bosnia showed, not for the first time, the gap between the rhetoric of self-determination and democracy and its translation into practice in the domestic arena.

Self-determination is a human right:[80] when it calls for secession and leads to war it comes into collision with the desire of international society to preserve the sovereignty of states.[81] For instance, the issues involved in the recognition of Croatia and Bosnia in 1991 and, subsequently, Serbia's treatment of Kosovar Albanians, NATO's intervention in Kosovo and international reactions to the wars in Chechnya in 1994 and 1999 revealed the problems of promoting democracy and safeguarding minorities in post-communist countries after their independence.[82] This is largely because there is no simple way out of the dilemma of reconciling ethnic variety with the territorial integrity of many countries.

Noting the ethnically diverse populations in most countries and the potential of ethnic discord to tear states apart, Boutros-Ghali observed in 1992 that a commitment to human rights—with special sensitivity to minority rights—could enhance the stability of states.[83] Underlining the centrality of states in the post–cold war arrangement, the UN *Declaration on Minorities*[84] affirms that minority rights are best protected in a democratic framework based on the rule of law. Their safeguarding can contribute to the political and social stability of states; indeed the resolution is explicit that nothing can be done to impair the "sovereign equality, territorial integrity and political independence of States." Concerned at the growing visibility of ethnic conflict in Europe since 1989, regional organizations including the CSCE/OSCE and the Council of Europe have affirmed that democracy and the rule of law offer safeguards for minority rights. CSCE work stems from Principle VII of the *Helsinki Final Act* (1975) and includes the Concluding Document of the Vienna meeting (1989)[85] the *Copenhagen Document*, the *Charter of Paris for a New Europe* and the *Helsinki Document* (1992).[86] The *Copenhagen Document*, drawn up a year before the outbreak of the 1991 war in Yugoslavia, first asserted that pluralistic democracy and the rule of law were essential for the enjoyment of human rights and fundamental freedoms. Probably reflecting concern that ethnic division could overturn democracy, the *Copenhagen Document* affirmed that protection of the rights of minorities was part of universally recognized human rights and essential for peace, justice and democracy.[87] The UN *Declaration on Minorities*[88] includes minority rights within the ambit of human rights and identifies them as a subject of international cooperation. Article 14 of the *European Convention on Human Rights* (1950) and the *Framework Convention for National Minorities* are the Council of Europe's main contributions to the protection of minorities. The *Framework Convention* follows the trail blazed by the UN *Declaration on Mi-*

norities in stating that minorities have the right to establish and maintain free and peaceful contacts across frontiers with persons with whom they share an ethnic, cultural or religious identity or a common cultural heritage. At the same time it underlines the sovereign equality, territorial integrity and political independence of states. Both documents have attempted to ease the tension between individual and group rights.[89] The European Union has no general policy on minority protection within its borders, and the Treaty of European Union makes no reference to minorities.[90] But in 1994 member-states of the EU adopted by consensus the UN *Declaration on Minorities*.

Democracy, Ethnic Diversity and the Sovereignty of States

Minority rights are clearly on the post–cold war international agenda; they are an issue in relations between states. The CSCE *Geneva Report* affirms that minorities issues, "as well as compliance with international obligations and commitments concerning the rights of persons belonging to them, are matters of concern and do not constitute exclusively an internal affair of the state."[91]

Yet international instruments cannot depart from the principle of the sovereignty of states,[92] and all endorse the territorial integrity of states. The UN *Declaration on Minorities* is against "any activity contrary to the purposes and principles of the United Nations, including sovereign equality, territorial integrity and political independence of States."[93] The OSCE High Commissioner on National Minorities has affirmed that he cannot function without the political support of OSCE member-states. It is they who will transform his recommendations into policies. This, and the need to appear impartial, means that the HCNM "is not an instrument for the protection of minorities or a sort of international ombudsman who acts on their behalf. This is reflected in his title: he is the OSCE High Commissioner ON National Minorities and not FOR National Minorities."[94] Minorities have duties as well as rights, and he urges them to integrate into the society in which they live rather than to appear isolationist. The OSCE seeks solutions to minority problems within the framework of the state itself.[95]

The UN *Declaration on Minorities* and the CE *Framework Convention for National Minorities* emphasise transfrontier cooperation between local and regional authorities without prejudice to the territorial integrity and constitution of each state. The *Framework Convention*[96] also suggests cross-border contacts between people belonging to the same ethnic group. In 1997 the Congress of Local and Regional Authorities of Europe deemed *the region*, bearing witness to Europe's diversity, "as an essential component of the State."[97] The CE *European Charter for Regional or Minority Languages* (1992) underlines that minority languages are to be protected but not to the detriment of the official languages and the need to learn them. The promotion and protection of minority and regional languages are based on the principles of democracy and cultural diversity and are to be implemented "within the framework of national sovereignty and territorial integrity."[98] Regional self-government entails loyalty toward the state to which regions belong, "with due regard to its sovereignty and territorial integrity."[99] It is in this context that transfrontier exchanges or contacts between users of the same language in neighboring countries are to be encouraged.[100] The inference is that such stable uncontested borders are necessary for a borderless Europe.

The redressal of minority grievances to preserve the territorial integrity of countries has been a longstanding international concern. The suggestion that ethnic stability should be forged through democratic means symbolizes an attempt to reconcile conflicting ideals of self-determination, democracy, minority rights and the sovereignty and territorial integrity of states. What are the chances of success? Since the end of the Second World War what has been the experience of democracies such as Spain, India and Sri Lanka in handling ethnic variety? The next chapter takes up these questions.

NOTES

1. *Report* of CSCE Meeting of Experts on National Minorities, Geneva, 1–19 July 1991, referred to hereafter as *Geneva Report*.

2. HCNM's address, 23 May 1993.

3. John Breuilly, *Nationalism and the State*, 2nd ed. (Manchester: Manchester University Press, 1993).

4. See chapter 2.

5. John Dunn, "Conclusion," in John Dunn, ed., *Democracy: The Unfinished Journey, 508 B.C. to A.D. 1993* (Oxford: Oxford University Press, 1992), p. 246.

6. Boutros-Ghali's address to the World Conference on Human Rights, Vienna, 14 June 1993, *UNHR*, p. 442.

7. These priorities would be questioned by some former Soviet republics such as Belarus, Kazakhstan and Uzbekistan, which have shown marked authoritarian trends since 1991, but even they pay at least lip service to democracy and human rights.

8. Between 1989 and 1996, it is estimated that 95 out of 101 armed conflicts were internal wars. International Institute for Democracy and Electoral Assistance, Stockholm, *Democracy and Deep-Rooted Conflict: Options for Negotiators* (Stockholm: International Institute for Democracy and Electoral Assistance, 1998), p. 14.

9. Anita Inder Singh, "Democracy and Ethnic Diversity: A New International Priority?" *The World Today*, vol. 52, no. 1 (January 1996): 20–22.

10. Articles 5.2 and 6.2.

11. More recently the OSCE and CE have sought to find ways to reconcile cultural differences through democracy so that diversity becomes the norm. Rapporteur's report, *Culture and Conflict Prevention*, Joint OSCE-CE Conference, Bergen, 21 May 1999.

12. Para. 40

13. Emphasis mine.

14. Assimilation is based on the idea of the superiority of the dominant culture. It aims at the achievement of homogeneity within the state by ensuring that minorities discard their culture in favor of the dominant culture. UN *Special Study on Racial Discrimination in the Political, Economic, Social and Cultural Spheres*, E/CN.4/Sub.2/307/Rev.1 (New York: United Nations, 1971), referred to hereafter as *UN Special Study*.

15. How they did so in the former Yugoslavia and USSR is discussed in chapter 3.

16. See among others, *The International Protection of Minorities Under the League of Nations*, E/CN.4/Sub2/6(1947), and C. A. Macartney, *National States and National Minorities* (London: Oxford University Press, 1934).

17. See the discussion in Connor, "Nation-Building or Nation-Destroying?" pp. 29ff.

18. Pluralism is defined as a policy that seeks to unite different ethnic groups in a relationship of mutual interdependence, respect and equality, while allowing them to retain their distinctive ways (*UN Special Study*). Patrick Thornberry adds that pluralism signifies the idea of unity within diversity; *Minorities and Human Rights Law* (London: Minority Rights Group, 1991), p. 8.

19. Whether the concepts of a "pluralist nation" or a "multinational democracy" would have the same meaning as "civic nationalism" remains to be seen. Anthony Smith argues that civic nationalism is neither as tolerant nor as unbiased as its self-image suggests, for civic nationalisms often demand surrender of ethnic community and individuality, the privatization of ethnic religion and the manipulation of the ethnic culture and heritage of minorities within the borders of the national state. Anthony D. Smith, *Nations and Nationalism in a Global Era* (Cambridge: Polity Press, 1995), p. 101. See also Alfred Stepan, "Modern Multi-National Democracies: Transcending the Gellnerian Oxymoron," *Oxford International Review*, vol. 8, no. 2 (spring 1997): 19–29.

20. Preamble to the *European Charter for Regional or Minority Languages* (1992).

21. Armenia, Georgia, Moldova, Estonia, Latvia and Lithuania refused to sign the Union Treaty in 1991. For a discussion of nations not demanding secession in some other parts of the world see, for instance, Michael Keating, "Stateless Nation-Building: Quebec, Catalonia and Scotland in the Changing State System," *Nations and Nationalism*, vol. 3, part 4 (October 1997): 689–717.

22. More generally, the idea of democratic governance as an emerging principle of international law is likely to influence the international community in the foreseeable future. Thomas Franck, "The Emerging Right to Democratic Governance," *American Journal of International Law*, vol. 86, no. 1 (January 1992): 46–91.

23. Alvin Rabushka and Kenneth Shepsle, *Politics in Plural Societies: A Theory of Democratic Instability* (Columbus, Ohio: Merrill, 1972). Axel Hadenius, *Democracy and Development* (Cambridge: Cambridge University Press, 1992) disputes the claims of Rabushka and Shepsle. There is more debate in Arend Lijphart, *Democracy in Plural Societies: A Comparative Exploration* (New Haven: Yale University Press, 1977); Larry Diamond and Marc Plattner, eds., *Nationalism, Ethnic Conflict and Democracy* (Baltimore: Johns Hopkins University Press, 1994); Juan Linz and Alfred Stepan, *Problems of Democratic Transition and Consolidation: Southern Europe, Southern American, and Post-Communist Europe* (Baltimore: Johns Hopkins University Press, 1996), pp. 3–27.

24. See chapter 4.

25. John Stuart Mill, *Considerations on Representative Sovereignty* (London: Longman, Roberts and Green, 1865), pp. 230, 232–33.

26. Lord Acton, *Essays on Freedom and Power* (Boston: n.p. 1948), p. 186.

27. Ernest Gellner, "Homeland of the Unrevolution," *Daedalus*, vol. 122, no. 3 (summer 1993): 153.

28. See Geir Lundestad, ed., *The Fall of the Great Powers: Peace, Stability and Legitimacy* (Oslo: Scandinavian University Press, 1994), pp. 394–95.

29. Linz and Stepan, *Problems of Democratic Transition*, p. 16.

30. Ibid.; Diamond and Plattner, *Nationalism, Ethnic Conflict and Democracy*; and my "Democracy and Ethnic Diversity."

31. Part of the problem is defining what constitutes "success" in handling ethnic diversity. Does it mean that people should have no ethnic identity or interests or that there should be no ethnic violence, no demands for secession? The first seems unrealistic; partition or secession, if carried out peacefully, would not create security problems; violence creates domestic and sometimes regional instability.

32. Eric Nordlinger, *Conflict Regulation in Divided Societies* (Cambridge, Mass.: Center for International Affairs, Harvard University, 1972); Joseph Montville, ed., *Conflict and Peacemaking in Multiethnic Societies* (Lexington, Mass.: Lexington Books, 1991); Hurst Hannum, *Autonomy, Sovereignty and Self-Determination: The Accommodation of Conflicting Rights*, rev. ed. (Philadelphia: University of Pennsylvania Press, 1996); Ruth Lapidoth *Autonomy: Flexible Solutions to Ethnic Conflicts* (Washington, D.C.: United States Institute of Peace Press, 1997); Uri Ra'anan et al., *State and Nation in Multi-Ethnic Societies: The Breakup of Multinational States* (Manchester: Manchester University Press, 1991).

33. Robert Dahl, *Democracy and Its Critics* (New Haven: Yale University Press, 1989), p. 199.

34. Vernon Bogdanor, "Forms of Autonomy and the Protection of Minorities," *Daedalus*, vol. 126, no. 2 (spring 1997): 66.

35. Timothy Sisk, *Power Sharing and International Mediation in Ethnic Conflicts* (Washington, D.C.: United States Institute of Peace, 1996).

36. On Spain and India, see chapter 2 On Finland's accommodation of the Åland Islands, see J. Barros, *The Åland Islands Question: Its Settlement by the League of Nations* (New Haven: Yale University Press, 1968); and Max Engman, "Finns and Swedes in Finland," in Sven Tägil, ed., *Ethnicity and Nation-Building in the Nordic World* (London: Hurst, 1995), pp. 179ff. On South Tyrol see Anthony Alcock, *The History of the South Tyrol Question* (London: Michael Joseph/Graduate Institute of International Studies, Geneva, 1970).

37. The prevalence of this perception and the breakup of the Soviet Union belied yet another boast of the Communist Party: that "fraternal cooperation" was the hallmark of relations between the peoples of the Soviet Union.

38. Martin Rady, "Nationalism and Nationality in Romania," in Paul Latawski, ed., *Contemporary Nationalism in East-Central Europe* (Basingstoke: Macmillan, 1995), p. 129.

39. Frances Millard, "Nationalism in Poland," in ibid., p. 116.

40. Andreas Kappeler, *Russland als Vielvölkerreich* (Munich: Verlag C. H. Beck, 1993).

41. Mark von Hagen, "The Russian Empire," in Karen Barkey and von Hagen, eds., *After Empire: Multi-Ethnic Societies and Nation-Building: The Soviet Union and the Russian, Ottoman, and Habsburg Empires* (Boulder, Colo.: Westview, 1997), pp. 65–66. See also the essays in Karen Dawisha and Bruce Parrott, eds., *The End of Empire? The Transformation of the USSR in Comparative Perspective* (Armonk, N.Y.: M. E. Sharpe, 1997).

42. Richard L. Rudolph and David F. Good, eds., *Nationalism and Empire: The Habsburg Monarchy and the Soviet Union* (New York: St. Martin's Press, 1992).

43. Michael Doyle, *Empires* (Ithaca: Cornell University Press, 1986).

44. Support or reliance by the state on one nationality implies lack of legitimacy and

lack of support from other nationalities. Some will doubtless question this assertion. For example, a case has been made in the South Asian context that the British enjoyed legitimacy. Quoting Sir Firoz Khan Noon, a former Pakistani prime minister, that "whoever could conquer a country was accepted as its legitimate ruler," Anthony Low states that the British governed India "with the acquiescence of the better-off peasantry." (D. A. Low, *Eclipse of Empire* [Cambridge: Cambridge University Press, 1990], p. 4.) To Dominic Lieven, such a view "smacks somewhat of the causes of legitimacy under Brezhnev. Coercion first, a legitimacy partly born of acceptance of the inevitable second, but a careful eye on the working class's material interests too." ("Empires, Russian and Other," in Marco Buttino, ed., *In a Collapsing Empire: Underdevelopment, Ethnic Conflicts and Nationalisms in the Soviet Union* (Milan: Feltrinelli Editore, 1993), pp. 89–103. A loyalist Muslim politician, knighted for his support of the Raj, would have elicited disagreement from Gandhi or Nehru, who spent eleven and nine years, respectively, organizing a nationalist movement that sought independence for India. One could look further afield. In the Eastern Europe of the cold war era, Havel in Czechoslovakia or Walesa in Poland would probably question the notion that collaborators confer legitimacy on foreign overlords. The point will probably be long debated. In this century, international law has recognized one main test of legitimacy—a multiparty election. No imperial ruler—and few authoritarian rulers—ever contested such an election.

45. On the part played by minorities in international relations and law, see Patrick Thornberry, *International Law and the Rights of Minorities* (Oxford: Clarendon Press, 1991), and idem, *Minorities and Human Rights Law*, and "Self-Determination, Minorities, Human Rights: A Review of International Instruments," *International and Comparative Law Quarterly*, vol. 38, part 4 (October 1989): 867–89; Alexis Heraclides, *The Self-Determination of Minorities in International Politics* (London: Frank Cass, 1991); Hurst Hannum, *Autonomy, Sovereignty and Self-Determination: The Accommodation of Conflicting Rights*; Catherine Brölmann, René Leféber and Marjoleine Zieck, eds., *Peoples and Minorities in International Law* (Dordrecht: Martinus Nijhoff, 1993); Jennifer Jackson Preece, *National Minorities and the European Nation-States System*; C. A. Macartney, *National States and National Minorities* and Alfred Cobban, *The Nation-State and National Self-Determination* are still worth reading.

46. Francesco Capotorti, *Study on the Rights of Persons Belonging to Ethnic, Religious and Linguistic Minorities* (New York: United Nations, 1991), pp. 10, 54.

47. *Convention on the Prevention and Punishment of the Crime of Genocide* (1948), Article 2.

48. Article 1 (3). See also Article 55(c).

49. Article 5.

50. Article 30.

51. Article 5.

52. Articles 2 and 4.

53. Article 2.

54. Articles 2 and 26.

55. Referred to hereafter as the *European Convention on Human Rights*: Article 14.

56. They included the Finno-Swedish agreement on the Åland Islands (1922) and the Austro-Italian agreement on the South Tyrol (1946). Hungary entered into agreements with Slovakia (1995) and Romania (1996) on the rights of Magyar minorities in those two countries. The Russo-Ukrainian Treaty (1997) respects the territorial integrity of both states.

57. Vernon van Dyke, "The Individual, the State and Ethnic Communities in Political Theory," in Will Kymlicka, ed., *The Rights of Minority Cultures* (Oxford: Oxford University Press, 1995), pp. 31–55; Will Kymlicka, *Multicultural Citizenship: A Liberal Theory of Minority Rights* (Oxford: Clarendon Press, 1995). On how some post–Communist states have tried to reconcile individual and group rights see Tamara J. Resler, "Dilemmas of Democratization: Safeguarding Minorities in Russia, Ukraine and Lithuania," *Europe-Asia Studies*, vol. 49, no. 1 (January 1997): 89–106.

58. BBC *Selected World Broadcasts (SWB)* EE 2509 15 January 1996, C/2, and EE/ 2510, 16 January 1996 C/5. See also Denis Deletant, "The Role of *'Vatra Romaneasca'* in Transylvania," in RFE/RL *Research Report*, vol. 2, no. 5 (1 February 1991): 28–37. The Hungarian-Slovak Treaty (1995) and Hungarian-Romanian Treaty (1996) make no reference to the collective rights of Magyar minorities.

59. Jean Manas, "The Council of Europe's Democracy Ideal and the Challenge of Ethno-National Strife," in Abram Chayes and Antonia Chayes, eds., *Preventing Conflict in the Post-Communist World: Mobilizing International and Regional Organizations* (Washington, D.C.: Brookings Institution, 1996), p. 130. Interestingly, the same point was made more than half a century ago in the Indian context by the Indian National Congress before independence. The Congress rejected calls by the Muslim League for communal representation on the grounds that it would deepen communal division. The political chasm between the Congress and the Muslim League proved unbridgeable, and it led to the partition of British India in 1947. After independence the Indian constitution provided for individual *and* group rights, and India's political institutions have accommodated minorities at the local, regional and national levels with considerable success. Yet India has also been scarred by recurrent outbreaks of communal violence and no less than three demands for secession in the last ten years. If there is any "lesson" from the Indian experience, it is probably that there is no blueprint for minorities problems.

60. Kymlicka, *Multicultural Citizenship*, pp. 69ff.; Ephraim Nimni, "Marx, Engels and the National Question," in Kymlicka, ed., *The Rights of Minority Cultures*, pp. 57–75. Walker Connor, *The National Question in Marxist-Leninist Theory and Strategy*. (Princeton: Princeton University Press, 1984), has a good bibliography of works by Marxist theorists.

61. For example, Samuel Huntington, "Political Development and Political Decay," in Claude E. Welch Jr., ed., *Political Modernization: A Reader in Comparative Political Change* (Belmont, Calif.: Wadsworth Publishing Co., 1967), p. 243–44; Alec Nove, "The Soviet Model and Underdeveloped Countries," in ibid., pp. 366–67; Samuel Huntington and Clement Moore, *Authoritarian Politics in Modern Society: The Dynamics of Established One-Party Systems* (New York: Basic Books, 1970), p. 515. Perceptions of events may be shaped by political needs or simply by the *zeitgeist*. In the post–cold war world, many would have said that the strong-arm methods used by the Soviets to "solve" their nationalities problems resulted in human rights abuses.

62. Article 3.

63. Article 3(2).

64. Yves Beigbeder, *International Monitoring of Plebiscites, Referenda and National Elections: Self-Determination and Transition to Democracy* (Dordrecht: Martinus Nijhoff, 1994).

65. Article 21(3) and Article 25 respectively.

66. Article 3 of Protocol 1 additional to the ECHR.

67. Linz and Stepan, *Problems of Democratic Transition*, pp. 366–67, 382.

Practical and Conceptual Dilemmas 25

68. See chapters 4 and 5.

69. The right to freedom of association is articulated in Article 20 of the *Universal Declaration of Human Rights*, Article 22 of the *International Convention on Civil and Political Rights*, Article 11 of the *European Convention for Human Rights*, paras. 6 and 32.6 of the *Copenhagen Document* and Article 7 of the CE *Framework Convention for National Minorities*.

70. "The people," like democracy, have not been defined in international law.

71. *UNHR*, pp. 143–46.

72. Ibid., pp. 229ff. See also the introduction by Boutros-Ghali to *UNHR*, pp. 5–47.

73. Rosalyn Higgins, "Responding to Individual Needs: Human Rights," *Problems and Processes: International Law and How We Use It* (Oxford: Clarendon Press, 1994), p. 95.

74. Iraq was the exception in 1991, and this was largely because the West wanted to embarrass Sadaam Hussein. See James Mayall, "Non-Intervention, Self-Determination and the " 'New World Order,' " *International Affairs*, vol. 67, no. 3 (July 1991): 421–29. The international community did not intervene militarily to stop human rights abuses by the Russian army in Chechnya between 1994 and 1996 and between 1999 and 2000, but NATO intervened in Kosovo ostensibly to uphold the values of democracy and human rights. See chapter 4.

75. For a fuller discussion of these points see R. J. Vincent, *Human Rights and International Relations* (Cambridge: Cambridge University Press, 1986); Hedley Bull, *The Anarchical Society*, pp. 79–80; Mayall, "Introduction," to James Mayall, ed., *The New Interventionism, 1991–1994: United Nations Experience in Cambodia, Former Yugoslavia and Somalia* (Cambridge: Cambridge University Press, 1996), especially pp. 5–7; Hannum, *Autonomy, Sovereignty and Self-Determination*, pp. 104ff.

76. On Hungary, see Edith Oltay, "Minority Rights Still an Issue in Hungarian-Romanian Relations," and "Minorities as Stumbling Block in Relations with Neighbors," RFE/RL *Research Report*, vol. 1, no. 12 (20 March 1992): 16–20 and vol. 1, no. 19 (8 May 1992): 26–33, respectively.

77. See chapter 5.

78. Thomas Carothers, "Democracy and Human Rights: Policy Allies or Rivals?" *Washington Quarterly*, vol. 17, no. 3 (summer 1994): 109–20.

79. UN Commission on Human Rights resolution on Promotion of Democracy, E/CN.4/RES/1999/57, 27 April 1999.

80. Ibid.

81. Some groups may be too small to form viable independent states.

82. See chapters 3 and 4.

83. Boutros-Ghali, *An Agenda for Peace*, 2nd ed. (New York: United Nations, 1995), para. 18, p. 77. This chapter will not deal with the whole spectrum of human rights, only with those aspects embracing minorities.

84. UN *Declaration on Minorities*.

85. Principles 18 and 19.

86. Part IV, para. 24.

87. Para. 30.

88. Article 1.

89. UN *Declaration on Minorities*, Article 3, para. 2, and Article 8. See also 34 I.L.M. 351 (1995+), especially the preamble to the Framework Convention, Article 3, para. 1; Articles 17, 20, 21; Jean Manas, "The Council of Europe's Democracy Ideal and

the Challenge of Ethno-National Strife," in Chayes and Chayes, eds., *Preventing Conflict in the Post-Communist World*, pp. 99–144; and Klaus Schumann, "The Role of the Council of Europe," in Miall, ed., *Minority Rights in Europe*, pp. 87–98.

90. Maria Amor Martin Estébanez, "The Protection of National or Ethnic, Religious and Linguistic Minorities," in Nanette A. Neuwahl and Allan Rosas, eds., *The European Union and Human Rights* (The Hague: Martinus Nijhoff, 1995), pp. 133–63.

91. *Geneva Report*, Section II.

92. The views of international officials are a contrast to the opinions of some others. For example, Richard Falk argued that "sovereignty was becoming obsolete in the era of globalization." "Toward Obsolescence: Sovereignty in the Era of Globalization," *Harvard International Review*, vol. 17, no. 3 (summer 1995): 35.

93. Article 8(4).

94. HCNM, Warsaw report, 12 November 1997. Emphasis in original.

95. Ibid.

96. Article 17.

97. Recommendation 34 (1997) on the European Charter of Regional Self-Government, Appendix, Article 10.

98. Preamble, *Charter for Regional or Minority Languages*.

99. Recommendation 34 (1997) on the European Charter of Regional Self-Government, Appendix, Article 8.

100. Article 14 of the CE *Charter for Regional or Minority Languages*.

Chapter 2
Managing Ethnic Diversity Through Political Structures and Ideologies: The Experiences of the Soviet Union, India, Spain and Sri Lanka

THE QUESTIONS

The fall of the Iron Curtain provided the immediate inspiration for the international community's advocacy of democracy as the most desirable way of managing ethnically mixed populations, but it is too early to pass a definitive judgment on the extent to which post-communist states have succeeded in forging democratic state-nations. However, long before the management of ethnic variety was placed on the international agenda, the political structures of countries such as the USSR, Spain, India and Sri Lanka were designed to accommodate their ethnically heterogeneous peoples. This chapter will try to assess how far they were able to do so and what lessons their experiences might offer to post-communist countries.

Ethnic schisms posed the greatest threat to the political unity and territorial integrity of all the countries under discussion. The political system of each country reflected the ideals as well as the methods by which its rulers sought to handle ethnic diversity. The Soviet Union—an authoritarian state throughout its history—was regarded by many as a model for other multiethnic countries, as a stable if stagnant authoritarianism that had solved its "nationalities problem."[1] The prospect of its splintering into fifteen republics was almost unthinkable until it happened in 1991.

The democracies selected for discussion—one in Western Europe and two in South Asia—have been chosen for the following reasons. Democracy developed in these countries after the Second World War under very different circumstances. In India democracy building followed independence from the British

Empire in 1947. Democracy in Spain was forged after the death of General Francisco Franco in 1975. Unlike the old nation-states, such as Britain and France, where the state was consolidated before nation-making began, democracy in India and Spain was a method of building a new state while simultaneously coping with ethnic variety. So their experiences may have some relevance for post-communist countries, if only because they lend some credibility to the views that democracy *can* bear a transplant and that the absence of strong liberal traditions does not have to be a barrier to democracy.

Eyebrows might be raised at the selection of countries so diverse, but perhaps international instruments can be taken at face value. The international preference for handling ethnic diversity through democracy implies, among other things, that culture is not a barrier to democracy.[2] The only way to test this assumption is to assess the degree to which culturally different democratizing countries were able to accommodate ethnically mixed populations. International officials take the view that democracy is a universal right, but they know that essential elements of democratic governance must be reconciled with diverse cultural traditions. A discussion of the ways in which culture has affected the course of democratization in India, Spain and Sri Lanka is beyond the scope of this book. The assumption underlying this chapter is that culture may be a variable, but it is not necessarily the determinant of a country's success or failure in forging democracy or in handling ethnic diversity. In making the comparisons, Donald Horowitz's advice will be kept in mind. "There is no guarantee that any three cases of a given phenomenon will adequately represent the range of variables that go into the making of that phenomenon. This is particularly so when the three cases ... selected ... represent yet another variable: geographic distribution. Consequently, the attempt ... to extract some recurring principles ... is problematic."[3] And yet, some generalizations may emerge from a comparison. To study Soviet efforts from a broader perspective, I will juxtapose some aspects of the Soviet, Indian and Spanish experiences so that the similarities and differences between them can be compared in order to illuminate aspects that may not otherwise be apparent. For example, some scholars have argued that the federal architecture of the USSR institutionalized ethnic identities and demands which culminated in the breakup of that country.[4] But in many other countries, federal structures have moderated such demands and contained conflict.[5] Why did this not happen in the Soviet Union?

AUTHORITARIAN STATES

The Soviet Union

The call for democratic institutions to manage ethnic variety implicitly acknowledges that the Soviet Union failed to solve its nationalities problem—and rightly so. It also questions the assumption that nationalism had withered away under communism. No existing theory of nationalism or democracy is based on the Soviet experience, and the disintegration of the USSR questions many existing assumptions about nationalism and national integration not only in the Soviet Union but also in other multinational countries. First, the advocacy of democracy challenges a general idea that "strong," highly centralized states, using a great deal of coercion, are likely to modernize traditional, economically backward societies, stamp out insular prejudices and forge enlightened, progressive and developed nations.[6]

Second, the anti-Soviet, anti-Russian stance of non-Russian republics can be explained partly by the fact that the assimilationist policies of the Soviet state implied Russification, partly by discrimination against non-Russians and their relatively low representation in the highest organs of state. However, given the preponderance of Russians in the Communist Party of the Soviet Union (CPSU) and in the Soviet government, and also the official identification of Russia with the Soviet state, how can one explain why the government of the Russian Federation turned against the Soviet state in 1990–91 and dealt it the *coup de grace*?

Third, as most countries have multiethnic, multireligious, multilingual populations, the potential for secessionist claims by dissatisfied minorities exists in many of them. Yet the historical record suggests that secession is rarely the first demand of nationalists.[7] In the Soviet Union, not all the nationalisms were secessionist. Why, then, couldn't the Soviet state accommodate them? Theories about "elites" and "federalism" do not even raise these questions; one must probe further and ask whether the authoritarian ideology and nature of the Soviet state precluded reconciliation and accommodation. The question is important, if only because most post–Communist countries are multiethnic.

The Soviet case may be particularly instructive, as Soviet leaders claimed that they would launch a social, economic and ideological revolution from above and consolidate union. The state would be the precursor of social change; it would remake the environment, speed up the demise of national cultures and create a socialist culture, a new political idiom and even a new social and political Man. Today we know that Soviet-style authoritarianism, modernization and the command economy failed to cement union. The Soviet state could not carry out economic reform without renegotiating the terms of its existence, and the combination of political illegitimacy and economic disarray culminated in its collapse.

The rest of this section will outline the ideological basis of the economic, religious, educational and language policies of these countries. The elites of all countries sought to consolidate statehood. Soviet leaders hoped to create a new Soviet Man; Indian, Spanish and Sri Lankan leaders harbored no such ambition. A blow-by-blow historical account of the policies of so many countries is beyond the scope of this book, but an attempt will be made to outline results of policies, especially insofar as they gave rise to, or helped to contain, regional or nationalist sentiment that challenged existing states. Why did the ideology and political structures of the USSR preclude reconciliation between the center and the republics? To what extent and why have democracies like India and Spain been able to handle ethnic heterogeneity?

Ethnic Divisions in the USSR and their Significance

If an ethnic core, common language, historical memory and shared vision are essentials of nationhood, then the USSR defied most definitions of "nation." But it was not unique in this respect. Ninety percent of the world's states are multiethnic, and ethnicity and territory have rarely been congruent in history, but few countries had a population as ethnically diverse as the Soviet Union. More than one hundred groups were recognized as "nationalities," and many of them identified with one of the twelve religions officially recognized by the Soviet state. In spite of its heterogeneous character, it is arguable that the USSR met better than Yugoslavia, Switzerland or India, the conventional criteria for being judged a "nation" and for surviving as a multiethnic state.[8] In the Russian population the USSR had an ethnic core, and Russians dominated the ruling Communist Party. Russian, the official lingua franca, was spoken by the majority of Soviet citizens.

Consolidating Union: The Ideological Basis

Soviet conceptions of nationalism must be seen against the background of Communist ideology, which was simultaneously the source of legitimization of the Soviet state and its *leitmotif*.[9] Conceptions of nationalism have varied with territory and time. In many countries, developing among an ethnically diverse population a sense of common belonging and identity has been described as nation-making; in the USSR this was called "internationalism," while nationalism implied a parochial mentality, caught in a bourgeois time warp. To the "internationally minded" Soviet leaders, nationalism represented the nefarious attempts of the bourgeoisie to dampen the class consciousness of the population by obscuring class differences within each nation and by encouraging rivalry among the proletariat of various nations. Soviet leaders acknowledged that national rivalries could be utilized by communists to win the class struggle: those that came into conflict with the interests of the Communist Party would be crushed. For Soviet leaders from Lenin onwards, the term "internationalism" meant their conception of the Soviet Union as one country. They claimed that the dictatorship of the proletariat was the only regime capable of ensuring peaceful coexistence and cooperation among nationalities.

From the outset, Soviet leaders openly affirmed that the dictatorship of the proletariat would be based on unlimited force, not law. This dictatorship would abolish the parliamentary system of separation of executive and legislative powers; it would be unrestricted by any rules and based directly on violence. Throughout the existence of the USSR, the relationship between the state and the people was based on coercion. Terror was simultaneously one of the primary instruments of governance and an outstanding characteristic of the Soviet state.

To win over nationalities, the Soviet tactic was to promise all nations equality under the constitution. The USSR was an amalgamation of Union Republics, each named after a national group and theoretically having the right of secession. In reality, Soviet leaders had no intention of allowing any republic to secede.[10] Inspired by an ideology which made no distinction between state and society or any allowance for separation of powers, Soviet leaders assumed that all nations would accept the CPSU as the ruling party and that its leadership alone would make political decisions. Throughout the existence of the USSR, the CPSU was the supreme political force. "Democratic centralism" meant that decisions of the central leadership of the Party would be binding on lower bodies regardless of their national composition. The republican communist parties were subordinate to the Central Committee. The Party's control over all republican and local institutions signified the undermining of the authority of republican governments. This extreme centralization almost nullified any real federalism in the Soviet Union. The acknowledgment of cultural diversity did not imply acceptance of political and intellectual diversity; rather, the Soviets either assumed, or were determined to invent, a single will. They sought to do this by a combination of intellectual and social engineering. Under Stalin the state became the agent of revolutionary social and economic change. Every resource of the CPSU was deployed to transform the USSR into an industrialized world power and to forge a new political culture and a new political and social Man.[11]

Consolidating Union? Economic Policies

Economic ideas have primacy in Marxist-Leninist thinking, according to which the relationships of production constitute society's base. The Soviets sought to change prerevolutionary social structures by redistributing political and economic power. This was necessary both to modernize the USSR and to wipe out nationalism, which was a hangover from a society dominated by the bourgeoisie. Collectivization abolished private property, liquidated real or imagined *kulaks*, physically if necessary, organized peasants into collective farms and established state control over agriculture. It was also a means of breaking the will of the non-Russian peoples for self-determination and guaranteeing their subjugation under Stalin's dictatorship.[12]

Despite its successes the Soviet economy was running into difficulties by Khrushchev's time, and, as we shall see, in the late eighties it combined with the nationalities problem to bring about the collapse of the USSR. Yet the Soviet Union was not the world's only country with an inefficient economy or ethnic problems; and these factors alone cannot explain its disintegration. The dilemma was that its economy could not be reformed without a renewal of the relationship between Moscow and the Union Republics, implying the need for changes in the nature of the Soviet state itself. As we shall see, it is because these changes were too little and too late that the Soviet Union fell apart.

Social Engineering and Assimilation: Consolidation or Fragmentation?

Soviet religious, education and language policies were the most important instruments in attempting to create a single culture identified with the state and a central educational system run by the state and to make all citizens, regardless of linguistic background, speak a single "state" language. From Lenin onwards Soviet leaders envisaged that as the USSR advanced to communism, a process of *sblizhennie*, or rapprochement, of nations would be followed by their *sliyannie*, or complete assimilation and amalgamation. Though not explicitly stated, the idea was that there would be assimilation into the Russian culture.

The coincidence of ethnic and religious loyalties was regarded by Soviet leaders as a barrier to political integration.[13] Religion was a key issue in the party's ideological activity; it was an enemy which had to be routed. Eradicating religion was, above all, a political task, an essential element in the political struggle against all class forces hostile to the Communist Party itself. In the USSR the separation of church from state literally meant breaking the power of the church. The decision to grant citizenship and equality of rights to all minorities implied inspiration from a secular modernity; it also struck at the primacy of the Russian Orthodox Church. This did not mean good treatment or tolerance of all religions: whether in Russia or Central Asia, the constitutions of 1918 and 1924 granted freedom of religion and also the freedom to carry out antireligious activities, but the state banned schools run by religious organizations and confiscated land owned by the church.

This ideological engineering was accompanied by political pragmatism. The Kremlin's perceptions of the nationalities problem and its religious policies were linked. The special features of a particular religion, its attitude toward the state, the perceived extent of its adaptability to the social and political changes desired by Soviet leaders were all taken into account in framing policies towards religious groups. For example, in Central Asia, Union Republics were created to counter pan-Islamic and pan-Turkic sentiment; in Russia Soviet leaders from Stalin to Gorbachev made the Orthodox Church serve the interests of the state.

Education has been an instrument of political and social integration in many countries, including the Soviet Union. In 1924 a uniform educational structure was set up throughout the USSR, and over the next two decades millions of poor peasants were educated. One of the most important tasks of the Party was to erase the "nationalist" memory if it conflicted with the interests of the Soviet state, to revive it or to shape it in a manner that suited the interests of the state. History was rewritten; its guiding principle was not "bourgeois objectivism" but "the principle of . . . Communist Party-mindedness."[14] In addition, officially approved art, music and literature and state control over the mass media were expected to remove all vestiges of nationalism from the popular consciousness. Soviet citizens were expected to adopt official values and beliefs as personal commitments.

Marxist-Leninist theoreticians attached great importance to language as a controlling factor in the formation of national consciousness. From the twenties onward, the Kremlin was intent on establishing Russian as the "Soviet language," and in 1938 the study of Russian was made compulsory in all schools. As publishing was a state monopoly, it is significant that the number of publications in Russian far surpassed that in other Soviet languages. But in a manner not quite anticipated by Benedict Anderson,[15] the official monopoly of the printing press failed to create an "imagined Soviet community."

The generalization that can be made is that assimilation failed to create a new Soviet Man. Glasnost confirmed the limited attractions of "internationalism"; it also established the failure of the Soviet state to break the link between religion and nationalism. In terms of the practical needs of a multilingual state, the official desire to have a single lingua franca was understandable. The policy succeeded to the extent that most Soviet citizens spoke Russian. However, statistics for the year 1989 show that 84 percent of non-Russians identified with their native language, and only 48 percent spoke Russian as a second language.[16] Whether or how much a knowledge of Russian shaped a "Soviet consciousness" is another matter. The evidence is that the imposition of Russian alienated most non-Russians. In many republics even members of the CPSU worked to further the use of the titular language. In 1976 and 1978 protests against teaching in Russian in Tbilisi University took place in Georgia, and Moscow did not succeed in removing a reference to Georgian as the official language of the republic from the republic's constitution. In 1980 demonstrations were organized in Estonia to protest against the small number of publications in Estonian and to demand legal safeguards for the status of Estonian. After 1985 in almost every non-Russian republic there were protests against the suppression of local languages and cultures and official attempts at Russification; there were also demands that republican languages be given primacy in their republics. The scale of the demonstrations belied the Communist Party's claim that different languages and cultures had flourished under Soviet rule, and its boast that the Soviets had achieved the "union and consolidation of peoples with equal rights."[17]

Authoritarianism, Forces for Change and the Failure of Accommodation

One important lesson emerging from the history of the USSR is that support from "elites" of any society can never be a permanent guarantee of support and stability for a government. Societies and their elites are not static; ethnic identities and demands are in a constant state of flux. The key fact here is *change*. Politicians in any country, practicing the art of the possible, must take into account social, economic and other changes in their societies. The failure of the Soviet central leadership and Soviet political structures was that they failed to accommodate and manage the changing social and political forces that had become visible after 1985 and which were a consequence of Soviet policies.

One element of *divide et impera* by the Soviet regime was to use Russia against other republics in a number of ways and at several levels. Stalin invoked Great Russian nationalism in support of the Soviet state. Aware that ethnic delineation of territory could solidify ethnic identities, the Soviets sought to preempt this eventuality by encouraging migration of Russians to the non-Russian republics. During the fifties, Khrushchev's treatment of Kazakhs illustrated how ruthlessly the Soviet state was prepared to trample on minorities to advance its own interests. The massive Slav immigration into Kazakhstan under the Virgin Lands scheme turned the Kazakhs into a minority in their own republic. To achieve this, Khrushchev overrode objections by Kazakh party leaders, sacked local party officials and replaced them with Slavs.[18] At another level, the Kremlin made a show of fair play and recruited local Communists in the republics, and the republican First Party Secretary belonged to the titular nationality. But the Second Secretary was always a Russian, and was appointed by the center. Responsible for cadre policy, the Second Secretary's task was to select and deploy local party officials, neutralize the influence of the local First Secretary and prevent his building up a personal following.[19]

Gorbachev broke with the past in many ways, but he continued "pro-Russian" policies. The center under Gorbachev encouraged Russians in the Baltic republics to resist the political claims of the titular nationalities.[20] These Russian communities had support from sections of the military and the KGB. The official extolling of Russian virtues and the identification of "Russia" with the Soviet state only turned most non-Russians against the center and "Russia." The CPSU was dominated by Russians, and most non-Russians associated Russians with some of the worst excesses of the Soviet regime. During perestroika, when most non-Russians were demanding greater representation at the center, Gorbachev's Politburo after 1989 was the most Russified and the most Slavic in Soviet history: it included only one non-Slav, Eduard Shevardnadze. In 1986 the unprecedented appointment of a Russian, Gennadi Kolbin, as First Party Secretary in Kazakhstan ignited anti-Russian violence in Almaty. At another level, Gorbachev spurned demands from Uzbek party leaders for greater resources for the economic development of their republic while increasing the amounts invested in Russia. And at a time when every non-Russian republic was insisting on the use of its titular language as the official language, Gorbachev's first draft of the Union Treaty annoyed most republics by proposing that Russian should be the state language of the USSR. It is quite likely that Gorbachev, desperately trying to extract an agreement from dissident republican leaders, was more maladroit than sinister, but his attitudes savored of gross insensitivity to non-Russians and hardly endeared his policies to them.

The history of the USSR raises many questions about the extent to which the Soviet state could be identified with the Russian majority. To many people—Russians and non-Russians, foreign academics and policy-makers—the two were synonymous. Gorbachev's reference, in March 1991, to "a state that is 1000 years old"[21] stressed the continuity of the Tsarist and Soviet states as "Russian" and underlined the association of Russia with the Soviet state. Nevertheless, there may be a good case to heed John Dunlop's advice that "Russia" should not be equated with the Soviet state.[22] Political expediency motivated the Soviet state under Stalin to exploit great Russian nationalism, but Stalin and his successors also launched a systematic assault on Russian culture and the Orthodox Church. Not surprisingly, many Russian nationalists alleged that the Soviet state had destroyed Russian culture and that Russians had been the victims of Soviet rule. Russia's political luminaries have yet to agree upon or articulate in detail their country's identity as a "nation"; nevertheless, Boris Yeltsin, between 1989 and 1991, challenged the Kremlin's writ and represented the idea that the Soviet state was unresponsive to Russia's interests and that new political arrangements were necessary to protect them. In other words, he exposed the rift between Russia and the Soviet state even as he deepened that rift. Russia refused to pay taxes to the center; Yeltsin declared that all Soviet troops on Russian territory would be under the jurisdiction of the Russian Soviet Federative Socialist Republic (RSFSR).[23] August 1991 found Russia in revolt against the Soviet state, and this revolt made a decisive contribution to the collapse of the USSR.

Authoritarianism, Political Structures and Breakdown

Nevertheless, it is arguable that the emergence of separatist nationalisms in the Union Republics was not inevitable. The winds of nationalism blew through all republics, a storm in some, a mere breeze in others. Common to all non-Russian republics was resistance to Russification, but all non-Russian elites did not demand secession. In the referendum of March 1991 some 70 percent of all Soviet citizens wanted their republics to stay within the union. Before the coup in August 1991 voters in only six republics—the three Baltic republics, Georgia, Armenia and Moldova—opted for independence; in other republics they voted in favor of remaining in the union.

In an attempt to resuscitate an increasingly inefficient command economy, the center under Gorbachev decentralized power and sought to negotiate a new relationship between the center and the republics. After 1985 the monolithic ethos of the CPSU was challenged by criticism from within the Party and by popular sentiment in the republics. The Party leadership in Moscow acknowledged the demand for the autonomy of republican parties but responded by affirming the unitary principle in party organization. It refused to recognize a diversity of interests and opinions, so the question of its creating institutions to give that diversity expression or representation hardly arose. In the absence of such institutions, "federalization" of the Party would not have contained separatism in the USSR any more than it did in Yugoslavia. It is worth underlining that most national movements in the USSR were not secessionist and were led by communists, yet the Soviet leadership was unable to accommodate them.

The shortcomings of the Soviet brand of federalism were most apparent in the economy. The economic crisis faced by the Soviet Union after 1985 has been detailed elsewhere,[24] from the perspective of this book it is sufficient to see the ways in which Gorbachev was obliged to renegotiate the relationship between the center and the republics.[25] Gorbachev agreed to implement laws on economic sovereignty, but their implementation was blocked by central institutions and policy was paralyzed by jurisdictional disputes between Moscow and republican governments. The center could no longer "command" the economy; instead it confronted increasingly fractious republics on economic issues. The problem was that in the absence of mediatory institutions, differences between the center and republics expanded into conflicts, and conflicts in turn became irreconcilable.[26]

DEMOCRACIES

In contrast, a low-income country like India has faced three major secessionist movements during the last two decades, but at the same time a succession of minority governments has won parliamentary support for the most radical economic legislation in India's history. These minority governments have been coalitions of several political parties—something which would have been unthinkable in the Soviet Union. The example of India is analogous with that of post–Franco Spain, which has yet to succeed in defusing Basque secessionist demands but which has simultaneously seen the forging of political alliances between regional and national parties at the center, democratic consolidation, economic growth and increasing regional autonomy. Conflict, then, is a fact, a fundamental of Indian and Spanish politics, but so is consensus. Is it because their political structures proffer more alternatives and, thus, more opportunities to accommodate political, intellectual and ethnic diversity? And can the failure of the USSR to reconcile ethno-political differences be laid at the door of its authoritarian political system which did not offer these options?

In common with the Soviet Union, Spain and India have dominant majority communities, but their experiences do not bear out the pessimistic view that democracy "always" results in domination by the majority. And although India and Spain have been defined by their constitutions as unions, there has been a real division of powers between the center and regions. In contrast, the Soviet Union was described by its constitution as "A Federal State,"[27] but political power was concentrated in the hands of its Communist Party. The Soviet constitution recognized the country's ethnic diversity but did not create the political institutions through which its varied peoples could articulate their changing multiple identities and interests. Spain and India, on the other hand, have crafted political institutions within which it is possible for ethnic identities to coexist with, or even be transcended by, a more pluralist national identity.

The potential of democracy for handling ethnic variety stems from the opportunities it presents for building consensus. It offers different ways of dealing with change and conflict, and much depends on the choices made by leaders. The countries discussed below do have different forms of democratic government, but in the cases of India and Spain democracy has had some success in reconciling ethnic variety.

India: Democracy, Diversity, Consensus and Conflict

The desire of the political majority of Indians to forge an Indian nation was demonstrated during the independence movement against the British Raj. After 1947 the strategies of Indian leaders, especially Jawaharlal Nehru, were built on the idea that nations are made, not born.[28] Recognizing India's ethnic *mélange*, Indian nationalists defined the nation in secular and pluralistic terms to accommodate its religious, cultural and linguistic diversity. To them nonviolence, parliamentary democracy and secularism offered the most effective means of nation-building, for these implied that no single group could dominate the other. Nonviolence was not merely a reflection of some spiritual tradition or a necessity in a fragmented society in which there existed an enormous potential for violence; it was also a concomitant of democracy. India's nationalist leaders disliked the violent language of communism, the fact that communism did not seek to change by peaceful democratic pressures but by coercion, destruction and extermination. In contrast, they envisaged that universal adult suffrage would draw all communities and classes into the political process, that parliamentary democracy would afford a means of resolving political differences peacefully and that parliament would constitute the unity of the Indian people. India, asserted Nehru, could not be governed in any other way. In the nineties challenges by Hindu nationalist parties to secularism—and to the rule of law itself—proved him right, for they sharply exacerbated communal conflict.

India's political institutions have been created on the assumption of a plurality of identities, interests, ideas and the existence of political, social and intellectual differences within social or political groups. The recognition of this diversity is marked, not merely by a real division of powers between the center and regions, but by the constitutional authority of the Supreme Court to adjudicate in disputes between the center and regions and between the individual and the state. India has a multiparty system, and the Indian state is not synonymous with any ethnic, religious or linguistic group.[29]

India: The Absence of Uniformity

In India universal literacy and a uniform system of education remain seemingly unattainable. Education is largely a regional domain. Minority rights and cultural freedom have meant, among other things, that regional governments, religious and ethnic groups can set up schools with the medium of instruction and syllabuses of their choice. Given the fact that barely 3 percent of India's GNP is spent on education, New Delhi's inability to impose anything on regional governments and the discord among Indian leaders and intellectuals themselves on the substance of the Indian identity, the devising and implementation of a uniform system of education is fraught with political risks for any government that dares to attempt it. To the pessimists, India's education system reflects the confusion of the Indian identity and the ill-conceived priorities of Indian leaders; to the optimists, it represents yet another successful compromise between New Delhi and regional governments. One hopes that the optimists will be proved correct.

In India, as in the Soviet Union, secularism has also meant the separation of church from state, but it has never implied the rooting out of religion. Indian secularism is predicated on the assumption that every religion has its own morality; therefore the state must have its own set of values. According to Articles 25, 26 and 27 of the constitution, the state will not discriminate against or bestow patronage on any religion.

All citizens have liberty of faith, belief and worship with the right to be agnostic or atheist. Every religion denomination has the right to manage its own affairs and acquire property. Religious instruction is prohibited in state schools, but is allowed in private educational institutions. On religious issues one is confronted with several paradoxes in India. Merely identifying with a religion does not create political conflict, and election studies show that religious affiliation does not necessarily determine the choices made by voters. The Hindu-nationalist Bharatiya Janata Party (BJP) has yet to win a majority of votes or seats in parliament, and since 1997 it has only been able to form governments at the center by coalescing with regional parties. Religion will not endanger the stability of India just because politicians exploit it for political gains; it will endanger stability if they depart from nonviolent democratic norms and use force to achieve political goals. The destruction of the Babri Masjid mosque in 1992 by Hindu extremists and the violence against Christians in 1998 illustrate this. Breaking democratic norms leads to communal violence; practicing them makes it possible for Indians to possess simultaneously a religious and an all-India identity.

In India controversy over languages centered around three questions: What should be the official language? How long should English continue to be an official language? What should be the status of regional languages?[30] The Official Languages Act of 1967 laid down that Hindi and English would be used in parliament and in communication between the center and Hindi-speaking states and that English would remain the language of communication between the center and non-Hindi speaking states. Within states, the regional language would be used. This arrangement, known as the "three language formula," defused tension over the national language. The drawing of state boundaries on linguistic lines after 1956 satisfied the demand for linguistic states and recognition of the main regional languages as official languages eased friction over their status. Although India has not come up with any definitive solution to the language problem, perhaps the approach has not been altogether unrealistic.

India: Political Coalitions and Consensus

India is a union of twenty-nine states and seven union territories, which were created on a linguistic basis. Regional governments are elected, but the center has a substantial array of powers in relation to them. It controls the most lucrative sources of taxation and can declare an emergency in the whole or any part of India. The Indian parliament can nullify any legislation passed by a state legislature. However, certain subjects, including language, agrarian reform and education, are regional subjects. New Delhi can only enunciate a policy; its implementation depends on regional governments. The Congress—as the ruling party for most of the time until the end of the eighties—was a broad coalition representing several, sometimes conflicting, interests, which were frequently a hurdle in the way of implementing social and economic reform. However, the inclusive nature of the Congress widened its appeal to all classes and communities. In its heyday under Nehru the Congress was home to strong regional leaders whose presence in the party was viewed by him as essential to make the party truly representative of the political majority. The highhandedness of Indira and Rajiv Gandhi resulted in the decline of inner-party democracy and the marginalization of powerful regional leaders. But no amount of string pulling from New Delhi on the inept regional congressmen favored by the Gandhis could shore up the appeal of the party, and the Congress lost much of its grassroots support.

Regional and communal parties have sometimes formed coalitions with one another, sometimes with the Congress. They have also competed in all-India elections and been represented in parliament. The present Indian government, elected in October 1999, is a coalition led by the Hindu-nationalist BJP which includes regional parties. Unlike its two predecessors since 1996, it has a small majority in parliament. No single party in the coalition won a majority of the votes polled or seats in parliament. The inclusion of regional parties in the government has enhanced their sense of involvement in national issues, although the region has remained their main constituency. The significant point is that their representation in parliament and in the regional government or legislature has depended first and foremost on their electoral success. The political majority in India is quite distinct from the ethnic majority. It simultaneously transcends regional and communal identities while co-existing with them and reflects and reinforces the multiple identities of most Indians.

The Congress party held office at the center for most of the period after 1947. Its strength was its ability to be a broad ideological front encompassing political opinion from the left to the right of the ideological spectrum, and its success owed much to its appeal to Indians of all classes and communities. The term "power-sharing" does not adequately describe the very broad ideological and intercommunal coalition that has been the Congress party, its inclusiveness, and its political success, both at the all-India and regional levels. Since May 1996, most coalition governments have been led by the BJP. Two of these coalitions were minority governments. The latest, elected in September-October 1999, has a parliamentary majority, and its impact on center-state and communal relations is unpredictable.

Democracy has meant that Indian federalism has rested upon multiple centers of power and competing political identities. W. H. Morris-Jones described India as a "bargaining federalism,"[31] S.A.H. Haqqi and A. P. Sharma labeled it a "centralized federalism."[32] Debate over the nature of Indian federalism will continue; the crucial point is that India's democratic constitution has provided for the setting up of machinery to settle disputes, to strike bargains between the center and the states and between states. These include the Finance Commission, the Interstate Council and Zonal Councils. In addition, the center has retained leverage over the states because of their inability to draw up state plans and to raise the revenues needed for their own expenditures. This has made them dependent on transfers of revenue from the center.

India: Diversity, Centralization and Conflict

At the same time the political landscape has been scarred by outbreaks of communal violence, and during the last decade the Indian state has confronted demands for secession in Punjab and Kashmir. It also has had to defuse threats from Hindu nationalists to the rights and very existence of minorities in India. The Hindu-nationalist BJP or its supporters were behind communal violence against Muslims in the early nineties and against Christians in 1998, so the impact of its leadership of a national coalition on communal relations remains to be seen.

The political, social and economic factors underlying ethnic tensions in India are complex, but the themes of political insecurity and expediency recur. Electoral setbacks suffered by the Congress in the elections of 1967 (although it was able to form a government at the center) prompted Indira Gandhi's attempts to tighten New Delhi's grip over state governments. Her machinations only strained center-state relations, and damaged the consensus forged by Jawaharlal Nehru.

In Punjab and Kashmir the attempt to centralize went hand in hand with encouragement to Sikh extremists in the hope that they would counterpoise a moderate Akali party in Punjab.[33] It is significant that, until the seventies, the Akalis never had won a majority in Punjab and had been able to form a government in the state only by coalescing with other parties. Perhaps the shortsightedness of Indira Gandhi's tactics can best be summed up by saying that it was a case of encouraging extremists to checkmate moderates with the intent of strengthening Indira—who came to equate herself with "India." The strategy backfired and bequeathed to Indira Gandhi's successors a problem that took some ten years to overcome. The extremists resorted to force, which was met with force, denting the edifice of Indian democracy.

In Kashmir, Rajiv Gandhi's government rigged elections in 1987 with a view to defeating the National Conference, a moderate political party. In the light of the poor electoral performance of regional and communal parties in Kashmir, this ploy appears as mystifying as Indira Gandhi's machinations in Punjab. In regional and all-India elections held in 1967 and 1972, the Congress polled 53 and 55.4 percent of the vote respectively, while the National Conference obtained 46.2 and 47.3 percent respectively in the elections of 1977 and 1983. In a state in which some 90 percent of the population are Muslims, the performance of Muslim communal parties—the Muslim United Front and the Jamaat-I-Islami—was dismal. Together they obtained 7.2 percent of the votes in 1972, 3.6 percent in 1977, and 20 percent in 1987. Essentially, election results showed a fairly well functioning parliamentary democracy in Kashmir, and it is the deliberate distortion of democratic norms by Rajiv Gandhi's government that played a major role both in causing disillusionment with Indian democracy and in provoking separatism. Intervention by Pakistan, a fuller discussion of which is beyond the scope of this work,[34] also contributed to the uprising in 1989, and India still faces an uphill struggle in restoring normalcy to the state. Attempts to hold elections failed several times in the face of separatist threats, and, as in Punjab, the use of force by New Delhi and separatists raised doubts about the quality of Indian democracy.

There is another factor that has triggered separatist movements and communal violence in India. Indian elections have shown, time and again, that the ethnic and political nations do not necessarily coincide. Some regional and communal parties, therefore, have failed to achieve political preponderance, even within their chosen constituencies, and have been unable to form governments at the national and all-India levels. In other words, democracy has not always worked to the advantage of many communal and regional parties. Frustration at their continual inability to secure electoral majorities has led them to try to mobilize popular support through armed militancy.[35]

India illustrates that democracy is not an ironclad guarantee of success in managing ethnic diversity. The politics of accommodation have generally eased linguistic, religious and ethnic tensions in India; attempts to suppress pluralism or to use force to achieve political ends have exacerbated them. In other words, breaking democratic norms has dented consensus, while the conscious practice of democracy has enlarged the area of consensus. India's mixed experiences suggest that the choice of political means is at least as important as intellectually and politically pluralistic concepts of nation in maintaining consensus and keeping ethnic conflict at bay.

Spain: Consensus through Diversity?

Spain has been a sovereign state since the fifteenth century when the marriage of Ferdinand of Aragon to Elizabeth of Castile united several independent kingdoms.[36] Some 98 percent of the population are Spaniards, but a history of fissiparous tendencies always made Spain's leaders concerned for their country's political unity. After the seventeenth century Spain saw five civil wars—the first in 1640 and the last between 1936 and 1939. Since the early nineteenth century political and social division imposed a heavy burden on Spain's liberal traditions. There were conflicts between defenders of the Catholic Church and anticlerics, between votaries and practitioners of strong central and regional nationalists, between the industrial north and northeastern regions and the agricultural south, between left and right. The liberal constitution of 1876 set up a constitutional monarchy, but liberal politics were often interrupted. For example, in the twentieth century a military coup in 1923 overthrew the government formed under the constitution. The republic established in 1931 dissolved within five years in a civil war that ended with the installation of an authoritarian regime by General Francisco Franco in 1939. Thereafter Spain remained an authoritarian state until Franco's death in 1975.

Tussles over the distribution of powers between the center and the regions heightened concern for Spanish unity among Spain's leaders. Resistance to centralization reared its head time and again in Catalonia, Andalusia and Navarra. Franco saw the answer in a strongly centralized system of rule and attempted to impose the Spanish language, laud the glories of Spanish unity and stamp out any expression of regional identity. Catalonia was the only autonomous republic under the 1931 constitution. Any talk of devolution or federalism was frowned upon as separatist and was not tolerated. Economic policy-making was highly centralized, with the emphasis on national rather than regional development. These centralist policies only served to provoke Basque and Catalan nationalisms.

Making the transition from repressive centralization to democracy therefore was not easy. The overriding aim of Franco's successors was to create a political system that would allow Spain's diverse cultural and linguistic identities and interests to be articulated. Following his accession to power in 1975, King Juan Carlos stressed the unity of Spain and its "special regional characteristics as an expression of the diversity of peoples" that made up the country. The constitution recognized the existence of a common culture among all Spaniards, but the Autonomous Communities could promote regional cultures. This statement of intent signalled a departure from Franco's authoritarianism and strong centralization. Political democracy, linked with political and social rights, became the means through which regionalism would be simultaneously expressed and contained.

Spain's democratic constitution was framed in 1978. Based on consensus, it was endorsed in a referendum in which more than 60 percent of eligible voters participated. In the Basque country, 89 percent of those voting expressed approval of the constitution; in Catalonia, 88 percent. The constitution also had the support of all parties except the Basque separatists.

The overwhelming majority of Spain's citizens are Spaniards, Catholic by religion, and have Castilian as their mother tongue. The constitution recognizes the multinational and multilingual character of Spain's citizens and guarantees the right of self-government of its nationalities and regions. The term "nationalities" was used instead of the more controversial "nation." Politically, one of the most significant points of the constitution is its recognition that other "nationalities"—namely, the Basques, Catalans and Galicians—exist within the "one and indivisible Spanish nation." The preamble of the constitution proclaims the will of "the Spanish Nation" to "protect all Spaniards and peoples of Spain in the exercise of human rights, their cultures and traditions, languages, and institutions." Article 3(3) recognizes the richness of Spain's linguistic diversity as "a cultural patrimony which will be the object of special respect and protection." Article 3(1) defines Castilian as the official language, Article 3(2) affirms that the other languages of Spain "will also be official in the respective autonomous communities." Catalan, Galician and Basque are the other major languages. Spaniards have freedom of movement throughout the country. The church is no longer identified with the state. Article 16(3) lays down that there is no state religion, and the Law on Religious Freedom, passed in July 1980, conferred equal status on all religions, religious communities and churches.

Administratively, Spain is divided into municipalities and Autonomous Communities. There are seventeen Autonomous Communities, and they were created between 1979 and 1983, following protracted negotiations between the center and each individual region. The outcome was an unevenly decentralized political structure giving different levels of autonomy to different regions.

The constitution of 1978 took the sting out of Basque and Catalan nationalisms by giving Catalonia, the Basque region and Galicia special status as historic regions. Autonomous Communities are subdivided into provinces, and a province can achieve a degree of autonomy equivalent to that of a region by a local referendum if it wins a majority vote in favor from each of the region's provinces. In this way the constitution provides a mechanism for altering political arrangements in a democratic manner. Autonomy statutes can only be altered by regional and central authorities and must be passed by an absolute majority in regional parliaments, the *Cortes*, and by referenda. As in India, elections have shown that the alignment of territory and ethnicity do not necessarily stand in the way of the emergence of a strong sense of national identity embracing multiple identities.

A division of powers—*competencias*—exists between the center and the regions. The center has exclusive jurisdiction over thirty-one subjects, including defense, justice, foreign policy and the economy. The Autonomous Communities are responsible for education, health, housing, culture, agriculture and local transport. The Autonomous Communities have the power to levy their own taxes. However, it would be impolitic for them to raise the fiscal burdens of their populations, and only about 2 percent of their revenues come from regional taxes. They receive much of their revenue from "tax-sharing grants" from the central budget. In the event of conflict between national and regional law, the national law prevails. The *Cortes* may pass legislation even on subjects of regional competence. The Constitutional Court was created with a view to adjudicating in disputes between Madrid and the regions and between regions and, in a sense, safeguards the cultural diversity of Spain.

Basque separatism, which became visible in the sixties under Franco, has posed a problem for Spanish democracy First, the territories claimed by Basque separatists are divided between Navarra, Aquitania, part of Castile, Alva, Guipozcoa and Vizcaya and never constituted a political or administrative unit. A Navarrese identity also exists, and the Navarrese would reject a Basque state. In the circumstances it is difficult to define the Basque "people." Basque secessionists have yet to win an electoral majority on their home turf. As in India, electoral failure partly accounts for secessionist demands, backed by violence, and raises the question of how to handle a separatist group that refuses to be accommodated. Unlike New Delhi, which earned the opprobrium of many Sikhs and Kashmiris by resorting to force to suppress separatism in the Punjab and Kashmir, Madrid has left it largely to the regional governments to contain secessionist violence. This has probably been wise, as the center has not become the focus of enmity for the majority of Basques. While Basque separatists have not given up their struggle for a state, there have been no massive armed interventions by Madrid, and Spain's democratic institutions have suffered far less damage than India's.

Sri Lanka: What Went Wrong?

Sri Lanka illustrates what can go wrong when elected governments in a multiethnic country identify with the majority community.[37] Twenty-five percent of its population are Tamils, who are Hindu by religion. The Sinhalese majority are Buddhists. Most Tamils are concentrated in the Northern and Eastern Provinces, comprising 85 percent of the population in the former and 42 percent in the latter. Unlike India, Sri Lanka did not experience communal violence when it achieved independence from the British in 1948, and it witnessed a smooth transfer of power. Its governments gained legitimacy through elections but exploited communal feeling to reap political advantage. Until 1954, the two leading political parties, the United National Party and the Sri Lanka Freedom Party, favored the replacement of English by both Sinhalese and Tamil. But in 1954, the United National Party government bowed to pressure from religious and cultural revivalist groups and opted for Sinhalese as the state language. In 1956, S.W.R.D. Bandaranaike and S.J.V. Chelvanayagam, leaders of the Sri Lanka Freedom Party and Tamil Federal Party respectively, agreed on federal political structures. However, under pressure from the United National Party, Bandaranaike abrogated the pact. Between 1960 and 1977 the Sri Lanka Freedom Party and United National Party alternated as winners and losers in Sri Lankan elections. Competing for power in predominantly Sinhalese areas, both pandered to the communal sentiment of the Sinhalese and increasingly alienated Tamils.

A United Front government elected in 1970 brushed aside demands from Tamils that Tamil be given parity with Sinhalese as an official language. It also refused to grant more autonomy to Tamil areas. This stance accompanied a policy of increasing centralization, politicization of the bureaucracy and judiciary and discrimination against Tamils seeking entry into universities and government service. Communal violence had occurred intermittently in Sri Lanka, but it was not until 1983, some thirty-five years after independence, that Tamils began to fight for statehood and Sri Lanka descended into civil war.

The following stand out: discrimination against Tamils and their language, raising the status of Buddhism, strong centralizing tendencies, exploitation of and surrender to Sinhalese communal opinion by Sri Lankan governments. There is little sign of any thought being given to crafting a pluralist concept of nation in Sri Lanka. It is an almost classic case of how politicians in a democracy can make precisely those choices which provoke ethnic quarrels. Yet such choices are not the inevitable consequence of democracy, rather of how it can—but should not—be practiced. Sri Lanka's slide into civil war was the outcome of a combination of missed opportunities, broken or unfulfilled promises and misconceived policies.

SUMMING UP

The ideological rigidity of the Soviet state set the terms by which groups could assert their interests; it assigned to them fixed political roles. So it is quite logical that nationalism should have been the primary idea to replace a collapsing communism in all fifteen republics. In India, by contrast, multiple identities exist; they are not static but shifting in changing circumstances, and these shifts have been accommodated in different ways by political institutions at the local, regional and national levels.[38] This is analogous with developments in Spain. There, the transition to democracy was attended by the fashioning of new political arrangements that offered substantial autonomy to Catalonia and the Basque region, and the center and regions learned to cooperate with one another. Spanish and regional identities have coexisted; in fact, the electoral processes have facilitated their coexistence.[39] A unitary state such as Britain serves as another illustration of the existence of multiple entities.[40] The Soviet experience shows that "modernization," even when modernization is carried out through force, is no guarantee that a state will be able to forge a new national or supranational identity that will transcend loyalties to religion, language or region in a multinational country. The evidence is that authoritarian states, by their very nature, do not try to reconcile and accommodate political differences between different religious, ethnic or linguistic groups. Their propensity to divide and rule has usually exacerbated such differences, frequently to breaking point and in a manner that has threatened the territorial integrity of the authoritarian state itself.

In the twentieth century assimilationist policies generally alienated minorities, all the more so if the rulers identified with a single community. This applied to both authoritarian and democratic states. To name just two: the former Soviet

Union and Sri Lanka. The Soviet experience also showed that a state could claim to be "internationalist" and profess to be representing different national identities and interests but in practice associate with one national group. Merely recognizing cultural diversity and professing "internationalism" is not enough to win over the support of minorities if the state is perceived by them as identifying with one "nation." If ethnic groups do not have the chance to articulate their interests through political institutions or feel that they have little or no say in shaping their destiny, they are likely to rebel against the state.

What is interesting about the Soviet experience is that an attempt to exploit the nationalism of the dominant national group, and to associate the state with this nationalism—as the Soviet state tried to do with Russia—does not necessarily ensure the support of that group for the state or assure its survival. From this, it follows that winning over "elites" is not sufficient to sustain multiethnic states. Elites, their interests and identities are always in a state of flux. Policymakers have to contend not only with the problem of accommodating ethnic diversity or "elites" but also change. If it is a fact that the republican elites who demanded "sovereignty" or "independence" were a product of Soviet rule, it is equally clear that the Soviet state was unable to accommodate their demands and aspirations, which were also an outcome of its policies. So it is not at all certain that the existence of an ethnic core secures the legitimacy of a state or its survival.

The rules of the democratic game have to be accepted if ethnic stability is to be maintained. Much communal violence and separatism has arisen in India precisely when the center and regional or communal parties have broken the rules. The resulting disorder has taken long to curb; the use of force by both sides has blocked reconciliation and has damaged India's democratic political structures. The rigging of elections by the center in Kashmir also brought Indian democracy into disrepute.

Tugs of war between the center and regions are common in democracies, and the existence of a Constitutional Court, having the power to adjudicate in disputes between the center and regions, appears to be essential to maintain democratic institutions and practices. India and Spain both bear this out. In Sri Lanka, on the other hand, where the executive dominated even the judiciary, minorities literally had no court of appeal to which they could address their grievances.

The role of neighboring countries in exacerbating ethnic tensions may be significant. The onus for Tamil and Kashmiri separatism rests on Colombo and New Delhi, but India's encouragement, under Indira Gandhi, of Tamil separatism and Pakistan's claim to Kashmir and its encouragement of secessionist forces have fanned the conflicts in those areas. On the other hand, the inability of Colombo and the Tamils to sort out their differences, even after India has used its good offices in favor of a settlement which will preserve the territorial integrity of Sri Lanka, underlines the domestic origins of the conflict there. In contrast, Spain has been helped in its handling of its dilemmas in the Basque region by the absence of irredentist claims by France. The renunciation of territorial claims by neighboring countries can be an important factor in preventing or containing secessionist demands, and this point will be discussed at greater length with reference to post-communist countries in chapter 5.

Democracy is an arrangement for the articulation and mediation of differences; it may offer more possibilities to forge consensus, accommodate diverse identities and intellectual and social trends in multiethnic, multinational, multicultural societies than any authoritarian system. Democracy does not offer instant or definitive solutions to the dilemmas created by ethnic diversity—but, then, neither does any authoritarian system. The optimism of the international community may not be entirely misplaced, so long as it is remembered that democracy offers choices, the possibility of coping with changing interests and demands and of forging consensus.

NOTES

1. For example, Samuel P. Huntington, "Political Development and Political Decay," and Alec Nove, "The Soviet Model and Underdeveloped Countries," both in Claude E. Welch Jr., ed., *Political Modernization: A Reader in Comparative Political Change*, pp. 207–45 and 363–72 respectively; Hans Kohn, *The Idea of Nationalism* (New York: Macmillan, 1945); Samuel P. Huntington and Clement H. Moore, *Authoritarian Politics in Modern Society: The Dynamics of Established One-Party Systems*.

2. See for example Jacques Barzun, "Is Democratic Theory for Export?" in Joel H. Rosenthal, ed., *Ethics and International Affairs: A Reader* (Washington, D.C.: Georgetown University Press, 1995), pp. 39–57; Richard Schifter, "Is There a Democracy Gene?" *Washington Quarterly*, vol. 17, no. 3 (summer 1994): 121–27; Aung San Suu Kyi, "Freedom, Development and Human Worth," *Journal of Democracy*, vol. 6, no. 2 (April 1995): 11,15.

3. Donald L. Horowitz, "Making Moderation Pay: The Comparative Politics of Ethnic Conflict Management," in Montville, *Conflict and Peacemaking*, p. 451.

4. Teresa Rakowska-Harmstone, "The Dialectics of Nationalism in the USSR," *Problems of Communism*, vol. 23, no. 3 (May/June 1974): 1–22; Walker Connor, *The National Question in Marxist Leninist Theory*; Gregory Gleason, *Federalism and Nationalism: The Struggle for Republican Rights in the USSR* (Boulder, Colo.: Westview, 1990); and Gerhard Simon, *Nationalism and Policy Toward the Nationalities in the Soviet Union: From Totalitarian Dictatorship to Post-Stalinist Society*, trans. Karen Forster and Oswald Forster (Boulder, Colo.: Westview, 1991) argued that nationalism, representing the interests of regional elites, was the outcome of the modernization that was intended to do away with it.

5. See for example the collection of essays in Michael Burgess and Alain-G. Gagnon, eds., *Comparative Federalism and Federation: Competing Traditions and Future Directions* (New York: Harvester Wheatsheaf, 1993).

6. For a discussion of how the collapse of the USSR confounded both liberal and Marxist theories of modernization, Zvi Gitelman, "Development and Ethnicity in the Soviet Union," in Alexander Motyl, ed., *The Post-Soviet Nations: Perspectives on the Demise of the USSR* (New York: Columbia University Press, 1992), pp. 220–39.

7. Walker Connor, "Ethno-Nationalism and Political Instability: An Overview," in Hermann Giliomee and Jannie Gagiano, eds., *The Elusive Search for Peace: South Africa, Israel, Northern Ireland* (Cape Town: Oxford University Press, 1990), pp. 9–32; and Donald Horowitz, *Ethnic Groups in Conflict* (Berkeley and Los Angeles: University of California Press, 1985).

8. Other developments in the USSR also lead us to question some assumptions about "nation." The strident anti-Russian tones of Ukrainian nationalism, before and after the dissolution of the USSR, confute assumptions that racial, cultural and linguistic closeness or "assimilation" bind different peoples together. Contrary to the expectations of Hélène Carrère d'Encausse, *Decline of an Empire: The Soviet Socialist Republics in Revolt* (New York: Newsweek Books, 1979), who predicted that "Islamic" nationalism would trigger the breakup of the USSR, the nationalisms of the Central Asian republics were not secessionist. In the Soviet Union ethnic schisms did not necessarily lead to calls for independent statehood; political cleavages were not necessarily congruent with social, religious and ethnic divisions.

9. In writing the following sections, I have found four interpretative accounts helpful. Leszek Kolakowski, *Main Currents of Marxism: Its Rise, Growth and Dissolution, Vol. 2, The Golden Age*, trans. P. S. Falla, (Oxford: Oxford University Press, 1981), pp. 467ff., and idem, *Main Currents of Marxism; Its Rise, Growth and Dissolution, Vol. 3, The Breakdown*, trans. P. S. Falla, (Oxford: Oxford University Press, 1981), pp. 1ff., 77ff., 117ff.; Connor, *The National Question in Marxist-Leninist Theory and Strategy*; Richard Pipes, *The Formation of the Soviet Union: Communism and Nationalism 1917–1923*, rev. ed. (Cambridge, Mass.: Harvard University Press, 1964).

10. Pipes, *Formation of the Soviet Union*, p. 45; Robert Conquest, *Soviet Nationalities Policy in Practice* (London: The Bodley Head, 1967), pp. 116–18; Aryeh Unger, *Constitutional Development in the USSR: A Guide to the Soviet Constitutions* (London: Methuen, 1981), pp. 43–44, 86–87, 203.

11. Robert Tucker, *Stalin in Power: The Revolution from Above, 1928–1941* (New York: W. W. Norton, 1990), pp. 44–65.

12. Gerhard Simon, *Nationalism and Policy*, pp. 148ff., 315ff.

13. Walter Kolarz, *Religion in the Soviet Union* (London: Macmillan, 1961); Pedro Ramet, *Cross and Commissar: The Politics of Religion in Eastern Europe and the USSR* (Bloomington: Indiana University Press, 1987); Bohdan R. Bociurkiw, "Nationalities and Soviet Religious Policies," in Lubomyr Hajda and Mark Beissinger, eds., *The Nationalities Factor in Soviet Politics and Society* (Boulder, Colo.: Westview, 1990), pp. 148–74.

14. Conquest, *Soviet Nationalities Policy*, p. 79.

15. Benedict Anderson, *Imagined Communities: Reflections on the Origin and Spread of Nationalism* (London: Verso, 1983).

16. Barbara Anderson and Brian Silver, "Some Factors in the Linguistic and Ethnic Russification of Soviet Nationalities: Is Everyone Becoming Russian?" in Hajda and Beissinger, eds., *The Nationalities Factor in Soviet Politics and Society*, p. 96.

17. Cited in Conquest, *Soviet Nationalities Policy*, p. 13.

18. There was also an economic dimension to this policy. Khrushchev wanted to transform untilled steppe in Kazakhstan and southwestern Siberia into new grain producing regions. Russian and Slavic "volunteers" were sent to cultivate lands where the Kazakhs had bred livestock for centuries. For the Kazakhs the Virgin Lands scheme

represented a colonization that threatened their very survival. Martha Brill Olcott, *The Kazakhs* (Stanford: Hoover Institution Press, 1987), pp. 225–29.

19. Connor, *The National Question in Marxist-Leninist Theory and Strategy*, p. 301.

20. Gail W. Lapidus and Victor Zaslavsky, with Philip Goldman, eds., *From Union to Commonwealth: Nationalism and Separatism in the Soviet Republics* (Cambridge: Cambridge University Press, 1992), pp. 12–13.

21. Speech of 15 March 1991, reported in *Foreign Broadcast Information Service, [Daily Bulletin], Soviet Union (FBIS-SOV)*, 18 March 1991.

22. John Dunlop, *The Faces of Contemporary Russian Nationalism* (Princeton: Princeton University Press, 1983), p. 286.

23. An analysis of Yeltsin's motives is beyond the scope of this book, but it may be worth remembering that Yeltsin did not run for the Russian presidency promising to dismantle the USSR, and he was willing to sign the Union Treaty, which would have increased the powers of Union Republics.

24. Anders Åslund, *Gorbachev's Struggle for Economic Reform*, 2nd ed. (Ithaca: Cornell University Press, 1991); Marshall Goldman, *What Went Wrong with Perestroika* (New York: W. W. Norton, 1991).

25. This account is based largely on Donna Bahry, "The Union Republics and Contradictions in Gorbachev's Economic Reform," *Soviet Economy*, vol. 7, no. 3 (July/September 1991): 215–55.

26. Stephen White, Graeme Gill and Darrell Slider, *The Politics of Transition: Shaping a Post-Soviet Future* (Cambridge: Cambridge University Press, 1993), pp. 57–58; Stephen Kux, *Soviet Federalism: A Comparative Perspective* (New York: IEWS, 1990), pp. 79–82.

27. Chapter 8 of the Soviet constitution of 1977 was headed "A Federal State," while Article 70 seemingly reconciled the best of all worlds by describing the USSR as "an integral, federal, multinational state." Richard Little, *Governing the Soviet Union* (London: Longman, 1989), p. 350.

28. For a very selective reading list on this see G. Parthasarathi, ed., [Nehru's] *Letters to Chief Ministers, 1947–1964*, 5 vols. (New Delhi: Jawaharlal Nehru Memorial Fund, 1985–90); Ravinder Kumar, *Essays in the Social History of Modern India* (Delhi: Oxford University Press, 1983), especially pp. 1–68; Sumit Sarkar, *Modern India 1885–1947* (Delhi: Macmillan, 1983); Sunil Khilnani, *The Idea of India* (London: Hamish Hamilton, 1997).

29. For example, Paul Brass, *The Politics of India Since Independence* (Cambridge: Cambridge University Press, 1990), pp. 36ff.; Sunil Khilnani, "India's Democratic Career," in Dunn, ed., *Democracy: The Unfinished Journey*, pp. 189–205.

30. For instance, see Brass, *The Politics of India Since Independence*, pp. 135ff., Rajni Kothari, *Politics in India* (Delhi: Orient Longman, 1970).

31. W. H. Morris-Jones, *The Government and Politics of India*, 2nd ed. (London: Hutchinson University Library, 1964).

32. S.A.H. Haqqi and A. P. Sharma, "Centre-State Relations: A Study of Structural Processual Determinants," in K. Bombwall, ed., *National Power and State Autonomy* (Meerut, India: Meenakshi Prakashan, 1964), pp. 42–47.

33. See among others Mark Tully and Satish Jacob, *Amritsar: Mrs. Gandhi's Last Battle* (London: Johnathan Cape, 1985); Robin Jeffrey, *What's Happening to India? Punjab, Ethnic Conflict, Mrs. Gandhi's Death and the Test for Federalism* (Basingstoke: Macmillan, 1986); Y. K. Malik, "The Akali Party and Sikh Militancy: Move for Greater

Autonomy or Secession in Punjab," *Asian Survey*, vol. 26, no. 3 (March 1986): 345–62; and Paul Wallace, "The Sikhs as a 'Minority' in a Sikh Majority State in India," in ibid., pp. 363–77; Paul Brass, "The Punjab Crisis and the Unity of India," in Atul Kohli, ed., *India's Democracy: An Analysis of Changing State-Society Relations* (Princeton: Princeton University Press, 1988), pp. 169–213.

34. But see Sumit Ganguly, *The Origins of War in South Asia: Indo-Pakistani Conflicts since 1947* (Boulder, Colo.: Westview, 1986), and idem, "Explaining the Kashmir Insurgency: Political Mobilization and Institutional Decay," *International Security*, vol. 21, no. 2 (fall 1996): 76–107.

35. Sudipto Kaviraj, "Crisis of the Nation-State in India," in John Dunn, ed., *Contemporary Crisis of the Nation-State?* (Oxford: Blackwell, 1995), pp. 115–29.

36. This account is based largely on Audrey Brassloff, "Spain: The State of the Autonomies," in Murray Forsyth, ed., *Federalism and Nationalism* (Leicester: Leicester University Press, 1989), pp. 24–50. Daniele Conversi, *The Basques, the Catalans and Spain: Alternative Routes to Nationalist Mobilization* (London: Hurst, 1997), pp. 140ff., 247ff.; Juan Linz, "Spanish Democracy and the *Estado de las Autonomías*," in Robert A. Goldwin, Art Kaufman, and William A. Schambra, eds., *Forging Unity Out of Diversity: The Approaches of Eight Nations* (Washington, D.C.: American Enterprise Institute for Public Policy Research, 1989), pp. 260–303; Linz and Stepan, *Problems of Democratic Transition and Consolidation*, pp. 87–115.

37. This account is based largely on Urmila Phadnis, "Sri Lanka: Crises of Legitimacy and Integration," in Larry Diamond, Juan Linz, and Seymour Martin Lipset, eds., *Democracy in Developing Countries. Vol. 3, Asia* (Boulder: Colo.: Lynne Rienner Publishers, 1989), pp. 143–85; A. Jeyaratnam Wilson, *The Breakup of Sri Lanka: Tamil-Sinhalese Conflict* (London: Hurst, 1988); S.W.R. de A. Samarasinghe, "The Dynamics of Separatism: The Case of Sri Lanka," in Ralph R. Premdas, S.W.R. de A. Samarasinghe, and Alan B. Anderson, eds., *Secessionist Movements in Comparative Perspective* (London: Pinter, 1990), pp. 48–70; James Manor, *The Expedient Utopian: Bandaranaike and Ceylon* (Cambridge: Cambridge University Press, 1989).

38. James Manor, "India: The Misconceptions and the Reality," *The World Today*, vol. 47, no. 11 (November 1991): 193–96.

39. Brassloff, "Spain," pp. 24–50; Juan Linz and Alfred Stepan, "Political Identities and Electoral Sequences: Spain, the Soviet Union and Yugoslavia," *Daedalus*, vol. 121, no. 2 (spring 1992): 123–39; Michael Keating, "Spain: Peripheral Nationalism and State Response," in John McGarry and Brendan O'Leary, eds., *Politics of Ethnic Conflict Regulation* (London: Routledge, 1993), pp. 204–5.

40. Has Northern Ireland been the exception to this rule? There is room for debate on this point. Brendan O'Duffy observed that the problem in Northern Ireland centered on conflicting national identities, but the British government's overriding emphasis upon security policy at the expense of substantial social and economic reforms was the primary obstacle to the achievement of lasting regulatory mechanisms. Brendan O'Duffy, "Containment or Regulation? The British Approach to Ethnic Conflict in Northern Ireland," in McGarry and O'Leary, eds., *Politics of Ethnic Conflict Regulation*, pp. 128–50. Does the accord of December 1999 mark a change from this policy, and will it stabilize Northern Ireland?

Chapter 3

Self-Determination, Democracy, Minorities and Sovereignty: The Issues Raised by the Collapse of Yugoslavia and the USSR

"Ministers have assessed developments in Eastern Europe and the Soviet Union . . . [and] adopted the following guidelines on the formal recognition of new states in Eastern Europe and in the Soviet Union. . . .

—respect for the provisions of the Charter of the United Nations and the commitment subscribed to in the Final Act of Helsinki and in the Charter of Paris, especially with regard to the rule of law, democracy and human rights

—guarantees for the rights of ethnic and national groups and minorities in accordance with the commitments subscribed to in the framework of the CSCE

—respect for the inviolability of all frontiers, which can only be changed by peaceful means and by common agreement"

European Community (EC) *Declaration on the Guidelines for the Recognition of New States in Eastern Europe and in the Soviet Union*, 16 December 1991

THE INTERNATIONAL REPERCUSSIONS OF THE COLLAPSE OF YUGOSLAVIA AND THE USSR

The EC's Declaration on recognition of the successor states to the erstwhile Yugoslavia and Soviet Union tended to give the impression that a commitment to democracy and respect for minority rights by the new states decided the issue of their recognition. But could the Declaration be taken at face value? Or did it camouflage the inability of international officials to shape events in Yugoslavia and the USSR? And did political contingency, arising from the disintegration of both states, force the hand of the international community?

Whatever the answers to these questions, one thing stands out. Internal developments in the two *authoritarian* states revealed their failure to accommodate their ethnically mixed populations and provoked demands for secession. This chapter will show why. At least partly because declarations of independence, secession and diplomatic recognition transformed domestic quarrels into international conflicts, the international community stressed democratic rule to manage ethnic diversity in the post–cold war world.

The end of the cold war, with its rigid bipolar structures, ideological simplicities and seeming certainties, opened the door to an unpredictable new world order. Three communist states—Czechoslovakia,[1] Yugoslavia and the Soviet Union—splintered into twenty-two new countries, but would all the new states become democracies? Envisaging the sovereign state as the "fundamental entity of the international community," Boutros-Ghali echoed the expectations of many that the post–cold war world would see the enhancement of peace and the securing of justice and human rights and that the time to redesign the international order had come.[2]

This would prove to be easier said than done. The issues of "self-determination," "minorities" and "democracy" showed up the difficulties of refashioning the post–cold war order as the dismantling of Yugoslavia and the USSR raised the specter of widespread ethnic turbulence. Yugoslavia began to unravel in June 1991; the Soviet Union two months later. The international community was unprepared for the plethora of problems thrown up by their disintegration, and it was against a background of political contingency and conceptual ambiguity that the implications of "self-determination" and "democracy" in the former Yugoslavia and Soviet Union had to be faced.

To add fuel to the fire, minorities in the breakaway territories of Croatia, Bosnia, Moldova, Georgia, Azerbaijan and Georgia disengaged themselves from calls for independence made by the majority communities and asserted their own right to self-determination, implying sovereign statehood. Insurgent minorities in the Krajina, the Republic Srpska, Nagorno-Karabakh, Abkhazia and the Trans-Dniestr contested the sovereignty and challenged the legitimacy of the governments of the seceding republics. Rebellious minorities thus raised the old question—dormant in Europe since 1945—what constitutes a "people"?

Not surprisingly, the wars in the former Yugoslavia and Soviet Union also revived some old controversies. When should international recognition be accorded to seceding nations? Was it when secessionist nationalists were able to demonstrate that they controlled the territory they claimed and enjoyed a monopoly of force over it?[3] Or when the majority of the population residing in a territory voted for independence? And did such a vote imply that the governments of breakaway territories would reflect the wishes of "the people" even if minorities elected to secede from the seceding entity? What did the democratic

THE FORMER YUGOSLAVIA

Democracy and Belated Recognition: Slovenia and Macedonia

In April 1990, the first multiparty elections since the Second World War were held in Yugoslavia.[4] Parties in all republics professed to be "democratic," probably because "democracy" at that time was a vogue word for escaping from the "Oriental prison" of the communist bloc and "joining Europe," "civilization" and "the West." In most republics the elections were won by secessionist and/or exclusivist nationalist parties or coalitions. In Slovenia the electoral success of a separatist coalition in 1990 did not presage conflict, partly because the titular nationality comprised 88 percent of the population and, more important, because ethnic groups were not quarreling over territory. In a plebiscite held on 23 December 1990, 88.5 percent of voters chose to leave Yugoslavia. Following Slovenia's declaration of independence on 25 June 1991, the Yugoslav People's Army moved in but failed to crush secessionist forces.[5]

The Slovenian authorities swiftly took over the republic's border posts and made known their intention to preserve human rights and basic freedoms "for all persons on the territory of the Republics of Slovenia regardless of their national affiliation."[6] A case for international recognition could be made on the grounds that Slovenia was in control of its borders and had made a commitment to protect the rights of its minorities, but the international community did not recognize Slovenia at this stage.

Similarly, Western countries were slow to recognize Macedonia, although it met their conditions for recognition.[7] In 1991 Macedonians were 67 percent of its population; Albanians 21 percent, Turks 4.8 percent and Serbs 2.7 percent. Other communities comprised about 7 percent. A referendum to decide the issue of independence on 8 September 1991 was boycotted by the Albanian minority, but most voters favored leaving Yugoslavia, and the government of President Kiro Gligorov declared Macedonia an independent state. Anxious to conciliate minorities and to win diplomatic recognition for Macedonia, Gligorov offered Albanians five cabinet posts. But neither "the people's choice" of independence nor Gligorov's olive branch to minorities earned Macedonia diplomatic recognition. Greece alleged that Macedonia would foment irredentism in Greek Macedonia and insisted that Macedonia change its name. A constitutional amendment clarified that Macedonia harbored no territorial ambitions, and Gligorov made known his willingness to enter into an agreement with Athens which would guarantee the Greco-Macedonia border, but Greece spurned these overtures. In January 1992 the Badinter Commission[8] was satisfied that Macedonia had met EC criteria for recognition and that the use of the name "Macedonia" did not imply territorial claims against another state.[9] But in contrast to the alacrity with which Croatia was recognized at the beginning of 1992,[10] international recognition was still not forthcoming for Macedonia. Russia recognized Macedonia in August 1992 on the grounds that it was concerned about the security and stability of all Balkan countries. However, it was not until April 1993, after Greece assented, that Macedonia was recognized by EC countries and accorded UN membership. Political expediency rather than the democratic principle decided the issue of Macedonia's recognition.

Dubious Democracy and Swift Recognition: Croatia and Bosnia

The attitudes of Croatian and Bosnian leaders toward their Serb minorities provided Slobodan Milošević with a pretext to rally Serbs to a vision of "Greater Serbia" and to incite Serb minorities in Croatia and Bosnia to revolt, even as he unleashed war in order to consolidate his political supremacy.[11]

In 1989 Croats made up 81 percent of Croatia's population, Serbs 12 percent. Serbs constituted some two-thirds of the population in the Krajina, which bordered Bosnia-Herzegovina, but the area was essentially an ethnic patchwork. Led by Franjo Tudjman, who dreamt of uniting all Croats in a single Croat state, the Croatian Democratic Union captured two-thirds of the seats in parliament after fighting the 1990 elections on a platform of favors for the majority nationality and discrimination against minorities. Such an attitude did not endear itself to Serb minorities, who wanted to be treated on an equal footing with the Croat "nation." Once in power the Croatian Democratic Union manipulated the symbols of democracy to justify the creation of an ethnic state in which the dominant "nation" rather than the individual had sovereignty. Minorities were assured of equal treatment and cultural autonomy, but in practice the official policy was to dismiss Serbs from their jobs on the grounds that they were overrepresented in "sensitive" areas, such as the administration and the media, and little was done to conciliate them or to offer them protection from communal violence.[12] All this went against the grain of the CSCE *Copenhagen Document* and *Charter of Paris*, which had called for the protection of minorities through a democratic system of governance based on the rule of law, but no outside power appears to have pleaded with Croatia to adopt a more liberal stance towards its minorities. Croatia's brand of ethnic discrimination also presented Milošević with an opportunity to exploit the fear and discontent of its Serbs.

Earlier, in October 1990, Serbs in the Krajina had proclaimed the establishment of a "Serb Autonomous Republic of Krajina" and on 28 February 1991 declared its independence. Then, barely a week before the Croatian referendum on independence in May 1991, they held their own plebiscite, in which they voted to remain part of Yugoslavia. This was the setting in which Croatia, like Slovenia, declared independence on 25 June 1991. To make matters worse, Serbs in Western Slavonia, where they comprised just under 30 percent of the population, proclaimed the establishment of the "Serb Autonomous Republic of

The Collapse of Yugoslavia and the USSR 55

Western Slavonia" in August 1991. Serbs and Croats took up arms: the Serb minority to sever Serb areas from Croatia; the Croatian government to preserve the existing borders of Croatia.

Bosnia was a veritable republic of minorities, with Muslims comprising approximately 44 percent of the population, Serbs 31 percent and Croats 17 percent. Serbs were concentrated in eastern Bosnia, Croats in Herzegovina. But the three communities were interspersed throughout Bosnia, and in twenty-three out of its ninety-nine municipalities none was in a majority. As in the Bosnia elections of 1918 and 1923, voting in the 1990 elections followed ethnic lines, and polling results reflected the absence of a composite "Bosnian" nationalism. An intercommunal coalition government was formed, but the winning parties tried to consolidate power at local, regional and national levels by expelling individuals belonging to "other" ethnic groups from official positions.[13]

Bosnian Serbs in the Republic Srpska boycotted the referendum on Bosnian independence held between 29 February and 1 March 1992, in which 99 percent of those participating opted for independence. President Islam Izetbegović declared Bosnia-Herzegovina an independent state on 3 March. Less than a month later, on 27 March, Bosnian Serb leaders proclaimed the independence of the Republic Srpska of Bosnia-Herzegovina. With Serb minorities repudiating through the ballot box, the political and moral authority of the Croatian and Bosnian governments, could it be said that the "people" of Croatia and Bosnia had voted for independence?

Did Democratic Principles Shape the International Response?

Neither state practice nor international law offered ready answers. What was clear was that neither gave minorities the right to self-determination. Resolution 1541(XV) of the UN General Assembly (1960)[14] was explicit that the right to self-determination applied to the people of a territory as a whole and that ethnic groups within seceding territories had no right to self-determination. The initial response of the international community toward the Croatian and Slovenian calls for independence was conservative, and the United States, the EC and the CSCE all stressed the principle of territorial integrity. For the CSCE the question was not one of settling disputes between states, but of easing tensions between them.

Whether "democracy" shaped the West's response to Croatia's call for independence is questionable. As Yugoslavia unravelled inexorably in the summer of 1991, member-states of the EC tried to agree on terms for recognizing Slovenia and Croatia. The EC rightly proceeded on the assumption that Yugoslavia was in a state of dissolution, but with the Yugoslav army occupying one-third of Croatia and with Serb minorities rejecting the authority of its government, Croatia was hardly in control of its territory. The EC was divided, with Germany pushing for early recognition in the name of self-determination.[15] Searching for a policy that would bear the stamp of "European unity" the EC decided, on the advice of the Badinter Arbitration Commission, that recognition of the breakaway republics of Yugoslavia should be in accordance with the principle of *uti possed itis*.

This practice developed in Latin America in the nineteenth century. When Spanish colonies attained independence, their boundaries as independent states followed the colonial boundaries. The principle did not apply to the Versailles settlement or to the partition of British India, Palestine and Cyprus. It assumed significance during African decolonization in the sixties. Endorsed by Resolution 1514 (1960)[16] of the UN General Assembly and by the Charter of African Unity in 1963, *uti possed itis* came to constitute a general principle of international law, implying that the territorial state defined the people. It was applied by the EC to the recognition of Croatia and Bosnia in 1991 on the grounds that in ethnically diverse areas the preservation of borders would prevent fratricidal wars. The calculation had turned out to be wrong in many African countries; in Yugoslavia the "fratricidal wars" were escalating when the EC announced its terms for recognition on 16 December 1991. In adhering to the principle of *uti possed itis* the Badinter Commission[17] stated that self-determination for Serbs in Bosnia and Croatia implied the safeguarding of human and minority rights by the governments of those two seceding entities. Individuals could choose the ethnic, religious or linguistic community to which they wished to belong.[18] Accordingly, the EC also stipulated that the seceding republics must give guarantees on minority rights. But even before the Badinter Commission submitted its report on 11 January 1992, Germany recognized Slovenia and Croatia on 23 December 1991. Badinter advised that Croatia had yet to ensure adequate protection for minorities, but he favored recognition, and the rest of the EC countries and the United States kept step with Germany.

Boutros-Ghali had feared that selective recognition of individual republics would "fuel an explosive situation, especially in Bosnia."[19] He turned out—unfortunately—to be right. International recognition of Croatia and Slovenia formalized Yugoslavia's dissolution and made Bosnia's call for independence inevitable. The Badinter Commission deemed that in the absence of a referendum "the will of the peoples of Bosnia-Herzegovina to constitute [the republic] as a sovereign and independent State cannot be held to have been fully established."[20] This left the Bosnian government with little choice but to conduct a referendum in which 99 percent of the electorate backed the demand for independence. But the referendum was boycotted by Bosnian Serbs, who had already conducted their own plebiscite in November 1991, and on the day of the Bosnian referendum they threw up barricades around Sarajevo. Bosnian Serb and Croat minorities, egged on by Belgrade and Zagreb respectively, made known their intention to challenge the authority of any Bosnian state and the boundaries of Bosnia as they stood in March 1992. In the circumstances, only a massive international intervention, capable of effectively disarming sections of the population and deterring aggrandizement by Serbia and Croatia, could have preserved the territorial integrity of Bosnia. Indeed Izetbegović knew that Bosnia "could not protect its independence without foreign military aid."[21] Nevertheless,

EC countries and the United States went ahead with recognition, which was destined to lead the international community into a long, drawn-out engagement to shore up the fledgling Bosnian state.

Did diplomatic recognition create new states, given that the sovereignty of two out of the four seceding republics of Yugoslavia was contested by the largest minority groups living there? In the cases of Croatia and Bosnia the answer would appear to be in the affirmative, but what were the alternatives in the face of state collapse? In the summer of 1991 the international community showed no inclination of staging any military intervention which might have altered the reality on the ground, so the Badinter Commission was in one sense only recommending the most expedient option available.[22] Resolutions declaring the unacceptability of annexations of territory or changes of borders by force were passed by an extraordinary ministerial meeting of the EC and the UN Security Council in August 1991. Endorsed by the Peace Conference on Yugoslavia in October, these resolutions had little meaning in the face of events which the international community could not steer.

THE FORMER SOVIET UNION

Democracy and Belated Recognition: Estonia, Latvia and Lithuania

Calls for self-determination in the former Soviet Union stirred worldwide interest, partly because it was a superpower and the West's archenemy in the cold war, partly because most would have found the prospect of its disintegration inconceivable, partly because "self-determination" and "sovereignty" had several connotations in that country. Declarations of sovereignty were not necessarily calls for statehood. Between June and December 1990 demands for "sovereignty" were made by Russia, Ukraine, Belarus, Azerbaijan, Kazakhstan, Kyrgyzstan, Turkmenistan, Tajikistan and Uzbekistan, but in the referendum to test popular support for the USSR on 17 March 1991, the overwhelming majority of voters in these republics favored preservation of the union.

To the Baltic republics, however, "sovereignty" implied independence. In the spring of 1990, Estonia, Latvia and Lithuania called for the restoration of their statehood, invoking international law to justify their demands. They had broken away from the Romanov empire in 1917, and their independence was recognized by the USSR in 1921. But they were annexed by the Soviet Union in 1940 under the terms of the Molotov-Ribbentrop Protocols of August 1939. In the eighties all three Baltic republics alleged that the Protocols, as well as their annexation by the USSR, were illegal,[23] and they demanded that their sovereignty be restored. Their claim was reinforced when more than 70 percent of their populations voted for independence. This was of significance in Estonia and Latvia, where non-Balts—mostly Russians—comprised 38 and 48 percent of the population respectively. In referenda held in March 1991, 77.83 percent of the electorate in Estonia and 73.68 percent in Latvia expressed a wish for independence. The substantial "proindependence" vote, in itself, did not mean that the majority of Russians supported the call for independence, but enough of them did to sustain the claims that the "people" of Estonia and Latvia had elected to leave the Soviet Union.

Even when it was clear that the "people" of the Baltic republics had chosen independence, an antipathy to changes of borders, as well as the hope that Mikhail Gorbachev would pilot the Soviet Union toward democracy, dissuaded the West from according them recognition, although most Western countries had never recognized their incorporation into the USSR. American officials let it be known that the practice of the United States had been to establish formal relations with "the lawful government of a state once that government was in effective control of its territory and capable of entering into and fulfilling international obligations." When they were "satisfied" that Lithuania could meet these requirements, Washington would establish diplomatic ties.[24] Barely three weeks before the August coup George Bush warned against "suicidal nationalism" in the republics and asserted that the United States would maintain "the strongest possible relationship with the Soviet Government."[25] When the USSR fell apart in August 1991, it was the Russian Federation which seized the diplomatic initiative and recognized Lithuania, Estonia and Latvia on 24 August 1991.[26] Western countries accepted the *fait accompli* and followed suit, welcoming the restoration of the sovereignty and independence of the Baltic republics. This stance enabled them to distinguish the claims of Estonia, Lithuania and Latvia for independence, for which there was some sympathy in the West, from similar demands by Georgia and Azerbaijan, which had little support in Western countries.

The fact that many Russians endorsed the demand for independence[27] meant that the campaigns for independence in Estonia, Latvia and Lithuania did not give rise to ethnic hostilities. This was in contrast to two other Union Republics—Georgia and Moldova—which refused to sign the Union Treaty. Minorities in these republics disassociated themselves from the independence movements, claimed their own right to statehood and tried to achieve it by force of arms.

Dubious Democracy and Slow Recognition: Georgia, Azerbaijan, Moldova

Georgia boycotted the referendum on the future of the Soviet Union in March 1991 and held its own referendum for independence. Ninety-nine percent of Georgians favored departing from the USSR, but the international community did not accord Georgia recognition. This was to some extent understandable. Any Georgian demand for independence would give rise to complications because Georgia's Abkhaz and Ossetian minorities participated in the union referendum on 17 March and expressed their desire to remain in the USSR.[28] The political division between Georgians, Abkhazians and Ossetians stood revealed.

A history of discrimination by Georgian governments against Abkhazian and Ossetian minorities[29] did much to explain the antagonisms between Georgians and Abkhazians and between Georgians and Ossetians in the nineties and brought to the forefront the tension between "self-determination" and "democracy." Georgia had broken away from the disintegrating Romanov empire in 1918 and was an independent state until 1921, when it was conquered by the Bolsheviks. Exclusivist nationalist policies had been carried out by the Soviet authorities since the thirties. Georgianization of education and political institutions and promotion of Georgian history had started even while the Georgian Communist Party was in power. In 1922 Abkhazia became an Autonomous Republic, Ossetia an Autonomous Region. These political structures gave Abkhaz and Ossetian minorities some protection from Georgian dominance. However, from the thirties onward the Georgian administration put pressure on the republic's minorities to assimilate into the majority population. All Abkhaz and Ossetian language schools were closed, and their alphabets were Georgianized. Georgian historians claimed that the Abkhaz had displaced the "original" Georgians from Abkhazia and were "outsiders."[30] Tension between Georgians and Abkhazians and Georgians and Ossetians simmered throughout the Soviet era.

Aggrieved at discrimination by Georgian authorities, the Abkhaz demanded union with the RSFSR in 1978. The Kremlin tried to mollify the Abkhaz by transforming the Sukhumi Institute of Pedagogy into the Abkhaz State University and to increase the number of Abkhazians enrolled in higher education. These measures only intensified the fears of Georgians about *their* status as a minority in the USSR and fuelled their resentment against the Abkhaz. Ethnic ill will deepened when the Abkhaz Supreme Soviet declared the sovereignty of Abkhazia in August 1990, and a month later the South Ossetian Supreme Soviet proclaimed South Ossetia to be a sovereign republic, with a view to uniting it with the North Ossetian Autonomous Soviet Socialist Republic (ASSR) within the RSFSR. The Georgian parliament delivered a sharp riposte by abolishing South Ossetia's autonomous status and dismissing its parliament, an act which triggered war between Georgians and Ossetians.

In October 1990 the electoral triumph of Zviad Gamsakhurdia, the Georgian nationalist leader, did little to lessen ethnic acrimony. He won 54 percent of the Georgian vote in October 1990 and continued the Soviet policy of Georgianization. His government claimed that groups like the Ossetians, who had settled in Georgia "recently," had no right of residence and could not be given equality of status with the Georgians. Minorities held ex-officio posts in the Supreme Soviet presidium but were not represented in the Georgian parliament.

Gamsakhurdia's attitude toward Georgia's minorities was merely one strain in a highly autocratic style of governance. The media were heavily censored; the president exercised strict control over the Ministries of Justice and Defense, and the KGB was recreated as a separate ministry. An emergency was declared without being ratified by the republican Supreme Soviet, as required by law. Gamsakhurdia effectively held all the reins of power in his hands and refused to enter into a dialogue with representatives of minorities; his authoritarianism and exclusivist nationalism went together. So when 87 percent of Georgians voted for their republic's independence in March 1991, Abkhazian and Ossetian minorities felt their very survival was at stake.

At the same time it is hard to say that the Abkhaz claim to self-determination was founded on democratic principles. The Abkhaz were only 17 percent of the population in Abkhazia, which at once raised the question about the wishes of the Georgians, who comprised 46 percent of the region's population. Probably motivated by anti-Georgian sentiment and fearful that democratic elections would lead to a shift in power away from the Abkhaz to Georgians,[31] Abkhaz leaders supported the coup in August 1991.[32]

The Abkhazian and Ossetian demands for secession were provoked by Gamsakhurdia's overall attempts to centralize authority, but his strong-arm methods precipitated a civil war among Georgians as well. By the time the Soviet Union was dissolved in December 1991, his brand of intolerant nationalism and coercive rule had sparked three wars in Georgia—between Georgians and Abkhazians, between Georgians and Ossetians, and among Georgians themselves. The Soviet Union had ceased to exist, but Gamsakhurdia's government, which had demanded secession, did not hold sway over Georgia's territory. Meanwhile, the vote for independence in March 1991 had not won Georgia international recognition even as late as December 1991. Western officials did not know how to grant recognition to the breakaway state in the face of the prevailing political turbulence. It was the return of Eduard Shevardnadze[33] to Tbilisi on 6 March 1992, his appointment as chairman of a newly created State Council and acceptance of Western conditions that prepared the ground for recognition of Georgia by the EC on 23 March and by the United States a day later. But promises to abide by democratic norms would not necessarily make for an easy transition to democracy, as the West would discover time and again in Georgia and in other former Soviet republics.

The international community always sought a political settlement within Georgia's existing borders, and at no time was it willing to recognize Abkhazia and South Ossetia.[34] After the dissolution of the Soviet Union in December 1991, Moscow's policy was complex. Russian arms supplies to the Abkhaz and Osset helped them to score military victories over Georgia. These successes were exploited to put pressure on Georgia to join the Commonwealth of Independent States (CIS) and to remain within Russia's sphere of influence. But Moscow never supported independence for Abkhazia and Ossetia and put its weight behind maintaining the territorial integrity of Georgia. Old fashioned power politics, rather than concern for self-determination or democracy, guided its attitudes toward the secessionist movements in Georgia.

International commitment to the democratic principle was again put to the test in the Armenian-dominated enclave of Nagorno-Karabakh in southwestern Azerbaijan. Both Armenia and Azerbaijan made historical claims to Nagorno-Karabakh; each saw the territory as the cradle of its nation. Ceded by Iran to the Tsarist empire in 1829, Nagorno-Karabakh was transferred by the Bolsheviks to Azerbaijan after the Russian revolution. Armenia never accepted the decision. The Bolsheviks then gave Nagorno-Karabakh to Armenia but returned it to Azerbaijan in 1921. The Armenians—some 77 percent of the population in Nagorno-Karabakh—resented the decision, and ethnic animosity prevailed under Soviet rule.

The independence of Armenia and Azerbaijan in December 1991 transformed the conflict in Nagorno-Karabakh from a domestic Soviet issue into a protracted interstate war. But the chronology suggests a conflict with its origins in the Soviet era fanned by extreme nationalisms on both sides. Nationalism and conflict preceded democratization and undoubtedly made it difficult for democracy to gain ground. One looks in vain for any signs of adherence by any side to democratic norms.

The immediate causes of the conflict can be traced back to the demand in October 1987 by Armenian demonstrators in Yerevan for the incorporation of Karabakh in Armenia. A vote by the Karabakh *soviet* in favor of union with Armenia in February 1988 precipitated a spontaneous outbreak of communal violence. As the fighting spread, streams of refugees fled the area to take shelter in their "kin" republic. Moscow responded by placing the area under a special administration in January 1989 but was unable to bring the situation under control. In August, Karabakh deputies declared the independence of the enclave. In September an announcement by the Supreme Soviet of Azerbaijan that Azeri would be the official language of the republic triggered an escalation of hostilities. Unable to stem the spiral of violence, Moscow returned the area to Baku in November. This only provoked Armenia into laying claim to Nagorno-Karabakh in December 1989.

Neither the Soviet authorities nor the Azeri or Armenian governments acted with impartiality. The Azeri authorities ordered the Interior Ministry troops to abstain from intervention in the Baku riots in 1990. In 1991 Soviet troops helped the Azeri authorities to deport Armenian villagers from areas between Nagorno-Karabakh and Armenia, while Yerevan connived in raids on Azeri villages. Following the collapse of the coup in August 1991, the Supreme Soviet of Azerbaijan voted for independence and in November Baku abolished the autonomous status of Nagorno-Karabakh. Only a month later the parliament of Nagorno-Karabakh formally announced that the republic was a separate political entity, and in a referendum held in December 1991 the majority of the population of Nagorno-Karabakh voted for independence from Azerbaijan. Meanwhile, Yerevan raised the banner of "self-determination," implying sovereign statehood for Nagorno-Karabakh rather than its annexation by Armenia. Azerbaijan insisted on preserving its territorial integrity, but Baku's control over the enclave was tenuous.

Azerbaijan was recognized in March 1992 by the West, although Nagorno-Karabakh was a *de facto* republic.[35] Once again, the West came to terms with an accomplished fact and recognized a state whose sovereignty was under siege by secessionist minorities in return for assurances of democratic conduct. But Azerbaijan's history as an independent state shows that democracy will be slow to take root there. Nagorno-Karabakh has never been recognized by the international community: International organizations, including the UN and the OSCE, favor the preservation of the territorial integrity of "all States in the region."[36]

In Moldova, political division between Russians in the Trans-Dniestr put a question mark over the legitimacy of any Moldovan claim to sovereign statehood. In 1989[37] Moldovans (ethnic Romanians) comprised 64.5 percent, Ukrainians 13.8 percent, Russians 13 percent, and the Gagauz 3.5 percent of Moldova's population. The majority of Russians lived in the Trans-Dniestr region, with its capital in Tiraspol, while the Gagauz mostly inhabited the southern districts of Moldova, especially around the town of Comrat.

Conditions for conflict in the Trans-Dniestr were laid under Soviet rule. The Trans-Dniestr was part of Ukraine until 1940, when it was joined with Bessarabia, which had been hived off by Stalin from Romania under the Molotov-Ribbentrop Protocols to form the Moldovan Soviet Socialist Republic (*SSR*). Under Soviet rule hundreds of thousands of Slavs, mostly Russians, settled in the republic; the majority worked in industrial and military establishments, and socioeconomic division came to coincide with political division.

Two factors drove deeper the political rift between Russians and Moldovans in the eighties. The first concerned language. As Russian was the official Soviet lingua franca Moldvans felt that their own language had been relegated to second-class status by the Soviet authorities. The Cyrillic script was introduced to the Moldovans of Bessarabia in 1944, but most Russians in the Trans-Dniestr did not know Moldovan. The immediate provocation to Russians was the recommendation, in September 1988, by the Moldovan Supreme Soviet, for the adoption of Moldovan as the official language and transition to the Latin script. In August 1989, the Moldovan Supreme Soviet adopted a law making Moldovan the official language and reinstating the Latin script. These measures only alarmed Moldova's Russian minorities in the Trans-Dniestr who perceived any advantage to the Moldovan majority to be detrimental to their interests. The Moldovan government tried to pacify Russian minorities by announcing that Russian would be the language of interethnic communication but failed to assuage their fears.

Second, some influential Moldovan intellectuals sought unification of Moldovan with Romania and the leading nationalist coalition, the Popular Front of Moldova, campaigned for independence and the promotion of Romanian culture. The year 1989 saw demonstrations by the Gagauz and Russian minorities against such measures, and in November 1989 the Gagauz declared the establishment of a Gagauz SSR. In January 1990 the Russian-dominated city of Tiraspol voted to become independent. Fears of minorities were intensified in June 1990, when thousands of Romanians crossed the border, which had been closed, and called for reunion with Moldova. In September 1990 the Russian-led government of the Trans-Dniestr declared that only Soviet laws would be valid on its territory.

There seemed to be little meeting ground between the Moldovan authorities and the Russian minorities in the Trans-Dniestr. Demonstrations in Chisinau manifested strong popular opposition to the signing of the Union Treaty by Moldova. In March 1991 the Gagauz and Russians in the Trans-Dniestr voted for the preservation of the union, unlike the Moldovans who boycotted the referendum. The political division between Moldovans and Russians was evident again in August 1991, when most Russians in the Trans-Dniestr supported the coup, while Chisinau denounced it as illegal and antidemocratic and proclaimed the independence of Moldova on 27 August. In contrast, Russian leaders in the Trans-Dniestr declared the region's independence from Moldova and announced their intention to uphold the values of the Soviet Union—that, too, in the aftermath of the coup. Thus Moldova emerged as an independent state with its sovereignty challenged by Russian and Gagauz minorities who were not necessarily motivated by a commitment to democracy.

Dismantling the Soviet Union: A Domestic Event

The EC Declaration of 16 December 1991 conveyed the impression that the West took the initiative in preparing the ground for democracy in post-Soviet states. In fact, the rulers and peoples of the former USSR—and Yugoslavia—dismantled their countries and presented the international community with a new agenda. Russia led the world in recognizing the Baltic republics in the last week of August 1991. For the most part, other Soviet republics were recognized *after* the formal dissolution of the USSR and the founding of the Commonwealth of Independent States by Russia, Ukraine and Belarus on 8 December 1991. The three founder-members of the CIS proclaimed their intention to build democratic, law-based states. The Agreement on the Creation of a Commonwealth of Independent States[38] upheld the principles of nonintervention in the domestic affairs of states, protection of the ethnic, cultural, linguistic and religious identities of minorities and the right to self-determination. This did not imply the right to secession from the new states—the Agreement underlined the inviolability of existing frontiers of the seceding Union Republics.

On 12–13 December, Uzbekistan, Kyrgyzstan, Kazakhstan, Turkmenistan, Tajikistan, Armenia, Azerbaijan and Moldova announced their intention of joining the CIS but made no commitment to setting up democratic political structures. On 13 December the Russian *duma* annulled the 1922 treaty which had established the Soviet Union, thus formally dissolving the Soviet state. Russia, Belarus, Ukraine, Kazakhstan, Kyrgyzstan, Tajikistan, Turkmenistan, Uzbekistan, Moldova, Armenia and Azerbaijan announced the establishment of the CIS on 21 December.[39] For all former Soviet republics, CIS membership signalled a break with their past and an attempt to acquire a new identity in the post–cold war world which their independence was helping to create.

Was Recognition of Former Soviet Republics Inspired by Democratic Principles?

No referenda for independence were held in Russia, Belarus, Moldova, Tajikistan, Kazakhstan and Kyrgyzstan, but all these republics received international recognition. The chronology shows that, except for Azerbaijan and Uzbekistan, most Union Republics had conducted referenda before the United States[40] and EC announced their terms on 12 and 16 December respectively.[41] The closest that the international community came to recognizing a seceding Soviet republic on the basis of a popular vote was the recognition of Ukraine by Canada, Poland and Hungary on 2 December, just one day after Ukrainians elected for statehood in a referendum. In no other case did the "people's choice" of independence inspire recognition of seceding Soviet territories.

Member-states of the EC recognized Ukraine on 26 December 1991, after it had accepted their conditions for recognition, including respect for human and minority rights and existing international borders. On the same day the United States recognized Russia, Armenia, Kazakhstan, Belarus and Kyrgyzstan. Washington also recognized the independence of the remaining republics but stipulated that the establishment of diplomatic ties would depend on their meeting its conditions on human rights and democracy. Satisfied that they had done so, the United States opened embassies in Moldova, Azerbaijan, Tajikistan, Turkmenistan and Uzbekistan on 15 March 1992. At best, international officials appeared to be setting standards for recognition; they had no idea whether and how the criteria would be put into practice.

The collapse of the Soviet Union, like that of Yugoslavia, took the world by surprise. Georgia, Moldova, Azerbaijan, Croatia and Bosnia were recognized, although the legitimacy of their governments was challenged by their minorities at the time of recognition. The idea of "progressive dissolution" of the USSR, marking the inevitable triumph of the Helsinki principles,[42] glosses over the fact that the Helsinki Accord was intended to legitmize the post-1945 division of Europe, not to erase it. Also, as James Mayall has observed in a different context, such an idea "gives disproportionate emphasis to the forces of continuity in world politics at the expense of developments which may occur only once, yet signal a fundamental change."[43] Since 1991 events in the former communist bloc have demonstrated, time and again, that it is domestic actors who play the primary roles in building democracy and that outside intervention is of secondary importance.

Postscript: The Democratic Principle and Recognition of New States

Self-determination, connoting the will of the people, was not the main criterion for recognizing states that emerged from the former Yugoslavia and USSR. As minorities in Croatia, Bosnia, Georgia, Azerbaijan and Moldova first voted for independence and then resorted to force to detach themselves from the seceding nations, they carved out the gap between the rhetoric of self-determination and democracy on the international stage and its implementation in the domestic arena. This was not because *all* nationalists were bigoted and intransigent but because ethnic variety frequently made it hard for self-determination and democracy to be reconciled with the territorial integrity and political unity of many countries. To this day the international community has not recognized a right of secession stemming from the right to self-determination, and at the beginning of 2001 the "correct" response to calls for self-determination in Montengro and Kosovo eludes international policy-makers.

The "international community" itself is not a magic wand for conjuring up the "right" policies. The wisdom of recognizing Croatia and Bosnia when their Serb minorities had challenged their authority, when Croatian and Bosnian nationalist leaders had failed to give satisfactory assurances of their intention to protect minority rights and did not enjoy a monopoly of force over the territories they claimed, will long provoke intense debate about whether diplomatic recognition created new unstable states or whether state collapse forced the international community on to uncharted waters. At the same time, international officials showed no inclination to accept the idea of statehood for rebellious minorities within the seceding entities, although some minorities expressed their wish for independence through the ballot box.

International officials continued to uphold the principle of the territorial integrity of states. Where this did not turn out to be feasible, then, as American attempts in 1996 to prevent the severance of Herzog-Bosna from a reconstituted Bosnian state and the subsequent Western opposition to the secession of Kosovo suggested, they at least tried to maintain old internal boundaries as the new frontiers of any seceding states. However, no outside authority could impose frontiers, and parties to wars of secession redrew international borders through trial by combat.

If the boundaries of most former Soviet republics have remained stable it is because most of them agreed between themselves to preserve the frontiers they inherited in 1991.[44] But international officials failed to persuade Serbia and Croatia to refrain from territorial expansion. And the establishment of diplomatic ties between Serbia and Croatia in the autumn of 1996 suggested that their common inability to win the war, rather than respect for existing borders, induced both to conform, by a long and tortuous route, to the principle of *uti possiditis*.

Regional and international organizations will try to reconcile self-determination with political unity by stressing the protection of minority rights through democratic practices and institutions. But self-determination, connoting the right to secession, will continue to come into conflict with international law. Illiberal states are just one aspect of the dilemma: what can the international community do with illiberal minorities? The democratic principle in itself was never a sufficient condition for recognition of the states that emerged out of the former Yugoslavia and USSR. All the criteria enunciated by the EC in December 1991 were not in place when the new countries were recognized.

The tension between the sovereignty of states and their international obligations, on the one side, and the desire of the international community that human rights and democracy should preserve that sovereignty, on the other, prevailed after 1991. "Post-Milošević" Serbia underlines the point. Will the electoral triumph of democratic forces in the Serbian elections of December 2000 be sufficient to defuse "democratic" demands for "self-determination" in Kosovo and Montenegro which could lead to the dismemberment of Serbia? How the international community tried to narrow the gap between the domestic and international dimensions of democratization in post-communist Europe is discussed in the next chapter.

NOTES

1. The dissolution of Czechoslovakia took place peacefully, so it had little international impact. Milica Bookman, "War and Peace: The Divergent Breakups of Yugoslavia and Czechoslovakia," *Journal of Peace Research*, vol. 31, no. 2 (1994); 175–87.

2. Boutros-Ghali, *An Agenda for Peace*, p. 41.

3. According to the Montevideo Convention of 1933 a state must possess a defined territory, an independent government, a permanent population and the capacity to conduct relations with other international entities.

4. Robert Hayden, "Constitutional Nationalism in the Formerly Yugoslav Republics," *Slavic Review*, vol. 51, no. 4 (winter 1992): 654–73.

5. Glenny, *The Fall of Yugoslavia*, p. 87.

6. *Foreign Broadcast Information Service* (*FBIS*), *Daily Report, Eastern Europe*, 25 June 1991, p. 36.

7. On the recognition of Macedonia see Duncan Perry, "The Republic of Macedonia and the Odds for Survival," RFE/RL *Research Report*, vol. 1, no. 46 (20 November 1992): 12–19.

8. Named after the French lawyer Robert Badinter and appointed by the London (Carrington) Conference on Yugoslavia in November 1991.

9. Opinion 6, 11 January 1992, 31.I.L.M.1992, pp. 1507–1512.

10. See p. 56 of this chapter.

11. Tim Judah, *The Serbs: History, Myth and the Destruction of Yugoslavia* (New Haven: Yale University Press, 1997).

12. See Tudjman's statement in BBC *Selected World Broadcasts* (SWB), 27 August 1990, EE/0853, B11 to B12. Commenting on the preponderance of Serbs in the police forces in Serb-majority areas, including Knin, Josip Boljkovac—then Croatia's Minister for Internal Affairs—stated, "This structure has to be changed, which we are doing in

accordance with our needs." Ibid., EE/0844/, B10. Warren Zimmerman, *Origins of a Catastrophe* (New York: Times Books, 1996), pp. 74–76, 95, 120, 132, 139, 152–53, corroborates these accounts. See also the U.S. State Department, *Country Reports on Human Rights Practices for 1991. Report Submitted to the Committee on Foreign Affairs, House of Representatives and the Committee on Foreign Relations* (Washington, D.C.: U.S. Senate, February 1992), p. 1322; Opinion 5 of the Badinter Commission, 31 I.L.M. 1992, p. 1505; *The Unfinished Peace: Report of the International Commission on the Balkans* (Washington, D.C.: Carnegie Endowment for International Peace, 1996), p. 106, and Glenny, *Fall of Yugoslavia*, pp. 121–24.

13. Good histories of Bosnia include Robert Donia and John Fine Jr., *Bosnia and Hercegovina: A Tradition Betrayed* (London: Hurst, 1994) and Noel Malcolm *Bosnia: A Short History* (Basingstoke: Macmillan, 1994).

14. United Nations General Assembly, 15th session, Resolution 1541 (XV), 15 December 1960.

15. Beverley Crawford, "Explaining Defection from International Cooperation: Germany's Unilateral Recognition of Croatia," *World Politics*, vol. 48, no. 4 (July 1996): 482–521.

16. United Nations General Assembly, 15th session, Resolution 1514 (XV), 14 December 1960.

17. Opinions 2 and 3 of the Badinter Arbitration Committee, 31 I.L.M. 1992, pp. 1497–1500.

18. 31 I.L.M. 1992, pp. 1501–3.

19. Cited in Marcus Tanner, *Croatia: A Nation Forged in War* (New Haven: Yale University Press, 1997), p. 271.

20. 31 I.L.M. 1992, pp. 1501–3.

21. Cited in Roland Rich, "Recognition of States: The Collapse of Yugoslavia and the Soviet Union," *European Journal of International Law*, vol. 4, no. 1 (1993): 51.

22. Martin Rady, "Self-Determination and the Dissolution of Yugoslavia," *Ethnic and Racial Studies*, vol. 19, no. 2 (April 1996): 387.

23. See Alexander Yakovlev's address to the USSR Congress of People's Deputies on 23 December 1989. A resolution passed by the Congress on 24 December 1989 stated that it deemed "the secret protocols to be legally invalid and null and void from the moment of their signing." BBC *SWB*, SU/0650, 30 December 1989, C1 to C10.

24. Cited in Halperin and Scheffer, *Self-Determination*, p. 28.

25. Ibid., p. 29.

26. The Soviet Union was not legally dissolved until December 1991, but after the failure of the August coup the Russian Federation was the *de facto* power.

27. See chapter 5.

28. Cf.Serbs in Bosnia and Croatia.

29. Stephen Jones, "Georgia: The Trauma of Statehood," in Ian Bremmer and Ray Taras, eds., *New States, New Politics: Building the Post-Soviet Nations* (Cambridge: Cambridge University Press, 1997), pp. 505–43; Ronald Suny, "Transcaucasia: Cultural Cohesion and Ethnic Revival," in Hajda and Beissinger, eds., *The Nationalities Factor in Soviet Politics and Society*, pp. 228ff.

30. This happened at a time when most non-Russian alphabets were Cyrillicized.

31. Darrell Slider, "Democratization in Georgia," in Karen Dawisha and Bruce Parrott, eds., *Conflict, Cleavage and Change in Central Asia and the Caucasus* (Cambridge: Cambridge University Press, 1997), pp. 156–98.

32. The chronology reveals the extent of political division between Georgians, Abkhazians and Ossetians. In December 1990 the South Ossetian parliament voted to leave Georgia and declared the sovereignty of South Ossetia. Several Abkhaz and Ossetian districts boycotted the referendum on Georgian independence in March 1991 but took part in the Union referendum and opted to remain in the USSR. On 21 December 1991 the South Ossetian Supreme Soviet declared independence from Georgia, and in the January 1992 referendum, 99 percent of South Ossetian voters endorsed secession from Georgia. In April 1992 the South Ossetian parliament wanted the region to be placed under Russian sovereignty. In February 1994 the Abkhaz parliament declared independence from Georgia.

33. Shevardnadze held various positions in the Georgian government and Soviet Communist Party before becoming Soviet Foreign Minister in 1985. He held this post until 1990. Between 1992 and 1995 he was Chairman of the Supreme Soviet of Georgia and Head of State; since 1995 he has been President of Georgia.

34. United Nations Security Council, 3268th meeting, Resolution S/RES/858; 24 August 1993; 3332nd meeting, Resolution S/RES/896; 31 January 1994; 3354th meeting, S/RES/906, 25 March 1994; 3488th meeting, S/RES/971, 12 January 1995; 3680th meeting, S/RES/1065, 12 July 1996; 3707th meeting, S/RES/1077, 22 October 1996; 3851st meeting, S/RES/1150, 30 January 1998; 3972nd meeting, S/RES/1225, 28 January 1999, para. 3.

35. Nagorno-Karabakh now functions as an independent state with its own president, parliament, army and communications with the outside world. Elizabeth Fuller, "Caucasus: Karabakh—A Quasi-Independent State—South Ossetia's Status Unclear," RFE/RL *Research Report*, July 1998.

36. United Nations Security Council, 3205th meeting, Resolution S/RES/822, 30 April 1993, and 3313rd meeting, S/RES/884, 12 November 1993.

37. Daria Fane, "Moldova: Breaking Loose from Moscow," in Ian Bremmer and Ray Taras, eds., *Nations and Politics in the Soviet Successor States* (Cambridge: Cambridge University Press, 1993), pp. 121ff.

38. Vera Tolz and Iain Elliott, eds., *The Demise of the USSR: From Communism to Independence* (Basingstoke: Macmillan, 1995), especially pp. 393–94.

39. "Charter of the Commonwealth of Independent States," in ibid., pp. 397–409.

40. James Baker, then American Secretary of State, called upon the seceding republics to make a commitment to democracy, free trade, free markets and respect for human rights. Cited in Halperin, *Self-Determination*, p. 30.

41. Referenda to decide the issue of independence were held in Lithuania on 9 February 1991, Latvia and Estonia on 3 March 1991, Georgia on 30 March, Armenia on 21 September, Turkmenistan on 26 October, Ukraine on 1 December, Azerbaijan and Uzbekistan on 29 December 1991.

42. Antonio Cassese notes that the EC Declaration of 16 December 1991 began with an affirmation of the principles of the *Helsinki Final Act* and the *Charter of Paris*, "in particular the principle of self-determination. By these words the Twelve intended to emphasize that they regarded the progressive breaking up of the two States [Yugoslavia and the Soviet Union] as a realization of the *political principle* of self-determination and as a historical process furthered by the concept that each people should freely choose its international political status." Cassese, *Self-Determination*, pp. 266–67. Italics in original.

43. Mayall, "1789 and the Liberal Theory of International Society," *Review of International Studies*, vol. 15, no. 4 (October 1989): 299.

44. See chapter 5.

Chapter 4
Reconciling the International and Domestic Dimensions of Democracy

It is important that the parties are as much as possible interested in outside involvement.
> Max van der Stoel, Warsaw address, 23 May 1993[1]

Democratization processes in general will take root in a society only if a number of conditions are met. First and foremost, there must exist the political will—both at the government level and in the community of citizens at large—to move towards a more democratic approach to government.
> Boutros Boutros-Ghali, 7 August 1995[2]

THE LIMITS OF INTERNATIONAL INTERVENTION

If the splintering of Yugoslavia and the USSR indicated that force is no guarantee for the survival of states or that an amicable political divorce is usually a chimera, then alternative ways of maintaining domestic stability needed to be explored. The intertwining of the issues of self-determination, minorities and democracy in the post–cold war world was unprecedented. The political, economic and military causes of the disintegration of the USSR and Yugoslavia were vastly complex, but there is no doubt that demands for self-determination by Estonia, Latvia and Lithuania and by Slovenia and Croatia respectively eroded the legitimacy of these states and dealt them the *coup de grace*. However, their collapse did not signal the end of the sovereign state as the keystone of the international edifice; rather it highlighted new assertions of sovereignty.[3]

Meanwhile, the secessionist wars in Croatia, Bosnia, Azerbaijan, Georgia and Moldova raised the specter of ethnic mayhem in the former communist bloc and of endless demands for self-determination leading to the forced redrawing of state frontiers. All these wars had domestic roots, and that is a major reason why international officials stressed the importance of internal policies in maintaining regional stability and recommended democracy as the way to manage ethnically diverse populations.

Moreover, the obstacles faced by the UN, the EC/EU and the Implementation Force (IFOR) in Bosnia highlighted the limits of what could be achieved by international intervention and underlined domestic stability as a prerequisite for regional and international security. In some measure these difficulties inspired the advocacy of democracy as the means by which internal and international peace could be maintained.

Given the fact of ethnic variety in most countries and the impracticality of every "nation" achieving statehood, minority and human rights are a means to enhance domestic and international peace. The conundrums—aggression, genocide and refugees—faced by the international community in Yugoslavia had their origins in its troubled history and in the failure of its successor states to guarantee minority and human rights.

For the second time in the twentieth century the wars that attended the breakup of Yugoslavia and the Soviet Union made minorities issues in Eastern Europe an international priority; they also led to a reformulation of the principles underlying international society. And the collapse of communism left democracy as the only ideology with worldwide appeal that could legitimize states. But how could the international and domestic dimensions of democracy be reconciled? In 1999 NATO's intervention in Kosovo raised a new question. Intended to reverse ethnic cleansing by Serb forces, uphold the values of democracy and human rights and establish a multiethnic democratic Kosovo, could the end result be exactly the opposite: that is, an Albanian nation-state in Kosovo created under the auspices of NATO and the UN as the Kosovo Liberation Army (KLA) tried to become the *de facto* government and Serbs fled the province?[4]

DEMOCRACY AND SOVEREIGNTY: SOME QUESTIONS

Democracy refers to a country's system of governance, but the international community has not left post–communist states to their own devices. Since 1991 European regional organizations, especially the OSCE and Council of Europe, have set in motion new mechanisms to facilitate diplomatic intervention, sometimes to end conflicts,[5] sometimes to persuade governments of the need to accommodate their ethnically mixed populations through democratic practices and institutions. How has such intervention been reconciled with the sovereignty of states in the post–cold war era?

International interest in protecting minority rights through democracy is partly inspired by a desire to preserve the sovereignty of states, the inviolability of borders and international stability. Minority rights are not a license to break up states. Democracy is seen as the best means of searching for a compromise between the often conflicting claims of order and justice. But democracy implies outside scrutiny of the internal conduct of states and an intrusion into their sovereignty, and the wars in Chechnya and Kosovo brought the issue into the limelight once again in very different ways. This chapter will address three questions arising from attempts to reconcile the international and domestic aspects of democratization in the former Yugoslavia and Soviet Union. First, what mechanisms have been set up by European regional organizations to safeguard minority rights through democracy, and have such mechanisms have been regarded by states as an infringement of their sovereignty? Second, how did the international community try to promote security through democratic principles in Chechnya and Kosovo? Third, to what extent does international engagement in elections—that essential precursor of democracy—contribute to ethnic amity and the strengthening of democracy in the former Yugoslavia and USSR?

PROMOTING MINORITY RIGHTS THROUGH DEMOCRATIC PRINCIPLES: THE ROLE OF INTERNATIONAL ORGANIZATIONS

The UN, OSCE, Council of Europe and EU have all cooperated with one another in trying to impress upon post-communist states the desirability of protecting minority rights through democracy. The UN, however, does not possess any enforcement mechanisms. Until the 1990s, reviews of the record of states in implementing minority rights were carried out by the Human Rights Committee, the Committee of Education, Social and Cultural Rights, the Committee on the Elimination of Racial Discrimination and the Committee on the Elimination of Discrimination Against Women. The Subcommission on the Prevention of Discrimination and Protection of Minorities and the Optional Protocol to the International Covenant on Cultural and Political Rights (1976) created a quasi-judicial mechanism for alleged violations of minority rights by giving the Human Rights Committee the authority to investigate individual complaints and to issue decisions, but these decisions had no legal force. In July 1995 the Economic and Social Committee created a Working Group, a subsidiary of the Subcommission on the Prevention of Discrimination and Protection of Minorities, to review the implementation of the UN *Declaration on Minority Rights*.[6] The UN General Assembly urged states to enforce the Declaration and called upon the UN High Commissioner for Human Rights to engage in dialogue with governments with a view to promoting implementation of the Declaration.[7]

The Council of Europe and the OSCE have been most actively engaged in persuading and advising post-communist states to enforce minority rights through democratic rule. A range of instruments has been devised to help states to fulfill their commitments on minority rights. These instruments have included the submission of voluntary reports by states about their enforcement of international norms on minority rights, mediation—especially by the OSCE—between disputing parties, reviews of the implementation of minority rights by the

Council of Europe and OSCE rapporteur missions. Any international standards on minority rights limit state sovereignty in theory, but international organizations have generally avoided conferring semi-independent or international status on minorities or territorial units which could challenge or reduce the authority of states.[8]

INTERVENTION THROUGH DIALOGUE: THE COUNCIL OF EUROPE

Despite the post–cold war emphasis on human rights, states, not individuals, are subjects of international law. But the *European Convention on Human Rights* gave citizens recourse to the European Court on Human Rights. The Council of Europe possesses a quasi-judicial system of enforcing human rights. The *European Convention on Human Rights* contains an elaborate procedure for the arbitration and judicial review of disputes over the implementation of human rights. However, the power to enforce decisions lies not with the Court but with the Committee of Ministers of the CE. Countries can be suspended for not complying with human rights standards: for example, Greece and Turkey were suspended in 1993, and in May 1999 Ukraine was threatened with suspension if it failed to abolish the death penalty.

The ambition of many countries to join the Council of Europe and the EU has given these organizations some leverage in persuading states to make a commitment to democracy and safeguard minority rights. Democracy implies outside surveillance of the internal behavior of states, and *in much of post-communist Europe this has taken place with the consent of states.* Since 1989 the Council of Europe has admitted democratizing states on the basis of commitments to comply with international norms on human rights, democracy and the rule of law. Its conditions for admission are the main way in which it imposes democratic procedures on its members. *The protection of minority rights is not the only criterion for admission*, and each request for admission is considered on its merits. For instance, the admission of Croatia and Russia in 1996 are especially controversial given Zagreb's discriminatory policies against its Serb minorities, its tardiness in implementing the Dayton Agreement and its frequent lack of cooperation with the International War Crimes Tribunal for Yugoslavia.[9] In the case of Russia human rights violations by the Russian army in Chechnya between 1994 and 1996 led to the interruption of Russia's application for membership of the CE, but Moscow's desire to engage with Europe enabled the CE to put pressure on the Russian government to make a commitment to fulfilling international human rights norms.[10] Russia also agreed to OSCE mediation with Chechen rebels. Defending their stance, CE officials argued that dialogue was the best way of influencing states[11] and encouraging reconciliation between minorities and governments. However, the question long will be debated whether conditions for admission were relaxed for Russia and Croatia. One thing is certain: there is no uniform way of applying the conditions.

Moreover, membership of the CE is more or less a prerequisite for admission into the EU. The *Council-Commission-European—Parliamentary Declaration on Human Rights* (1977) requires aspiring EU entrants to sign the *European Convention on Human Rights* and accept the right of individual petition. This is a component of the *acquis communautaire*,[12] the Maastricht Treaty and the Europe Agreements[13] signed by post–communist countries. The aim is to put moral and political pressure on states to safeguard minority rights through democracy.

In common with the UN and the OSCE, the Council of Europe also favors the protection of minority rights[14] without strengthening secessionist forces, but in principle international instruments on minority rights limit the sovereignty of states. States ratifying the CE *Charter for Regional or Minority Languages*[15] submit triennial reports to the Secretary-General on the measures taken by them to promote regional or minority languages. These reports are examined by a committee of experts who forward their opinions, together with comments by the states concerned, to the CE's Committee of Ministers. The Secretary-General of the CE makes a biennial report to its Parliamentary Assembly on the application of the Charter by signatory states. At another level, the Standing Conference of Local and Regional Authorities of Europe is entrusted with creating conditions in which ethnic communities straddling frontiers might form Euroregions to bridge legal barriers on subjects of common interest, such as education, culture and the environment. For example, Poland, Ukraine, Slovakia, Hungary and Romania formed the Carpathian Euroregion to advance cooperation in the cultural and scientific fields and to look afresh at their historical ties.

The Committee of Ministers also monitors implementation of the CE *Framework Convention for National Minorities*.[16] States that have ratified the Convention present reports on enforcement measures taken by them. The implementation of minority rights is discussed in the CE Committee of Ministers and the Parliamentary Assembly, which has also sponsored projects to ease tensions between communities in the areas of education, culture, regional and local government.

Minority rights were also to be safeguarded through the Pact on Stability in Europe (Stability Pact) signed under EU auspices in March 1995. The Pact was intended to create a favorable climate for the strengthening of democracy, the enhancement of respect for human rights and the identities of peoples and the promotion of economic development. Emphasis was laid on bilateral resolution of disputes by neighboring countries. Initially two regional round tables were established: one for the Baltic countries, one for Central and East European countries. The OSCE is responsible for monitoring the implementation of the Pact. A third Stability Pact, dealing with the Balkans, was presented at the EU meeting in Cologne on 10 June 1999. Like its predecessors it seeks to promote democracy, ethnic amity and economic prosperity and to preserve the territorial integrity of states in the Balkans. The Stability Pacts reflect once again the hopes of European policy-makers that democratic rule will usher in lasting peace in areas with considerable potential for ethnic strife.[17]

INTERVENTION THROUGH DIALOGUE: THE OSCE

During the cold war the CSCE[18] reviewed the compliance of member-states in enforcing human rights norms on an *ad hoc* basis. The CSCE suggested norms at a series of conferences held at Helsinki (1973–75), Belgrade (1977–78) and Vienna (1986–89). More specialized meetings in Ottawa in 1985 and Berne in 1988 supplemented these conferences. Discussion of the extent to which states were implementing human rights served as an opportunity to highlight human rights abuses and, consequently, as a pretext to put pressure on them to reform, but there was no procedure by which enforcement could be monitored systematically. In 1990 the Office for Democratic Institutions and Human Rights (ODIHR) was established to promote the new priorities of the OSCE. These priorities included the consolidation of common democratic values and the prevention of conflict through dialogue, the monitoring of the human rights situation in countries and assistance in the building of civil society. Through diplomacy the OSCE tried to persuade states to abide by human rights norms and stressed that human rights, fundamental freedoms and the rule of law were an international concern. The most important instruments of its diplomacy on minorities issues were the Human Dimension Mechanism, the High Commissioner on National Minorities (HCNM) and Missions.

The term "human dimension" refers to the commitment made by OSCE member-states to respect human rights, uphold the rule of law, advance democratic principles and build democratic institutions. The Human Dimension Mechanism grew out of the *Vienna Document* (1989), the *Moscow Document* (1991)[19] and the *Decisions of the Rome Council* (1993). Participating states exchange information, hold bilateral meetings and invite an OSCE mission of up to three experts to contribute to the resolution of a dispute on their territory. The Moscow mechanism was invoked by Russia with reference to Estonian citizenship laws, and Estonia invited an OSCE mission to suggest amendments which might inspire the confidence of their Russian-speaking minorities. In 1993 Moldova requested an OSCE mission to help sort out its differences with Russian minorities in the Trans-Dniestr. Annual Implementation Review conferences were outlined in the *Prague Document on Further Development of CSCE Institutions and Structures* (1992); states taking part in them investigated the enforcement of OSCE norms on human and minority rights. Again sovereignty was not an issue when states sought or welcomed intervention by the OSCE. It became a bone of contention when a state declined to cooperate, as did Serbia when it refused to give visas to an OSCE rapporteur mission to look into human rights violations on its territory and expelled three OSCE missions—in 1992, 1994 and 1999.

The OSCE appointed Max van der Stoel as its first High Commissioner on National Minorities in January 1993 to counsel governments on domestic legislation to accommodate minorities, to advise states and the OSCE Permanent Council on measures necessary to issue an early warning of tensions that could escalate into conflict and, so, to avert conflict. Van der Stoel described his brief thus: "The role of my office is to prevent fires caused by inter-ethnic tensions from breaking out in the first place. If there are signs of smoke, my job is to address the situation and try to put it out, or, if that fails, to raise the alarm."[20] The HCNM seeks to resolve ethnic conflicts and to work *with* states to craft long-term measures to promote and safeguard minority rights. His unique mandate is to handle primarily domestic conflicts having an international dimension.[21] He is exclusively charged with monitoring the enforcement of minority rights; his suggestions are not binding on governments, and he is aware that the ultimate responsibility for translating his advice into enforceable policies rests with states. He maintains confidentiality and impartiality and has scope for independent action. He makes clear that he is not acting on behalf of minorities and that the OSCE favors solutions to minority problems within the framework of existing states. Van der Stoel mediated in disputes involving Russian minorities in Estonia, Latvia, Lithuania, Ukraine and Moldova; he acted as a catalyst for the Hungarian-Romanian Treaty of 1996[22] and intervened with the government of Vladimir Mečiar to protect the rights of Magyar minorities in Slovakia. In Estonia and Latvia his diplomacy contributed to the liberalization of citizenship laws so that Russians who had settled in these countries after the Soviet invasion of 1940 could acquire citizenship more easily.[23] The HCNM advised the Ukrainian government to allow the use of the Russian language along with Ukrainian in state institutions, brokered negotiations between Kiev and leaders of the Russian minority in the Crimea and recommended autonomy for the Crimea within the constitution and territory of Ukraine. The willingness of so many countries to seek the HCNM's mediation or to listen to his counsel reflected the desire of governments for international help on minorities issues. In such cases sovereignty did not give rise to disagreement: the HCNM acted only with the agreement and cooperation of states. Van der Stoel saw his limited budget as his main problem; he was on the whole satisfied that OSCE member-states usually endorsed his recommendations and tried to carry them out.[24]

The OSCE also established Missions as an instrument of conflict prevention, crisis prevention and resolution in former communist countries. The size and mandates of the Missions varied, but for all Missions the strengthening of democracy and the rule of law were cardinal aims. Missions were set up in Macedonia, Ukraine, Albania, Central Asia, Estonia, Georgia, Latvia, Tajikistan, Moldova, Bosnia, Sandjak, Vojvodina and Kosovo. The Missions encouraged dialogue between representatives of minorities and their governments, collected information on human rights problems and tried to suggest remedies.

The Mission to Bosnia was established in December 1995 and advised the government on how best to implement the Dayton Agreement. Its democracy-building activities included judicial reform, the promotion of human rights and the enforcement of regional stabilization measures. The Mission contributed to the organization of general elections in 1996 and 1998, municipal elections in 1997 and national assembly elections in the Republic Srpska in November 1997.

The OSCE Mission to Croatia, established in April 1996, monitored the enforcement of Croatian legislation and agreements and commitments entered into by the Croatian government on the return of all refugees and displaced persons and the protection of minorities. Its work assumed special significance when the Croatian government took over Eastern Slavonia, Baranja and Western Sirmium from the UN, and it has not been helped by Zagreb's stalling on measures which would have made it easier for Serbs to return to their homes.

OSCE Missions to Serbia were not well received by the Serbian authorities. The Kosovo Verification Mission was the largest, most complex mission undertaken by the OSCE. Established in October 1998 in accordance with an agreement between the OSCE and Serbia its purpose was to monitor Serbia's compliance with UN Security Council resolutions 1160 and 1199,[25] to verify maintenance of the cease-fire, to help refugees and displaced persons to go back to their homes, supervise elections, establish new administrative structures and promote human rights and democracy. The recalcitrance of Serbia and the KLA brought on war in March 1999,[26] what was more surprising was the absence of any tip-off by the Kosovo Verification Mission about ethnic cleansing by Serb forces.

In the former Soviet Union the Mission facilitated a settlement of the Georgian-Ossetian conflict. It also sought to remove the sources of ethnic misunderstanding and to explore how the political aspirations of the Abkhazians could be reconciled with the territorial integrity of Georgia.

In Moldova the OSCE Mission counseled the government on the creation of a special status for the Trans-Dniestrian region as a starting point for the negotiations, and in July 1995 Russian leaders in the Trans-Dniestr and the Moldovan authorities agreed to renounce force. In May 1997 the Mission in Ukraine worked to promote free and fair elections and an independent media in the Crimea. It also helped leaders of the Russian minority in the Crimea to arrive at an agreement on the political status of the Crimea within Ukraine. OSCE Missions also advised the Estonian and Latvian governments on how to liberalize citizenship laws with a view to accommodating their Russian-speaking minorities.

Generally it can be said that, far from opposing international scrutiny of their performance in complying with international norms on minority rights, most post-communist states sought and welcomed OSCE mediation and monitoring of their record in enforcing international standards. However, some countries, such as Serbia and Russia, faced with secessionist threats and attempts by their Albanian and Chechen minorities to change borders through war, used all their military might to preserve their territorial integrity and initially resisted international intervention. As in 1991, international officials were inconsistent in their responses to the crises that unfolded from the secessionist wars in Chechnya and Kosovo in the second half of the nineties.

RECONCILING DEMOCRACY AND SOVEREIGNTY? CHECHNYA 1994 AND 1999

Many Chechens claimed that the demand for "independence" from post–Soviet Russia had its roots in a long history of enmity between Chechens and their "Russian" overlords. Repression by the Tsarist empire in the nineteenth century, by the Bolsheviks between 1918 and 1921 and the deportation of tens of thousands of Chechens between 1943 and 1944 all combined to forge a historical memory and imagination that inspired a move for independence from Russia in the early 1990s. The creation by the Bolsheviks of the autonomous *Oblast* of Chechnya in 1922 did not end the desire for independence: the Soviets faced rebellion in Chechnya in the 1930s.[27]

In 1989 Chechens were a majority—57 percent of the population—in their Autonomous Republic, and Russians made up about 12 per cent. In November 1990 the All-National Conference of Chechens declared the sovereignty of Chechnya, stating that Chechnya was willing to be the subject of the Union Treaty. The inference was that its status should be upgraded to that of Union Republic—that it was not calling for secession from the USSR—but the Soviet authorities turned down the demand.[28]

In November 1991, General Dzhokar Dudaev, then president of the Chechen republic, proclaimed its sovereignty and won an election on the platform of independence. Yeltsin's government contested the validity of the elections, issued a warrant for Dudaev's arrest and sent troops to Grozny. The Russian army was obstructed at Grozny airport by the Chechen National Guard, and the Russian parliament recalled the troops. But Moscow never recognized the legitimacy of the Chechen vote for independence and refused to negotiate with Dudaev. The outcome in December 1994 was the outbreak of a brutal war which resulted in more than 70,000 casualties and massive human rights abuses by Russian forces.

The United States and EU countries castigated Russia for the human rights violations by its army, but at no time were they willing to recognize the independence of Chechnya. Western governments were concerned that the disintegration of Russia would create chaos. The American State Department was clear that the United States had "no interest and the world has no interest in seeing a splintering or dismembering of the Russian Federation. That would be enormously destabilizing. It would produce the possibility of large-scale refugee flows"; it could have a domino effect throughout Russia. The State Department sympathized with Russia's attempt to control "a very crime-ridden and corruption-ridden province.[29] American policy-makers also drew analogies with the American Civil War, asserting that the Civil War had been fought on the principle that "no state had a right to withdraw from our union."[30]

The EU and Council of Europe expressed support for Russia's territorial unity while putting moral and diplomatic pressure on Moscow to end the war and make peace with the Chechens. On 15 December 1994 the European Parliament adopted a resolution stating that Chechnya was part of the Russian Federation. The EU made a distinction between human rights violations by the Russian army and support for a democratic government in Moscow and deemed that the latter deserved higher priority. EU officials criticized human rights abuses by Russian troops but perceived Yeltsin as the main democratizing force in Russia and wished to avoid isolating him diplomatically.[31]

However, Russia must realize that repression was not the best way to preserve its territorial integrity, and the EU and Council of Europe exerted diplomatic and moral pressure on Russia to end the war. The EU suspended negotiation of the Partnership and Cooperation Agreement with Russia, while the Council of Europe interrupted consideration of Russia's application for membership. Subsequently, Russia's military débacle and its wish to engage with Europe made it amenable to diplomatic intervention by the EU, Council of Europe and OSCE, and these organizations advised Moscow to make peace on the basis of democratic norms.

What "democratic principles" were invoked by European regional organizations to reconcile their opposition to demands for secession by Chechens with condemnation of human rights violations by the Russian army? How did they persuade both sides to work for a settlement?

European regional organizations urged Russian and Chechen leaders to negotiate. The Kremlin was persuaded to conduct free and fair elections in Chechnya in the belief that popular access to the ballot box would inspire Chechen confidence in Moscow's intention to govern democratically. In the aftermath of the polls, in which the Chechen leadership triumphed, the Kremlin and the regional government arrived at a compromise on the division of powers between Moscow and Grozny, based on the idea of political and intellectual pluralism and multiple centers of power in a democracy.[32]

The fact that both Chechen leaders and the Russian government accepted outside mediation and that the OSCE was able to broker a settlement suggest that dialogue did play a significant role in containing conflict, if only because Moscow had a real need for peace in Chechnya. Finding European regional organizations desirous of preserving Russia's territorial integrity, Moscow became more inclined to conciliate Chechen rebels. Chechnya between 1994 and 1996 illustrates how the OSCE used the twin principles of dialogue and democracy to end armed hostilities and to settle differences between Chechen rebels and Moscow. This was the first step toward enhancing domestic and regional security; whether it was sufficient is another story.[33]

CHECHNYA: POST-1999

Facing—or conniving with—a strident "Islamic" militancy, the regional Chechen administration was unable to maintain law and order. It also resorted to "Islamic" legal practices, which were condemned by European officials. In 1999 the Chechen parliament passed an "Islamic" constitution, intended to come into force in 2001. Lord Russell-Johnston, President of the Parliamentary Assembly of the Council of Europe, criticized this measure as being incompatible with both the *European Convention on Human Rights* and the Russian constitution. The Chechen government also allowed Wahabi militants from the neighboring republic of Dagestan to establish military bases on Chechen soil. In 1999 the Wahabis launched a war of independence from Russia and proclaimed the establishment of the "Islamic State of Dagestan." Terrorist action in Moscow alarmed the Kremlin as well as the international community. As in 1994, Russia retaliated with massive military force. Once again the EU and CE expressed concern over fresh human rights abuses by the Russian army in Chechnya but were explicit that they stood for the territorial unity of Russia. The EU presidency condemned "the declaration of the so-called Islamic state of Dagestan" and "recognized the territorial integrity of the Russian Federation."[34] Lord Russell-Johnston affirmed that the Russian government "can count on our support in the fight against terrorism."[35] For its part, Russia initially asked foreign countries to refrain from meddling in its internal affairs but eventually allowed an OSCE mission into Chechnya.[36]

Chechnya demonstrated—both in 1994 and 1999—that the domestic inclinations of states may be the most important factor in deciding whether sovereignty will be a subject of disagreement. Russia was not the first democratizing state to use force against violent separatists and to brush off international strictures on human rights abuses by its army. But in 1996 Moscow's recognition of the limits of what could be achieved through war rendered it willing to accept OSCE mediation. Its refusal, to date, to accept outside mediation in the 1999 war suggests that other, as yet unknown forces may be at play in the Kremlin. At the beginning of December 1999, threats by the International Monetary Fund to link economic aid to a more conciliatory policy in Chechnya were offset by statements by EU officials that isolation could provoke a domestic Russian backlash against the international community.[37] The 1999 war in Chechnya also reaffirmed the international community's continuing endorsement of the territorial integrity of states. In 1999 the war in Kosovo also underlined this point—but in a very different way.

DEMOCRACY AND SOVEREIGNTY: KOSOVO 1999

Eight years after the dissolution of Yugoslavia, the crisis in Kosovo showed yet again the difficulties faced by international officials in urging states to respect human rights and democratic norms and in reconciling the principles of territorial unity and self-determination.

Conflicting interpretations of history contributed to the war in Kosovo. In 1389 the Ottomans defeated the Serbs at Pristina and incorporated Kosovo into the Ottoman empire, where it remained until it was reconquered by Serbia following the Balkan war of 1913.[38] Both Serbs and Albanians in Kosovo regard the territory as the cradle of their respective "nations" and see themselves as descendants of its original inhabitants. The 1974 Yugoslav constitution granted Kosovo the status of Autonomous Republic and recognized the Kosovar Albanians comprising 90 percent of its population as a nationality.[39] In the political parlance of the former Yugoslavia this meant that unlike the Croats and Slovenes, Kosovar Albanians were not a nation and did not have their own national republic or the right to secede. In September 1991 the majority of Kosovar Albanians voted for independence, but their claim to statehood was not recognized by the international community, which wanted to preserve the frontiers of the seceding national republics as their new international borders. In contrast to the Serbs and Croats in Bosnia, the Albanians were not then in a position to mount an armed challenge to the sovereignty and territorial integrity of Serbia. The international community's attitude toward the Albanian demand for statehood mirrored its response to separatist demands by Serbs and Croats in Bosnia and Serbs in Croatia. International officials anticipated that minority and human rights would be protected by the successor states to the former Yugoslavia. In fact the Kosovar Albanians were repressed by Milošević, just as Croatian Serbs were discriminated against by the Tudjman administration. Again, at the Dayton Conference in 1995, the Kosovar Albanian claim to statehood was ignored.[40]

The 1974 Yugoslav constitution was also destined to antagonize the Kosovar Serbs. Equal rights granted to all communities under the constitution led to Kosovar Serbs being discriminated against. Four-fifths of official posts were reserved for Albanians, resulting in the "virtual Albanianization" of the provincial administration.[40] There was no spirit of compromise on either side. Making a bad situation worse, Milošević abolished autonomy for Kosovo in December 1989 and sacked many Albanians from its government. The combination of repression and discrimination exacerbated communal ill will.

The resentment of Kosovar Albanians was exploited by Sali Berisha, elected president of Albania in 1992. He fomented irredentism by claiming that all Albanians were one nation. Backing Albanian separatism in Kosovo, he encouraged the KLA, formed in 1993,[42] which carried out attacks on Serbs and insisted on independence.

Following Berisha's defeat in the 1995 Albanian elections, his successor, Fatos Nano, did not overtly aid the KLA and sought international mediation in defusing the tension there. International officials fretted. The presence of Albanian minorities in Macedonia and Montenegro conjured up visions of a simmering Balkan cauldron about to boil over, and Balkan states, including Bulgaria, Greece, Macedonia, Romania and Turkey, called for dialogue to end the crisis. Stressing respect for existing international boundaries, they condemned terrorism "in all its forms" and violence "as a means of repressing political ideas." The United States was against both independence and what Secretary of State Madeleine Albright described as "the untenable status quo"— a reference to the repression carried out by Serbian forces in Kosovo. The EU castigated both terrorism and repression of "non-violent expression of political views." Russia urged that the rights of Albanian minorities be observed in accordance with OSCE and UN standards and favored some form of autonomy within Serbia.[43] But even Ibrahim Rugova, the moderate Kosovar Albanian leader, demanded independence, while Milošević was adamant that talks on Kosovo could only take place on the basis of the existing Yugoslav constitution.[44] Moreover, Serbia would not brook outside intervention in Kosovo. Serbian voters endorsed their government's stance in a special referendum held on 8 April 1998. Belgrade's opposition to international infringement of Serbia's sovereignty thus earned popular legitimacy.

The irony was that Belgrade's resistance to international intrusion, underscored by a popular vote, put Serbia at odds with the OSCE's policy of seeking solutions to minority problems through democratic means. Warning Belgrade that the Kosovo crisis could adversely affect security in the Balkans, the OSCE asserted that Kosovo was not just Serbia's internal affair. Belgrade remained unmoved. As in 1991, the West was unable to devise a coherent policy for containing conflict, let alone a longer-term solution to ethnic dilemmas in the Balkans. NATO was undecided whether to deploy forces in Northern Albania and Macedonia to put pressure on Serbia to follow a more conciliatory policy toward its Albanian minorities, or whether intervention against Serbia could be misconstrued as Western backing for Kosovo's secession from Serbia.[45] *Deja vu!*

The first half of 1998 saw Serb forces and the KLA wrestling for control over the Drenica triangle, with the Serbian army finally reestablishing its hold over the area. But Belgrade's attempts to wipe out the KLA were attended by severe human rights violations. Serb forces targeted the civilian population and resorted to scorched earth tactics. By September 1998 a quarter of a million Albanians had been put to flight. The declining security situation led Western countries to step up the search for diplomatic and military solutions to the crisis. They held fast to the principle of the territorial integrity of Serbia even while denouncing human rights abuses by Serb troops.

In October 1998, the peace plan presented by Christopher Hill, the American ambassador to Macedonia, left both sides dissatisfied: the Serbs because it gave too liberal an autonomy to Kosovo, the Albanians because it fell short of independence.[46] Envisaging power-sharing between different national communities, the Hill plan only raised the prospect of political polarization and deadlock. The OSCE would supervise elections and a joint commission would coordinate implementation of the agreement. All parties were obliged to cooperate with the International War Crimes Tribunal in The Hague. International intervention to enforce the agreement was also envisaged. *Both* Belgrade and the KLA refused to compromise.

NATO threatened air strikes against Serbia in order to avert further humanitarian catastrophe. This failed to sway Belgrade, which had already rejected international intervention in Kosovo and secured popular support for its stance. In January 1999 Serbia demanded the removal of the OSCE Kosovo Verification Mission. But it was not until the killing of forty Albanians by Serb forces at Racak in the same month that the Contact Group—comprising the United States, the United Kingdom, France, Italy, Germany and Russia—convened a conference at Rambouillet in February 1999.

At Rambouillet the Contact Group sought to end the violence through dialogue and presented nonnegotiable terms to Serbia and the Kosovar Albanians.[47] The terms envisaged preservation of the territorial integrity of Yugoslavia and neighboring countries while upholding human rights and autonomy for Kosovo. NATO would enforce any agreement. The Contact Group came up against the KLA's demand for independence and Serbia's resistance to outside intervention in Kosovo. The Rambouillet draft tried to find a meeting point between these opposing objectives by leaving untouched the issue of Kosovo's future political status for three years and envisaged a "final settlement for Kosovo, on the basis of the will of the people, opinions of relevant authorities, each Party's efforts regarding the implementation of this Agreement, and the Helsinki Final Act." For very different reasons, Belgrade and the KLA made the same interpretation of this provision—and then reacted to it in dissimilar ways. To the KLA the terms implied a legal right to hold a referendum of the people of *Kosovo*. As Albanians comprised the majority in the province, the chances were that Kosovo could become independent under international auspices after three years. Initially the KLA welcomed this prospect. But Serbia saw the Rambouillet terms curbing its sovereignty and dug in its heels.

Belgrade rejected the Rambouillet proposals. So did the Kosovar Albanians, represented, for the most part, at the Rambouillet conference not by the elected government of Kosovo but by those closer to the more militant KLA.[48] In a last-ditch attempt at compromise the Contact Group convened another conference in Paris in March 1999. The terms presented by Serbia at Paris confirmed again that the political division between Contact Group and Belgrade lay in the nature of power to be exercised over Kosovo. Belgrade made clear that it would exercise federal functions in Kosovo, that the functions of the Kosovo assembly would be reduced and that there would be no Constitutional or Supreme Court in the province. No agreement on these lines was possible, so the Contact Group urged the Kosovar Albanians to accept the original Rambouillet draft. The prospect of a referendum at the end of three years which could result in independence for Kosovo induced the Kosovar Albanians to sign up. But Serbia would not budge. Having threatened to launch air strikes if the talks broke down, NATO was left with no option but to carry out its threat on 24 March 1999.

The NATO offensive was the first attack by the alliance on a sovereign state. It was justified as a humanitarian intervention, aimed at reversing ethnic cleansing of Albanians from Kosovo and upholding the principles of democracy and human rights.[49] The air strikes had the opposite effect. They provided Milošević with a pretext to throw out more than a million Albanians from Kosovo in an attempt to create an ethnically pure province. The details of this humanitarian catastrophe are beyond the scope of this book. What concerns us here is the question of whether NATO's defeat of Milošević augured the emergence of a democratic multiethnic Kosovo. The first signs were not encouraging. Albanian refugees returning home after the truce wreaked revenge on Serbs. It was now the turn of Serbs to flee Kosovo, as NATO forces were unable to protect them. The specter of an Albanian nation-state in Kosovo loomed large. If that were to become a reality, it would mean the defeat of NATO's long-term objective.

The wars in Chechnya and Kosovo proved that force is no remedy for ethnic discontent and violence, that democratic principles must be respected by governments *and* nationalists and that peace cannot be imposed on belligerents who see the chance of achieving their aims through war. Sovereignty became an issue because of human rights violations by the Serbian army in Kosovo. But the KLA also killed many Albanians, and whether its campaign for an independent Kosovo can be reconciled with the professed international aim of preserving the territorial integrity of Serbia is uncertain. Neither the Serbian government nor the KLA appeared committed to democratic principles. It is too early to say whether an EU–sponsored Stability Pact and economic largesse in the form of "Marshall Aid" for the Balkans will help to stabilize the region, whether Kosovo has ceased to be an area of disputed sovereignty or whether its territorial contours—and those of post-communist Europe—have been finalized.

NATO claimed that it was fighting for human rights and democracy in Kosovo, that it was waging war against the oppressive regime of Milošević and not the people of Serbia. But this glossed over the fact that Milošević had won three consecutive elections since 1991, and some European leaders realized that inflicting a military defeat on him would not guarantee the election of a liberal successor.[50] The international and domestic dimensions of democracy would still need to be reconciled. Despite international pressure Serbia refused to observe democratic norms or respect human rights. Nor could Belgrade or the Kosovar Albanians be dissuaded from waging war. Yet again Kosovo shows how the failure to abide by democratic standards can provoke secession and that the international community cannot foist democracy on those uninterested in practising it.

Intractable conflicts are less likely if states have a democratic orientation: this explains the interest of the international community in advancing democracy through free and fair multiparty elections. But to what extent have elections promoted democracy in the former communist bloc?

BUILDING DEMOCRACY: INTERNATIONAL
INVOLVEMENT IN ELECTIONS

Political choices made by citizens and rulers are the keys to the success of a country's transition to democracy. International officials know that it takes time for democracy to be fortified.[51] Meanwhile, democracy assistance[52] has been given by European regional organizations with a view to facilitating the holding of free and fair elections in the former communist bloc and, more generally, to help sustain democracy. That includes the transfer of specific expertise at the local and national levels to professional groups and associations and the promotion and building of civil society. It is still too early to measure the success of democratization in the former communist bloc.[53]

There can be no democracy without regular, free and fair multiparty elections. They allow all communities to choose their rulers and to participate in nation-building. Fairly conducted, polling can also assure minorities of the intention of their governments to rule democratically. International policy-makers have hoped that elections will bring about consensus and enhance domestic stability. To what extent have the conduct and results of elections in the former Yugoslavia and Soviet Union fulfilled this expectation?

International monitoring of elections in post–cold war Eastern Europe and the CIS has made them international events. Such monitoring is intended to deter manipulation and fraud by official agencies and to display international support for the triumph of democracy over authoritarianism in countries which, because of their fragile democratic traditions, were once considered incapable of ever achieving it. Election monitoring also underlines the involvement of the international community in the process of democratization.[54]

What are the criteria of the UN and European regional organizations for deciding that an election is free and fair? Election monitors take into account implementation of the law and of electoral regulations, the effectiveness and impartiality of the preelection arrangements, independence of the media, the nature of the campaign and the political environment leading up to election day, polling day itself, the final vote count, the announcement of the results and the handling of appeals and complaints.[55]

ELECTIONS—HARBINGERS OF DEMOCRACY AND
ETHNIC STABILITY?

Elections in the war-ravaged republics of the former Yugoslavia have not encouraged much optimism about either the future of democracy or ethnic equilibrium. Nowhere are the difficulties of bridging the gap between the international and domestic dimensions of democratization more evident than in Bosnia, where the international community has found itself buttressing a state unable to sustain its independence without international military support.

Bosnia has seen a unique attempt by the UN, OSCE, EU and NATO to lay the foundations of democracy in the former communist bloc; there, international organizations have gone farthest in simultaneously constructing democracy and a new state from scratch.[56] Elections in Bosnia were linked with the enforcement of the human rights provisions of the Dayton and the Paris Agreements[57] and the aim of municipal and national elections was to prepare the ground for new democratic political structures. International officials hoped to improve interethnic relations through democratization by fostering political and intellectual diversity, encouraging the development of a free media and strengthening democratic institutions and respect for human rights. In the long run they wish to build a civil society through dialogue,[58] reconciliation and the setting up of new democratic institutions.[59]

The task was daunting. The Dayton/Paris Agreement was actually a treaty between three of the five successor states to Yugoslavia—Bosnia, Serbia and Croatia. The Agreement recognized the legal sovereignty of the Bosnian state[60] while simultaneously creating two separate entities, the Federation of Bosnia-Herzegovina and the Republic Srpska, within this state. It also recognized three peoples—Bosnians, Serbs, Croats—miscellaneous others—two citizenships, two police forces and two armies. This complex setup itself reflected the quarrels and compromises that went into the making of the Dayton/Paris Agreement and foreshadowed difficulties in implementing it.

Provisions on democracy and human rights in the Dayton/Paris Agreement could be divided into two categories: those where enforcement would prepare the ground for the setting up of a new Bosnian state and those which would be implemented by a new Bosnian government. The first category included the return of some 2.5 million refugees and displaced persons to their places of origin with restoration of their property and the holding of elections in which Bosnian citizens could, if necessary, vote by absentee ballot in the municipality in which they had resided in 1991. The idea was to ensure the reversal of ethnic cleansing through polling. The Agreement also called for the identification and bringing to justice before the International War Crimes Tribunal of individuals suspected of war crimes. The performance of all these tasks was a necessary prelude to the "real," crucial and most difficult phase, which would come after the elections:[61] the creation of political institutions under the Bosnian constitution[62] and the enforcement of the human rights provisions of the Agreement.[63]

There are no local traditions or legal precedents to legitimize or popularize the articles on human rights in the Dayton/Paris Agreement. The constitution of Bosnia and its human rights provisions[64] have been framed with reference to the UN Charter and *Declaration of Human Rights* and international human rights agreements including the Genocide Convention, the *European Convention on Human Rights*, the International Covenants on Political and Civil Rights and on Economic, Social and Cultural Rights. The provisions represent an attempt to safeguard individual and group rights and include the rights to life and liberty, freedom of thought, conscience, religion, expression and liberty of movement and residence. The draft constitution of Bosnia names the institutions through which human rights will be implemented, including a constitutional court, an ombudsman, and a Human Rights Chamber. This takes us back to the origins of the war in Bosnia and the question of credible guarantees for the protection of minorities and human rights, in other words, the day-to-day workings of the reconstituted Bosnian state. In the long run, it is the ability of authorities—Bosnian or international—to enforce them that alone will inspire all communities with confidence and usher in a lasting peace.

Several paradoxes emerge from the story of the United Nations Protection Force (UNPROFOR) and IFOR missions in Bosnia and the difficulties IFOR, the OSCE and EU face in carrying out the Dayton Agreement. The long-term problem in Bosnia is to create a state that is both stable and democratic enough to enforce human rights. Human rights are the brainchild of the international community, but their implementation depends on states. Human rights are best protected by democracies, but democracy does not ensure respect for human rights.

DOES THE PEOPLE'S CHOICE ASSURE DEMOCRACY?

The implementation of the Dayton/Paris accord has highlighted many dilemmas of democratization. Because elections are the precondition for democracy, there is a tendency to equate the two. In fact, elections in themselves are not sufficient to forge democracy and, in some cases, have amounted to little more than political maneuvering.

Voter turnout in the Bosnian municipal elections in September 1997 was 70 percent. But the OSCE reported that, contrary to the Dayton/Paris Agreement, displaced persons could not return to their homes. Freedom of movement and media coverage were also restricted. Elections in the Republika Srpska were marred by the same flaws.[65] Nonetheless, elections remained the only way by which viable democratic institutions could be established.[66]

International policy-makers cannot influence the choice of voters, and frequently they have been embarrassed by the electoral triumph of illiberal nationalists. In September 1998 the ultranationalist Nikola Poplasen was elected President of the Republic Srpska. His refusal to appoint a prime minister capable of commanding a parliamentary majority led to his dismissal in March 1999 by Carlos Westerndorp, the EU high representative in Bosnia. The will of the people was clearly at odds with the ways in which international officials hoped to advance democracy.

Electoral rigging in Serbia brought intolerant nationalists to power on no less than three occasions. The Serbian presidential elections of 1997 could not be validated because the voter turnout was less than 50 percent and had to be rescheduled for 7 December 1997. There were widespread reports of electoral fraud, and some polling booths did not open at all. Nonetheless the Serbian authorities tabulated election results from these polling stations. Official records showed a turnout of almost 100 percent, with the candidate of the ruling Left Coalition obtaining almost universal approval.[67]

In the Croatian elections of 1993 and 1995, the Tudjman administration restricted access by opposition parties to the state media. In both Serbia and Croatia highly centralized governments censored the media and tried to curtail the independence of the judiciary by appointing "suitable" judicial officials. Ultranationalist ideology, privileging communal over individual rights, was used to legitimize the regime and its authoritarian tendencies.[68] Neither country displayed much tolerance toward minorities. Croatia "solved" the problem of having to win over dissatisfied Serb minorities in the Krajina and Western Slavonia by expelling most of them in August 1995 with the connivance of the United States.[69] Will the success of a liberal coalition led by Ivica Račan in the December 1999 Croatian elections see the emergence of a policy more tolerant of Serbs? At the start of 2001, it is too early to say. Meanwhile, Serbia repressed Albanians in Kosovo. For its part the KLA has hardly shown liberalism toward Kosovar Serbs, while the international administration in Kosovo has not been able to assure them security. Consequently, many Serbs have fled Kosovo even as the UN, buoyed by NATO, has tried to build the multiethnic, democratic Kosovo that NATO claimed was its objective. Will the triumph of more democratic forces in the Serbian presidential and parliamentary elections held in the last quarter of 2000 will act as a moderating influence over Serb and Albanian extremists in Kosovo?

The success of illiberal nationalists also meant that some governments did not honor their obligations on human rights. For example, Croatia frequently has refused to cooperate with the International War Crimes Tribunal on Yugoslavia and, short of threatening economic sanctions, there is little that the international community can do to secure Zagreb's cooperation or to ensure that Serb refugees can return to their former homes in the Krajina and Western Slavonia.

In the former Soviet Union elections have *generally* been free and fair in Lithuania, Latvia and Estonia, though somewhat less so in Russia and Ukraine. But Belarus, which was one of the founder-members of the CIS and one the first former Soviet republics to be recognized by the West, has shown little sign of observing democratic practices.[70] There the principle of the separation of powers has continually been violated. In 1996 President Lukashenko stopped the work of the Supreme Electoral Commission, which was overseeing the referendum to be held in November that year, although the commission had been elected by and was responsible to parliament. Freedom of association is now restricted, and the media is under state control.

In Armenia international observers concluded that the parliamentary elections of 1995 had not been conducted fairly and that the government had acted illegally and arbitrarily to ensure the success of its candidates. In the Armenian presidential elections, held in September 1996, the OSCE reported violations of electoral law and the falsification of election returns.[71] The presidential elections of March 1998 saw a repetition of these malpractices. Many polling stations were attacked, voters in rural areas were intimidated, and votes were bought. In 1998, as in 1996, the opposition refused to accept defeat on grounds of electoral fraud, which did not augur well for democracy in Armenia. The assassination of the Armenian prime minister, Vazgen Sarkissian, in October 1999 cast another shadow over the country's political stability and the future of its democracy.

Regular, periodic elections have been held in Moldova and Ukraine since their independence in 1991. The relatively good performance of Communists in parliamentary elections in Moldova and Ukraine in March 1998 aroused concern about the course of democratization in those countries, but the communists did not win majorities. The Communist Party in Ukraine polled 25 percent of the votes and won a quarter of the seats allocated by party, while in the single-member constituencies it won only 40 out of 225 seats. Leonid Kuchma won the presidential election in November 1999 on a strong anti-communist platform, though not without restricting the access of the opposition to the media.[72]

In Moldova the Communist Party won 30 percent of the vote in March 1998. It is likely that the vote represented a protest against economic hardship and declining public services, as well as a search for political alternatives, rather than a return to an authoritarian political system. In both countries the communists could only govern by entering into coalitions with other parties. This they were willing to do. In Moldova the Communist Party coalesced with the Centrist bloc. They did not demand the appointment of a communist as prime minister and continued the economic privatization program of the reformists. Winners and losers would appear to have accepted democratic electoral rules.[73]

Electoral procedures in all elections in Moldova and Ukraine have not always complied with international norms. For instance, the OSCE was critical of state control over the Ukrainian media during the presidential election campaign leading up to elections in October 1999.[74] However, changes of government and parliament have taken place as a consequence of election results. Democratic competition seems to be an accepted fact. But a civil society is still in the making, and consensus needs to be strengthened.[75]

Acceptance of the rules of the democratic game is significant in Moldova, given that it faced armed challenges to its legitimacy and unity from its Russian and Gagauz minorities, but their fears about their status in an independent Moldova appear to have been allayed, at least for the time being, by legislation on citizenship, language, human and minority rights. However, some Russian leaders in the Trans-Dniestr still entertain hopes of independence. It will be some time before democracy is well established in Ukraine, but its governments have, through a mixture of domestic legislation, political astuteness and hard work on relations with Russia, kept separatist Russian forces in the Crimea at bay.

In Russia presidential elections have been fought on the competing platforms of democracy and authoritarianism between two fundamentally political and economic systems. And voters have expressed a preference for the post-Soviet system to its authoritarian predecessor. Between 1990 and 1996 the balance between supporters and opponents of the new system remained stable. In the 1993 parliamentary elections the Liberal Democratic Party of Vladimir Zhirinovsky obtained 22 percent of the votes; in the 1995 parliamentary elections, the party's share of the vote plummeted to 11 percent, and in 1999 to just over 6 percent. The Communist Party emerged as the largest single party with 22 percent of the vote in 1995 and almost 25 percent in 1999. But most reformist parties fared well in the December 1999 polls, and for the first time since 1991 comprise a majority in the *duma*. The pro–Kremlin Unity Party, formed barely two months before the elections, looked set to give a strong lead for radical economic change. Vladmir Putin's electoral triumph in March 2000 raised hopes of the acceleration of democratization in Russia, but his political zigzags as president have cast a shadow over the future of Russia's nascent democracy.

What explains popular support for reform in all presidential elections since 1991? One possibility is that Russia's mixed electoral system encourages party fragmentation; another is that voters are expressing dissatisfaction with the hardships that have attended economic change. But in presidential elections the issues have been more clear-cut, and on those occasions voters have expressed their preference for the present system. Some thought that the most significant point about the 1993 parliamentary and 1996 presidential polls was that they had established elections as the only game in town.[76] Mid–1999 saw attempts by central and regional leaders to forge new political alliances for parliamentary elections at the end of the year.

The exception to this inchoate, sometimes messy but peaceful political to-ing and fro-ing is Chechnya. The 1996 elections in Chechnya, judged by the OSCE to be the most free and fair in post-Soviet Russia, did not result in ethnic and political stability, and the autumn of 1999 saw Russia mired in another war to preserve its territorial integrity.

"Irregularities" were reported in the Azeri presidential elections of June 1992 and October 1998,[77] parliamentary elections in Kyrgyztan in 1995 and elections to the Supreme Soviet of Kazakhstan in 1994. In Kazakhstan the façade of democratic legislative and constitutional provisions masks an authoritarian ruler. Voter turnout in the 1995 elections was 95.6 percent, and President Nursultan Nazarbaev won 95 percent of the vote. Such figures point to a manipulated electoral result.[78] More recently, in presidential elections held on 10 January 1999, the extent of malpractices, including restrictions on the right of association and assembly and access to the media, led to the OSCE's refusal to monitor the voting or to recognize the results.[79] There is little dialogue between the president and the opposition; civil society is very weak, and the rule of law and an independent judiciary hardly exist. In Uzbekistan, opposition parties have not been able to register. Seriously concerned at the undemocratic ban on two opposition parties in the December 1999 Uzbek elections, the OSCE refused to send a full monitoring mission.[80] In Central Asian countries civic traditions generally have been slow to take root, and political corruption only seems to have reinforced the apathy of the electorate.

SUMMING UP

The CE and OSCE have brought diplomatic and moral pressure to bear on former communist countries and encouraged the protection of minority rights through democratic rule. A meeting ground was found in the desire of many post-communist states to join the Council of Europe and the EU. Their aspirations to be "European" undoubtedly presented the Council of Europe with a lever to persuade them to govern democratically.

Many post–Communist countries sought the framing of international norms on minorities issues. They were also ready to accept OSCE mediation to defuse ethnic tensions. Countries signing the CE *Framework Convention for National Minorities* and the *Charter for Regional or Minority Languages* have voluntarily agreed to checks on their records in protecting minority rights. In such cases states and the international community have not been at loggerheads over sovereignty.

Russia at first invoked the argument of sovereignty to protest against international criticism of human rights violations by its army in Chechnya in 1994, but its military débacle made it amenable to OSCE mediation, which helped to end the war and to persuade both Moscow and Chechen rebels to engage in dialogue. Moscow also conducted elections to display its democratic intentions. But polling resulted in the establishment of an illiberal regional government, unable or unwilling to subdue Chechen separatism. With Russia waging another war in 1999 to bring Chechen rebels to heel, a shadow hangs over the possibility of any "democratic solution" to the crisis in Chechnya. The EU and Council of Europe endorsed Russia's attempts to stamp out terrorism in Chechnya, even as they have called upon Moscow and Chechen separatists to resolve their differences through dialogue. Once again Moscow resisted what it perceived as international meddling in its domestic domain but consented to an OSCE mission in Chechnya. What this mission will achieve is an open question.

Sovereignty became an issue in the case of Serbia, which expelled three OSCE missions and resorted to force against Kosovar Albanians. The intransigence of the KLA also contributed to war. Peace in Kosovo will only endure if both sides abide by democratic norms.

Much depends on that most important domestic aspect of democracy: elections and those they bring to power. Illiberal leaders are more likely to discriminate against minorities. Minorities, for their part, may be equally illiberal. No brief can be made for Milošević's repression of Albanians, but would a KLA government protect the rights of Serb minorities in Kosovo? And if it did not, what moral, political, military or economic levers could the international community use to influence the KLA to accommodate Kosovar Serbs through democratic norms? Similarly, how can the attempts by the regional Chechen leaders to introduce "Islamic" codes of justice and an "Islamic" constitution be viewed as "democratic" simply because they have been voted to power?

It is clear that elections in the former Soviet Union and Yugoslavia have not always ensured that minority rights will be safeguarded by elected rulers. In their different ways, polling results in Bosnia, Croatia and Serbia, the difficulties in carrying out the Dayton Agreement and the 1999 wars in Kosovo and Chechnya all illustrate that the tension between the sovereignty of states and their international obligations prevails. The election of illiberal leaders may prove to be one of the greatest obstacles to the reconciliation of the domestic and international dimensions of democracy.

However, this is not the universal picture. Truculent nationalists have not always been voted into office; nor have minorities in *all* post-communist countries been violent and secessionist. And ethnic division has not necessarily obstructed democratization or led to war.

NOTES

1. HCNM, Warsaw address, 23 May 1993.
2. UN doc. A/50/332, 7 August 1995.
3. For some recent debates on sovereignty, see Michael Ross Fowler and Julie Marie Bunck, "What Constitutes the Sovereign State?" *Review of International Studies*, vol. 22, no. 4 (October 1996): 381–404; Joseph Joffe, "Rethinking the Nation-State," *Foreign Affairs*, vol. 78, no. 6 (November/December 1999): 122–27; Gene M. Lyons and Michael Mastanduno, eds., *Beyond Westphalia? State Sovereignty and International Intervention* (Baltimore: Johns Hopkins University Press, 1995).
4. Michael Mandelbaum, "A Perfect Failure," *Foreign Affairs*, vol. 78, no. 5 (September/October 1999): 2–8; Adam Roberts, "NATO's 'Humanitarian War' over Kosovo," *Survival*, vol. 41, no. 3 (autumn 1999): 102–23; OSCE *Istanbul Summit Declaration*, 19 November 1999, para. 4.
5. Connie Peck, *Sustainable Peace: The Role of the UN and Regional Organizations in Preventing Conflict* (Lanham, Md.: Rowman and Littlefield, 1998).
6. United Nations General Assembly, 52nd plenary meeting, Resolution 1995/31, 25 July 1995.
7. United Nations General Assembly, 51st session, Resolution A/RES/51/91, 12 December 1996: and 52nd session, Resolution A/RES/52/123, 12 December 1997 respectively.
8. Did the West deviate from this norm at the Rambouillet conference on Kosovo?
9. *Implementation by Croatia of Its Commitments in the Framework of Accession to the Council of Europe*, CE doc. 7569, 27 May 1996; and CE press release, 28 January 1998.
10. *Honouring of Obligations and Commitments by the Russian Federation*, Parliamentary Assembly of the Council of Europe Information Department, doc. 8127, 2 June 1998.
11. Niels Helveg Petersen, "Vital Partnership: Russia in Europe," *Forum* (June 1996), pp. 6–8.

12. In 1993 the EU's council stipulated that Central and East European states would only be allowed to join the EU if they complied with its norms on making a commitment to democracy, the rule of law, human rights and safeguards for minorities. This was part of the *acquis communautaire*, reiterated in the Europe Agreements and the Maastricht Treaty of 1992.

13. Devised under Article 328 of the Treaty of Rome, Europe Agreements allow Central and East European countries to strengthen their political and commercial ties with the EU and stress the creation of institutions to facilitate political dialogue.

14. Klaus Schumann, "The Role of the Council of Europe," in Miall, *Minority Rights*, pp. 87–98.

15. Articles 15, 16 and 17.

16. Articles 24, 25 and 26.

17. For example, European Council *Presidency Conclusions*, Helsinki, 10 and 11 December 1999, DOC/99/16, dated 13 December 1999; OSCE *Charter for European Security* (Istanbul), 18–19 November 1999, para. 13; CE *Final Declaration of Conference on the Parliamentary Contribution to the Implementation of the Stability Pact for South-Eastern Europe, Sofia, 25–26 November 1999*; OSCE *Istanbul Summit Declaration*, para. 11.

18. The OSCE publishes a wide range of material on its activities, including the *Newsletter*, the reports of the ODIHR and documents.

19. See *Updated Consolidated Text on OSCE Mechanisms and Procedures*, OSCE Ref. SEC.GAL/92/98, 3 November 1998; and *Review of the Implementation of All OSCE Principles and Commitments*, Report of the Rapporteurs, OSCE Ref. RC(99)JOUR/10, 1 October 1999, Annex 1.

20. *Early Warning and Early Action: Preventing Inter-Ethnic Conflict*, Speech by HCNM at the Royal Institute of International Affairs, London, on 9 July 1999, HCNM.GAL/5/99,20 August 1999, referred to hereafter as HCNM, London address, 9 July 1999.

21. HCNM, Warsaw report, 12 November 1997.

22. See chapter 5.

23. Ibid.

24. HCNM, Warsaw and London addresses, 23 May 1993 and 9 July 1999 respectively.

25. United Nations Security Council, 3868th meeting, Resolution S/RES/1160, 31 March 1998; and 3930th meeting, Resolution S/RES/1199, 23 September 1998.

26. OSCE *Newsletter*, November 1998, January 1999 and February/March 1999.

27. In 1924 the Soviets created the Ingush Autonomous *Oblast*; in 1934 the Chechen and Ingush Autonomous *Oblasts* were combined to form the Chechen-Ingushetia Autonomous *Oblast* region. In 1936 it became an Autonomous Republic, which was abolished in 1944, and tens of thousands of Chechens were deported to Central Asia. Chechens were allowed to resettle in their homeland after 1968.

28. Good accounts of the 1994 war in Chechnya include Anatol Lieven, *Chechnya: Tombstone of Russian Power* (New Haven: Yale University Press, 1998); Jane Omrod, "The North Caucasus: Confederation in Conflict," in Bremmer and Taras, eds., *New States, New Politics: Building the Post-Soviet Nations*, pp. 96–107.

29. Cited in Gail W. Lapidus, "Contested Sovereignty: The Tragedy of Chechnya," *International Security*, vol. 23, no. 1 (summer 1998): 34, 36.

30. Cited in ibid., pp. 34, 35 n.62, 36.

31. Cited in Reinhardt Rummel, "The European Union's Politico-Diplomatic Contribution to the Prevention of Ethno-National Conflict," in Chayes and Chayes, eds., *Preventing Conflict in the Post–Communist World*, p. 203.

32. See BBC *Selected World Broadcasts*, SU2919/B1-B10, 15 May 1997. The European Parliament thought that "the course of negotiations chosen by the Russian Federation and Tatarstan can be utilized in the context of other zones of potential conflict between the center and the regions in Russia." Resolution A4–0134/95/ref, 15 June 1995, *Official Journal of the European Communities*, vol. 38.

33. See chapter 5.

34. Pesc/99/81–10561/99 (Presse 251). For further EU reactions see 2217th Council meeting, General Affairs, 15 November 1999, PRES/99/344; 2232nd Council meeting, General Affairs, 6/7 December 1999, PRES/99/390;2239th Council meeting, General Affairs, 24 January 2000, PRES/00/10;2243rd Council meeting, General Affairs, 14/15 February 2000, PRES/00/32.

35. CE Press statements, 28 September and 22 October 1999; PACE report on conflict in Chechnya, doc. 8585, 3 November 1999; PACE Political Affairs Committee report, doc. 8697, *Conflict in Chechnya—Implementation by Russia of Recommendation 1444* (2000), 4 April 2000; European Council, *Presidency Conclusions* Helsinki, DOC/99/16, 13 December 1999.

36. RFE/RL *Newsline*, 2 November 1999.

37. RFE/RL *Newsline*, 30 November 1999, and "Declaration on Chechnya," speech by Chris Patten, member of the European Commission, 19 November 1999, SPEECH/99/166.

38. A good history of Kosovo is Miranda Vickers, *Between Serb and Albanian: A History of Kosovo* (London: Hurst, 1998).

39. See especially Basic Principles, Articles 1 to 5 of the 1974 constitution; in William B. Simons, ed., *The Constitutions of the Communist World* (Germantown, Md.: Aalphen aan den Rijn and Sijthoff and Noordhoff, 1980), pp. 428, 444–45.

40. Christian Hillgruber, "The Admission of New States to the International Community," *European Journal of International Law*, vol. 9, no. 3 (1998): 509.

41. Vickers, *Between Serb and Albanian*, p. 180.

42. The KLA (*Ushtria Clirimatare e Kosoves*) was founded in 1993 and was associated with several attacks on Serb institutions. In November 1997 it publicly confirmed its existence as an army fighting for the independence of Kosovo.

43. Radio Free Europe/Radio Liberty (RFE/RL) *Newsline*, 3 and 6 March 1998.

44. Ibid., 11 and 12 March 1998, 25 June 1998.

45. Carl Bildt, "Déjà vu in Kosovo,"*Financial Times*, 9 June 1998. The American Defense Secretary, William Cohen, said that the United States "does not feel that it is imperative to use force to stop the violence in Kosovo." NATO intervention would be justified in terms of "collective defense" if violence created instability. RFE/RL *Newsline*, 12 June 1998.

46. Richard Caplan, "Christopher Hill's Road Show," *The World Today*, vol. 55, no. 1 (January 1999): 13–14.

47. Eight chapters of the draft envisaged a constitution for Kosovo, the maintaining of political and civil security, the holding and supervision of elections under OSCE auspices, the establishment of a constitutional court, a supreme court, district and municipal tribunals, and the creation of the office of an ombudsman. Citizens of Kosovo would enjoy the rights and freedoms enshrined in the *European Convention on Human*

Rights. Kosovo would send citizens to the Assembly of Serbia and have representation in the Serbian government, the federal Constitutional Court and the Serbian Supreme Court.

48. Marc Weller, "The Rambouillet Conference on Kosovo," *International Affairs*, vol. 75, no. 2 (April 1999): 227.

49. See the many NATO communiqués, especially the Statement on Kosovo, 23 April 1999; NATO Parliamentary Assembly Warsaw Plenary Declaration on Kosovo, 31 May 1999, AS.182.SA(99)1 rev.1; speech by NATO Secretary-General Janvier Solana on 21 June 1999. See also Max Jakobson, "Is Kosovo a Turning point?" *International Herald Tribune*, 31 August 1999.

50. See for example the statement by Maarti Ahtisaari, *International Herald Tribune*, 13 July 1999.

51. For recent debates on this see *Journal of Democracy*, vol. 10, no. 1 (January 1999).

52. See for example, *Activities for the Development and Consolidation of Democratic Stability, (ADACS), Synopses of Activities—1997 Russian Federation*, Council of Europe Document SG/INF(98)Iadd/Russia, 14 April 1998, Division for Pan-European Co-operation Programmes, Directorate of Political Affairs; *Activities for the Development and Consolidation of Democratic Stability, Joint Programmes between the European Commission (PHARE and TACIS) and the Council of Europe*, Council of Europe, Information Document ADACS/JP(98)1; *Assistance with the Development and Consolidation of Democratic Security, Cooperation and Assistance Programmes with Countries of Central and Eastern Europe, Annual Report 1996*, Council of Europe document SG/INF(97)1; European Commission, *Tacis Annual Report 1994*, Com(95)349 final, Brussels 18.7.95; European Commission, *The Tacis Programme Annual Report 1995*, Com(96)345 final, Brussels 18.7.1996; European Commission, *The Tacis Programme Annual Report 1996*, Com(97)400 final, Brussels 25.07.97; European Commission, *The Tacis Programme Annual Report 1997*, Com(98)416 final, Brussels 03.07.98; Pinto, D., *From Assistance to Democracy to Democratic Security* (Strasbourg: Council of Europe, n.d.).

53. Some of the debates on democratization in the former communist bloc can be followed in Mary Kaldor and Ivan Vejvoda, "Democratization in Central and East European Countries," *International Affairs*, vol. 73, no. 1 (January 1997): 59–82; Geoffrey Pridham and Tatu Vanhanen, eds., *Democratization in Eastern Europe: Domestic and International Perspectives* (London: Routledge, 1994); Geoffrey Pridham, Eric Herring, and George Sanford, eds., *Building Democracy? The International Dimension of Democratization in Eastern Europe* (London: Leicester University Press, 1994).

54. Beigbeder, *International Monitoring of Plebiscites, Referenda and Elections*; UNGA doc. A/50/332, 7 August 1995; ODIHR *Bulletins*, and OSCE Secretary-General's *Annual Reports* on OSCE activities.

55. For example, *Elections in the OSCE Region*, ODIHR Background Material for the Review Conference, Warsaw, 1 October 1996, REF.RM/1/96/Add.1, 11 October 1996.

56. The UN and OSCE sent monitors to Georgia and Nagorno-Karabakh but did not launch full-fledged operations in those areas. Russia has played the role of "peacekeeper" there, and its brief has not extended to building democracy.

57. The General Framework Agreement for Peace in Bosnia and Herzegovina was initialed on 21 November 1995 at the Wright-Patterson Air Force Base near Dayton, Ohio, and signed in Paris on 14 December 1995. All references are to the *General*

Framework Agreement for Peace in Bosnia and Herzegovina, Paris, 14 December 1995 (referred to hereafter as Dayton/Paris Agreement).

58. Robert Hayden, "The Partition of Bosnia and Herzegovina, 1990–1993," RFE/RL *Research Report*, vol. 2, no. 22 (28 May 1993): 1–14; Gilbert Reilhac, "Democracy—Key to Peace in Bosnia," *Forum* (March 1996): 9–11; David Chandler, "Democratization in Bosnia: The Limits of Civil Society Building Strategies," *Democratization*, vol. 5, no. 4 (winter 1998): 78–102; Ivo H. Daalder and Michael B. G. Froman, "Dayton's Incomplete Peace," *Foreign Affairs*, vol. 78, no. 6 (November/December 1999): 106–13.

59. OSCE *Newsletter*, February 1992, p. 4.

60. Referred to officially as the Republic of Bosnia-Herzegovina.

61. Carl Bildt, "When Force is not Enough," and "Extend the Brief on Bosnia," *Financial Times*, 8 December 1995 and 2 August 1996 respectively; Declaration by Flavio Cotti on elections in Bosnia-Herzegovina, CSCE Ref. c10/35/96.

62. Dayton/Paris Agreement, 35 I.L.M. 1996, Annex 4, pp. 117–25.

63. Annex 6, Dayton/Paris Agreement, 35 I.L.M. 1996, pp. 130–36.

64. An account of the war in Yugoslavia and the humanitarian intervention that it prompted, first by UNPROFOR and then by IFOR, are beyond the scope of this book. But see, among others, Adam Roberts, "Humanitarian War: Military Intervention and Human Rights" and Rosalyn Higgins, "The New United Nations and Former Yugoslavia," both in *International Affairs*, vol. 69, no. 3 (July 1993), pp. 429–49 and 465–83 respectively; Steven L. Burg, "The International Community and the Yugoslav Crisis," in Milton Esman and Shibley Telhami, eds., *International Organizations and Ethnic Conflict* (Ithaca: Cornell University Press, 1995), pp. 235–71; Spyros Economides and Paul Taylor, "Former Yugoslavia," in James Mayall, ed., *The New Interventionism*, pp. 59–93.

65. OSCE *Newsletter*, November 1992, pp. 1–2.

66. OSCE *Newsletter*, September 1997, p. 3, and OSCE/ODIHR *Bosnia and Herzegovina Municipal Elections, 13–14 September 1997*, ODIHR.GAL/22/97, 13 November 1997; and *Bosnia and Herzegovina Elections, 12–13 September 1998*, ODIHR.GAL/52/98, 30 October 1998.

67. OSCE/ODIHR *Republic of Serbia Parliamentary and Presidential Elections on September 21 and October 5, 1997*, ODIHR.GAL/10/97, 24 October 1997; *Republic of Serbia Rerun of the Presidential Election December 7 and December 21, 1997*, ODIHR.GAL/2/98, 10 February 1998.

68. Jill Irvine, "Ultranationalist Ideology and State-Building in Croatia, 1990–1996," *Problems of Post-Communism*, vol. 44, no.4 (July/August 1997): 30–43.

69. Leonard Cohen notes that American officials maintained that the Serbs had "involuntarily" left Krajina but were careful to distinguish such a mode of departure from ethnic cleansing. "Such a characterization really amounted, however, to a distinction without much of a difference." Leonard Cohen, "Embattled Democracy: Post-Communist Croatia in Transition," in Karen Dawisha and Bruce Parrott, eds., *Politics, Power, and the Struggle for Democracy in South-East Europe* (Cambridge: Cambridge University Press, 1997), p. 104.

70. For a recent discussion see Kathleen Mihalisko, "Belarus: Retreat to Authoritarianism," in Karen Dawisha and Bruce Parrott, eds., *Democratic Changes and Authoritarian Reactions in Russia, Ukraine, Belarus and Moldova* (Cambridge: Cambridge University Press, 1997), pp. 223–81.

71. For example, *Republic of Armenia Presidential Election, March 16 and March 30, 1998*, ODIHR Final Report, Ref. GAL/15/98, 16 April 1998.

72. Askold Krushelnycky, "Ukraine: Incumbent President Plays on Fears of a Communist Return," RFE/RL *Research Report*, 10 November 1999.

73. ODIHR Reports, *Republic of Moldova Parliamentary Elections, 22 March 1998*, (no other reference); *Republic of Ukraine Parliamentary Elections, 29 March 1998*, ODIHR.GAL/31/98, 2 July 1998; RFE/RL Endnote by Paul Goble, "When Communists Win Elections," 6 April 1998.

74. RFE/RL *Newsline*, 1 November 1999.

75. The impact of Moldova's relations with Russia and Romania on its ethnic issues needs to be explored, but see Neil Melvin, *Russians Beyond Russia: The Politics of National Identity* (London: The Royal Institute of International Affairs, 1995), pp. 56ff., and William Crowther, "The Politics of Democratization in Moldova," in Dawisha and Parrott, eds., *Democratic Changes and Authoritarian Reactions in Russia, Ukraine, Belarus and Moldova*, pp. 282–329.

76. Mathew Wyman, Bill Miller, Stephen White, and Paul Heywood, "The Russian Elections of December 1993," *Electoral Studies*, vol. 13, no. 3 (September 1994): 254–71.

77. See especially ODIHR *Presidential Election in the Republic of Azerbaijan, 11 October 1998*, ODIHR.GAL/55/98, 11 November 1998.

78. *Final Report: Evaluation of the Phare and Tacis Democracy Programme, 1992–1997*, p. 77

79. RFE/RL *Newsline*, 12 January 1999, and ODHIR *Republic of Kazakstan (sic) Presidential Election, 10 January 1999*, Ref. ODIHR.GAL/7/99.8 February 1999.

80. BBC Monitoring, "OSCE Refuses to Send Full Mission to Uzbek Elections," *Inside Central Asia*, no. 302, 22 November to 28 November 1999, pp. 1–2, and RFE/RL *Newsline*, 6 December 1999.

Chapter 5

On the Absence of War in the Former Communist Bloc: Magyar and Russian Minorities in Countries Neighboring Hungary and Russia

THE QUESTIONS

The suggestion by international organizations that ethnic diversity should be accommodated through democratic political arrangements assumes that nationalism does not inevitably lead to war and disorder.[1] This assumption questions the conventional wisdom on nationalism, democracy and war. But the wars that attended the collapse of Yugoslavia and the Soviet Union in Serbia, Croatia, Bosnia, Georgia, Moldova and Nagorno-Karabakh would seem to bear out the pessimistic views that nationalism and democracy are potent formulae for war, that democratizing countries go to war,[2] that ethnic conflict upsets democratization and that democratization in divided societies provokes ethnic battles.[3] Yet these wars have been the exception rather than the rule in post-communist Europe, and the international community may have a point. Despite the existence of ethnic nationalisms in all post-communist countries few wars have occurred within and between most of them. This salient fact leads to the main questions posed in this chapter: can the absence of war be explained by the domestic policies of governments toward their Magyar or Russian minorities or by their international relations with neighboring countries? And to what extent does democratization account for the absence of war? The focus will be on Hungary and Magyar minorities in Romania and Slovakia, and Russia and Russian minorities in Ukraine, Kazakhstan, Estonia and Latvia. Magyar and Russian minorities are the largest minority groups in Europe, and about one-tenth of all Russians and a quarter of Magyars live outside Russia and Hungary respectively. The treatment of Russian and Magyar minorities in all countries neighboring

Russia and Hungary respectively has engaged the attention of Moscow and Budapest. It has also aroused regional and international interest in relations between Russia, Hungary and their neighbors.[4] But on the whole Eastern Europe and the CIS have confounded expectations that those regions would become ethnic battlefields.

The majority of East European and CIS countries are weak states with fragile democratic traditions: some, like Slovakia, Romania, Croatia and Serbia have minorities concerned, even fearful for their future. The largest minorities were at one time former rulers of the territories or parts of the territories, which today comprise Slovakia, Romania, Bulgaria, Estonia, Latvia, Ukraine and Kazakhstan. Slovak and Romanian identities have been forged partly in opposition to Magyars. In the former Soviet republics the Russians were perceived as the overlords until very recently and came to be identified with repression, which in turn has done little to endear them to the peoples whose nationalisms were a reaction against Soviet rule and who achieved sovereign states in 1991.

The disintegration of Yugoslavia into civil war in 1991 raised fears about a similar scenario emerging from the breakup of the USSR. The Soviet Union's collapse led to predictions of more than one hundred ethnic conflagrations on its territory.[5] Ominous warnings were also sounded about the disintegration of Russia, its failure to democratize and its propensity to expand territorially, all of which were said to be the inescapable and inevitable outcomes of its history and culture.[6] Almost a decade after its emergence as a state, the Russian Federation has defied predictions that it would fall apart, despite secessionist movements in Chechnya and Dagestan and many a tug of war over revenues between Moscow and Autonomous Republics and Regions[7] and the occasional impression that it was fraying at the edges. Indeed the chances are that new coalitions between the center, republics and regions, and between the regions themselves, will actually help to hold it together.

Ethnic Nationalism Does Not Necessarily Cause War

For the most part the anticipated ethnic wars have yet to materialize in the former communist bloc. In Russia it is arguable that ethnicity was a necessary but insufficient condition for the war in Chechnya between 1994 and 1996 and that the war—and its end—probably owed less to ethnicity than to the vagaries of power politics in the Kremlin.[8] This does not imply that ethnic nationalism has passed into the mists of history. Extreme nationalists belonging to the preponderant ethnic group, denying the reality of the multiethnic, multicultural populations of their respective countries and advocating exclusivist or assimilationist policies toward minorities have at one time or another played the political field in all post–Communist countries. Russian politicians, whether in office like Alexandr Rutskoi as vice-president, or outside the government like Vladimir Zhirinovsky, have asserted Russia's right to change its borders with neighboring countries. But Zhirinovsky's electoral fortunes have waned over time. And in Hungary István Csurka called for the expulsion of minorities, but he obtained only 1.25 percent of the vote in 1994 and just over 5 percent in 1998. Nationalist coalitions led by Vladimir Mečiar in Slovakia or Ion Iliescu in Romania exploited ethnic divisions (along with other issues) to shore up their popular appeal and, until quite recently, fared well in their respective elections. It is possible that in Slovakia and Romania the depth of ethnic rifts slowed the pace of democratization. But it equally could be said that Mečiar and Iliescu manipulated ethnic sentiment with a view to deflecting attention from their authoritarian tendencies, which were mirrored, to some extent, in their attempts to centralize power and silence the media. The electoral defeats of Iliescu in November 1996 and Mečiar in September 1998 suggested that the use of nationalism as a rallying point in the face of incompetent and illiberal government may be limited. What accounts for Iliescu's electoral success in the winter of 2000? Since Constantinescu decided not to contest the elections it is hard to assess the extent to which Iliescu may have simply gained from Constantinescu's withdrawal. What is clear is that Romanian voters rejected the extreme nationalism represented by Corneliu Vadim Tudor.

When Have Nationalism and Democratization Led to War?

As the ethnic conflicts in the former Yugoslavia and Soviet Union have already been discussed at great length,[9] I will not go over the same ground but will now sum up the causes and consequences of the conflicts that have occurred, highlighting similarities and differences between warring and nonwarring countries and the extent to which nationalism and democratization might account for the absence of war.

The two neighbors of Russia which have been riven by war are Azerbaijan and Georgia. In neither country did the conflicts involve Russian minorities. The war in Nagorno-Karabakh concerned the fate of Armenian minorities in Azerbaijan; two conflicts in Georgia stemmed from the grievances of its Abkhaz and Ossetian minorities. Only in Moldova, in the Trans-Dniestr area, did war engage Russian minorities, and two factors made this conflict somewhat exceptional. Neither Moldova nor the Trans-Dniestr shares borders with Russia. Unlike in other nonwarring countries—Kazakhstan, Ukraine, Estonia and Latvia—the Russian minority in the Trans-Dniestr is only the second largest minority and the third largest ethnic group in Moldova, after Moldovans and Ukrainians. In 1992 the war in the Trans-Dniestr was precipitated by fears of the Russian minority that Moldova would unite with Romania. This did not happen, and the outcome was a strengthening of a territorial Moldovan nationalism.[10]

Ethnic nationalism certainly accounts in considerable measure for the wars between Serbs and Croats in Croatia, between Serbs, Croats and Muslims in Bosnia, between Serbs and Albanians in Serbia and between the Abkhaz and Georgians, but it also exists in practically all nonwarring countries. Certainly the "typical reasons" for ethnic conflict—which include the existence of ethnic and sometimes exclusivist nationalisms, centralizing tendencies in weak states, contested borders and contested territories, economic disparity and the need for economic modernization—are present in warring and nonwarring countries. But why have hostilities broken out only in a minority? All the nonwarring countries, like those that have experienced war, share a common legacy of communist rule, and ethnic enmities are part of that communist inheritance. But the past is not necessarily an "inevitable" prologue or precursor of war. It may undoubtedly explain why Estonia and Latvia have dragged their feet on the issue of citizenship for their Russian minorities, but it does not reveal why Balts and Russians or Magyars and Romanians have refrained from taking up arms against one another.[11] How can these different outcomes be explained?

Some generalizations can be made. The origins of all conflicts can be traced to domestic factors. Where war occurred elections often marked the first move toward democracy, but the ballot box did not secure the legitimacy of the secessionist nationalist movements. This is partly because the secessionist forces fought elections on exclusivist nationalist platforms, partly because they tried to put their ideas into practice after winning elections.[12] To the extent that democratization has brought intolerant nationalists into power, it has contributed to conflict as in Georgia, Bosnia, Croatia and Serbia. The relationship between democratization and war is, as Neil MacFarlane writes with reference to Georgia, "highly sensitive to context." Democratization did not cause nationalism, nor was it the main cause of conflict, but it created "a permissive condition," which provided the channels through which nationalist ideas could be articulated.[13] However, this same permissive condition also exists in all nonwarring countries so it cannot be seen as an adequate trigger of conflict.

Attempts to carry out assimilationist or discriminatory policies toward minorities only provoked demands for secession and failed to secure the moral and political authority of the governments concerned. Such policies intensified fears of minorities that their culture, identity and very survival were in danger. Aggrieved minorities saw statehood as the only way to preserve their "nation" and worth fighting for. Wherever secession was demanded, it was difficult to arrive at a compromise, and separatist nations and the state resorted to force to achieve their opposing aims: the state to preserve its territorial integrity, separatist nations to carve out a new state.

Perhaps nationalism was not the only cause of conflict—even in the former Yugoslavia, where an economic crisis and the inability of the national republics and the center to agree on economic reform contributed to its disintegration. It is also arguable that the ethnic tenor of Yugoslavia's nationalisms and the denial of citizenship to Serb minorities in Bosnia and Croatia tell only part of the story. Ethnic nationalisms can raise the political temperature, but they do not necessarily presage violence. The ethnic nationalisms of the Balts and Russian speakers in Estonia and Latvia and the friction over citizenship for Russians who settled there after 1940 did not spark armed hostilities before or after the breakup of the USSR. It is not merely that there was no consensus between the constituent republics of Yugoslavia or between communities in Bosnia and Croatia. In March 1991, even before the dismemberment of Yugoslavia, Milošević and Tudjman arrived at an understanding that Serbia and Croatia would divide Bosnia.[14] War in Bosnia was not "unforeseen" by all the parties to it. The expansionist ambitions of both Croatia and Serbia lit the ethnic tinderbox, and war became "inevitable" because it was the method of political choice.

In contrast, Hungary and Russia did not embark upon territorial aggrandizement. Evidently preferring diplomacy to war, they have requested international intervention time and again to assure equitable treatment for "kin" minorities in neighboring countries.

Again, the wars in Georgia and Nagorno-Karabakh owe something to the resentment caused by the transfer of populations under Stalin and the ethnic animosities to which they gave rise. But ethnic deportations also took place in Estonia, Latvia, Kazakhstan and Ukraine, which have not seen armed strife. That explanation may lie partly in history, partly in the reality that politics is the art of the possible and that factors as varied as geography and political interest are shaping their post–cold war political and economic orientation as much as "history"[15] or "memory" or interpretations of them by elites in the different countries. Estonia, Latvia, Kazakhstan and Ukraine can only preserve their statehood by accommodating their Russian minorities and forging territorial nations.

Geography Does Not Determine the Political Orientation of a Country

Any attempt to account for the absence of war in post-communist countries comes up against conceptual and methodological problems. Scholars and policymakers classify post-communist countries into different geographical and political categories. At one level all former Soviet republics are members of the OSCE. On another plane Kazakhstan is Central Asian. Estonia, Lithuania and Latvia are not members of the CIS: they are Baltic countries and regard themselves as "European," that is, as potential members of the EU. Georgia and Azerbaijan should also be European, since they are situated to the west of the Urals, but they usually are listed under "Transcaucasia," a kind of no man's land that neither Europeans nor Asians are in any hurry to claim as one of their own. However, Georgia's application, in 1999, for membership in the Council of Europe underlined its desire to be "European," and it was welcomed back into the European family of nations by the CE.[16] Geographically, Belarus and Ukraine are European, but Belarus's current leadership seems anxious to return the country to the Russian fold, while Ukraine's history, geography and political and economic vicissitudes have raised the question of whether its future lies with "Europe" or Russia.[17] And then there is the Eurasian Russia. The conventional wisdom is that "Russia will always be Russia"—whatever that means.

There is also much confusion in the political categories used to identify East European countries. Of the former Yugoslav republics, Croatia and Slovenia regarded themselves and were viewed by some in the West as being part of "Europe," which connoted to them and to their protagonists their possession of an innate talent for democracy. This glossed over or denied the authoritarian strands in the history of many European countries and also failed to explain why nationalists, known for their illiberal proclivities, were elected three times—in Croatia, which is a member of the Council of Europe, as well as in Serbia, which was not. In the CIS, Belarus is geographically European and has no significant ethnic tensions but seems unlikely to evolve into a democracy in the foreseeable future.

Democracy Has Not Been Consolidated in Nonwarring Countries

Multiparty elections are a precondition for democracy, for they imply intellectual choice. But multiparty elections in Yugoslavia in 1990 brought illiberal leaders to power. Elections in Russia since 1991 have been democratic. By contrast, elections to the Soviet Congress of Peoples Deputies in 1989 were not democratic.[18] No Soviet leader contested a multiparty election; many post-Soviet leaders have, and the post-Soviet presidents of Russia and Ukraine are the first democratically elected leaders in the history of their countries. Even where elections have been rigged, the idea of multiparty elections to attain, legitimize and cede power seems to be widely accepted.

"The question remains when democracy can be taken for granted." Juan Linz and Alfred Stepan say that democracy is consolidated when there is a consensus that it is "the only game in town" . . . "when all the political actors accept the idea that political conflict within the state will be resolved according to established norms, and that violations of these norms are likely to be both ineffective and costly."[19] Does such a consensus exist in post–communist countries? The Baltic countries are generally viewed as being democratic, but is there a consensus between Estonians and Latvians on the one side and Russians on the other? And in Russia, would Alexandr Lebed, Gennadi Zyuganov or Vladimir Zhirinovsky play by the rules of democracy if they came to power? The reality is that a consensus on the nature of the Russian state has yet to be forged. It is hard to see consensus emerging in Serbia, Croatia or Bosnia. However, in Hungary and the Czech Republic leaders were quick to assert their commitment to democracy. In these countries the rules of the game seem to be accepted and the chances are that democracy will be sustained. Constitutions in themselves are not everything; in the long run the spirit in which they are worked may have the greatest impact on the course of events. For instance, Kazakhstan's constitution defines it as a democracy, but Nazarbaev's style of governance suggests that this declaration of intent amounts to mere rhetoric.

Economic Hardship Has Not Necessarily Helped Illiberal Nationalists

Fears that economic hardship would stir political unrest, which would then be exploited by authoritarian forces to their advantage,[20] have not necessarily been borne out. The Romanian elections of 1997 and the Slovak elections of 1998 saw the triumph of liberal forces over communist-nationalist coalitions; in Russia, Zhirinovsky has so far failed to win power at the center. And in Serbia Milošević was unable, eventually, to rally nationalist sentiment in the face of dismal economic performance. The ghosts of "Weimar Russia" and "Weimar Eastern Europe" can be laid to rest. The road to economic advancement has been strewn with hardships—but for many democracy offers the only alternative to the economic cul de sac of the communist era.

Nationalism, Neighboring Countries and the Occurrence or Absence of War

The role of neighboring countries varies. Hungary, Bulgaria and Greece had a direct interest in events in Yugoslavia, but none encouraged irredentism. Hungary was concerned about the fate of Magyar minorities in Vojvodina; Bulgaria and Greece about Macedonia. Greece feared that Macedonia could stir up an irredentist movement across their common border. On the other hand the war in Nagorno-Karabakh was undoubtedly fuelled by Armenian irredentism. Serbian and Croatian expansionist aims contributed to the outbreak of war in Bosnia. Sali Berisha, as President of Albania between 1991 and 1997, incited Albanian separatism in Kosovo, but his successor, Fatos Nano, did not overtly continue this policy.

Russia has intervened militarily in Azerbaijan and Georgia, but in neither case were Russian minorities the cause. The role of post-Soviet Russia in the conflict has been discussed in other works;[21] here two points may be made. Russia helped Abkhaz forces to defeat Georgian forces in September 1992 and to secure *de facto* independence. Moscow's intention appears to have been to increase its clout over Tbilisi and to put pressure on Georgia to join the CIS.[22]

Eduard Shevardnadze thought that Georgia's interests would be best served through bilateral ties with Russia rather than through membership in the somewhat ineffective CIS. In June–July 1993 Russia and Georgia settled the dispute in South Ossetia, seemingly illustrating the wisdom of this stance. Seeing Georgia as a bridge between East and West, Shevardnadze, not wishing to be restricted to the confines of the CIS, was concerned to maximize Georgia's diplomatic options. But he underestimated Russia's determination to keep former Soviet republics under its thumb, and in September 1993 Georgia succumbed to Russian pressure and joined the CIS. Russia had abetted the Abkhaz claim to independence, and CIS membership offered Georgia "the last chance," as Shevardnadze put it, to save Georgia from disintegration. Since Georgia entered the CIS the Russo-Georgian relationship has improved. A Russian-led peacekeeping force has been stationed in Abkhazia since June 1994. Mediating in negotiations on the political status of Abkhazia, Moscow has stood for the preservation of the territorial integrity of Georgia. This reflects Moscow's commitment to maintaining the 1991 internal boundaries of the Union Republics as post-Soviet international boundaries.

The outstanding fact is that ethnic nationalism in most democratizing countries in Eastern Europe and the CIS did not lead to war. The following account about Magyar and Russian minorities in countries bordering Hungary and Russia respectively will bear this out.

HUNGARY AND MAGYAR MINORITIES IN NEIGHBORING COUNTRIES

Hungary's borders have changed several times and so has the content of its national identity.[23] Following the dismantling of the Habsburg empire in 1918, Hungary paid the price of defeat. Under the Treaty of Trianon in 1920, Hungary lost large sections of territory to the new states of Czechoslovakia, Yugoslavia and Romania and smaller areas to Poland and Austria. Some three million Magyars found themselves living in foreign countries. "Trianon Hungary" was just one-third of "Habsburg Hungary." Resentment at the harsh terms of the Treaty of Trianon motivated Hungary's alignment with the Axis powers in the Second World War, enabling it to recapture some of the territories it had lost. But in 1945, as in 1918, Hungary was penalized for being on the losing side and had to surrender the lands it had regained during World War II.

About 10 percent of Hungary's population are minorities, including Croats, Romanians and Slovaks. Since the eighties Hungary has stressed bilingualism and biculturalism rather than autonomy or self-determination as solutions to its minorities problems. Almost a quarter of all Magyars live in neighboring countries, including Serbia, Croatia, Ukraine and Slovakia, so it is not surprising that Hungary's relations with its neighbors revolve around the treatment of their Magyar minorities. In Austria, Slovenia and Croatia their small numbers render them politically insignificant;[24] it is in Romania and Slovakia that they are of greater consequence. Since the last years of the Kadar regime Hungary has contended that Magyars living outside its borders are an integral part of the Hungarian nation. However, Budapest was equally quick to assert that it could not give Magyar minorities any instructions and that its main tasks were to draw international attention to their problems and to work for a solution. Hungary thus "internationalized" the treatment of "kin" minorities in neighboring countries.[25]

However, minorities were not the only issue in Hungary's relations with its neighbors, and changes of leadership saw changes in the rhetoric on Magyar minorities. József Antall, Prime Minister between 1990 and 1994, claimed to be prime minister "in spirit" of fifteen million Magyars living throughout the world and found it "impossible to have good relations with a country that mistreats its Hungarian minority."[26] This appeared to echo the 1990 version of the Hungarian constitution, which stated that "The Republic of Hungary recognizes its responsibilities towards Hungarians living outside the borders of the country and shall assist them in fostering their relations to Hungary."[27] However, Hungary has not demanded any revision of borders as an answer to the problems of Magyars in neighboring countries; in fact it has not called for a redrawing of its international frontiers since their delineation by the Treaty of Paris (1947). Hungary has also reaffirmed its commitment to the 1975 Helsinki Accord, which underlined acceptance of existing borders. The 1990 version of the Hungarian constitution declares that the Hungarian state will safeguard the "independence and territorial integrity of the country as well as its frontiers determined by international treaties." Hungary has repudiated war as a means of "settling disputes between nations" and refrains from using force "directed against the independence or territorial integrity of other states, and from applying threats of violence."[28]

Hungary has relied on a number of international measures to defuse tension over minorities. It has undertaken to observe international human rights norms; it has also asked regional European organizations to frame them. Bilateral treaties with neighboring countries have further safeguarded the rights of Magyar minorities, and Budapest has demanded the codification of group rights on the plea that individual rights are not enough to protect the identities of minorities. Group rights would allow minorities to use their mother tongue in the administrative and judicial systems in areas inhabited by Magyars, the right to education in their mother tongue and the right to proportional representation at all levels of administration. With a view to reducing tension over minorities issues, Hungary has signed treaties with Ukraine (1991), Slovenia and Germany (1992), Croatia (1992 and 1995), Slovakia (1995) and Romania (1996). Of its neighbors, only Ukraine has accepted the concept of collective rights and territorial autonomy. Serbia, Slovakia and Romania, whose democratic credentials were not very strong, spurned the demand for collective rights on the grounds that international conventions underlined individual rights.[29]

Magyars in Slovakia

Ethnicity carved out the most significant fault line in Czechoslovakia since its birth in 1918 and continued to mark political division in independent Slovakia after its emergence as an independent state in 1992. Magyars found themselves in the new state of Czechoslovakia after the 1920 Treaty of Trianon and in Slovakia after the velvet divorce in 1992. Between the two world wars they had the right to establish their own organizations and schools and print their own newspapers, but in practice such activities were discouraged by the Czechoslovak authorities. Under the post–1945 communist regime Magyars had citizenship and were allowed to set up Hungarian-medium schools at least at the elementary level. But the Communist Party controlled and restricted public debate so that Magyars—like Czechs and Slovaks—could not openly articulate their demands and grievances. Following the Soviet invasion of Czechoslovakia in 1968, the Slovak government embarked on policies of homogenization.

Magyars comprise 10.76 percent of Slovakia's population; most inhabit the southern Danube basin in an area between the Bratislava[30] district and the Ukrainian border. They are a majority in two districts, Komarno and Dunajská Streda, where they comprise 72.20 and 87.23 percent of the population respectively. Talk of the partition of Czechoslovakia raised Magyar fears of discrimination in an independent Slovakia because Mečiar exploited ethnic sentiment and sought to forge a Slovak identity not only against Czechs but also against Magyars, and he depicted Magyars as threats to the national interests and territorial integrity of Slovakia. To some extent his nationalist rhetoric reflected an attempt to mask the inchoate Slovak national identity and the absence of a consensus on defining it. Neither before nor after the independence of Slovakia had Mečiar's Movement for a Democratic Slovakia ever won a majority of votes.[31] Mečiar consistently spurned a pluralist definition of the Slovak state that would embrace Slovaks and Magyars. Meanwhile, ultraright parties like the Slovak Nationalist Party called for the expulsion of Magyars from Slovakia. During his tenure as prime minister, talks between Slovak and Magyar parties never resulted in coalitions, and there was no interethnic party with a civic platform. That changed in 1998 with the election of Mikuláš Dzurinda, who offered Magyar parties seats in his government.

For their part, Magyar parties in Slovakia were not secessionist. This, together with agreement between Mečiar and Václav Klaus on the international boundaries of the post–1992 Czech Republic and Slovakia, largely accounts for the absence of war between them. The strongest Magyar party—Coexistence—favored the resolution of minority issues in a democratic federal system. In 1993, invoking the concept of collective rights, Coexistence called for the creation of an autonomous area on the Slovak-Hungarian border. All Slovak political parties rejected this demand. Following Mečiar's defeat in the elections of March 1994, a liberal coalition led by Josef Moravčik, dependent on Magyar parties for its political survival, reversed some discriminatory legislation against Magyars. But Moravčik's government only lasted until October 1994. Mečiar then returned to power with the support of the right-wing Slovak National Party and the neo-communist Association for Slovak Workers and continued with discriminatory policies against Magyars.

The constitution of Slovakia guarantees basic rights, but restrictions placed on bilingualism in 1990 remained in force. Hungary complained that the Slovak constitution failed to give minorities the right to establish and maintain schools in their mother tongues. Minority groups were not invited to participate in the drafting of the Language Law of 1994, which limited the use of minority languages in the public sphere, including schools, hospitals, the army and the media. In contrast, the Dzurinda government has promised the liberalization of language laws to accommodate the wishes of Magyar political parties.

The OSCE and EU were critical of discrimination against Magyars and their language in Slovakia. However, the desire of both Hungary and Slovakia to join the EU, the Council of Europe and NATO made them amenable to pressure from Western countries to settle their differences over minorities and renounce all territorial claims. The expectations of the EU were outlined in the 1995 Stability Pact, and the EU pressed Slovakia to sign a clause on the safeguarding of minority rights as part of its Europe Agreement. The Treaty of Friendship and Cooperation, signed between Hungary and Slovakia on 19 March 1996, affirmed the territorial inviolability of both countries.[32] Both countries affirmed compliance with the *Copenhagen Document*, the UN *Declaration on Minorities, Recommendation 1201* of the Council of Europe and the *Framework Convention for National Minorities*. The rights of minorities were designated as fundamental human rights and minorities were said to form "an integral part of the society and of the State" in which they lived. Both countries recognize their responsibilities to protect and foster the national, ethnic, religious and linguistic identities of minorities within their borders. Hungary and Slovakia undertook to support the teaching of Slovak and Hungarian respectively, to expand opportunities in educational institutions for the study of the cultures and languages of both countries.[33] Hungary and Slovakia agreed that the protection of minority rights fell within the ambit of international cooperation and was not merely a domestic affair of the states. Influenced by UN, OSCE and Council of Europe instruments on minority rights, the Treaty made clear that individuals could decide whether or not they belonged to a minority and that Hungary and Slovakia would not practice assimilationist policies.[34]

All political parties in Hungary have accepted the Treaty, but the Hungarian opposition criticized Gyula Horn for signing it without ensuring that mechanisms would be established to ensure that Slovakia would implement it.[35]

The desire to "join Europe" appears to have induced Mečiar's government to enter into the agreement rather than any commitment to building democracy or safeguarding minority rights, and it continued to restrict the use of Hungarian after the signing of the Treaty. Consequently, both NATO and the EU penalized Slovakia for its illiberal tendencies and its treatment of Magyars by excluding it from their lists of early candidates.[36] Ill feeling between Slovaks and Magyars endured, but with Hungary refraining from making irredentist claims, Magyar minorities renouncing secessionist demands and Hungary and Slovakia agreeing to respect each other's international borders, ethnic violence was averted. The more conciliatory policies followed by the Dzurinda government encouraged an improvement in ethnic relations. A language law allowing the use of minority languages in the public sphere was introduced in April 1999 and was welcomed both by the Hungarian government and the OSCE.

On the whole, the absence of war between Slovakia and Hungary is probably explained more by their mutual acceptance of international borders and the renunciation of all territorial claims than by democratization. Initially democratization brought illiberal rulers to power in Slovakia. Eventually, however, it also enabled voters to shift their political alignments to elect more liberal leaders in 1998. If this trend prevails it could well contribute to the strengthening of amicable interethnic ties.

Magyars in Romania

Magyars are 7.12 percent of Romania's population and comprise an absolute majority in two districts of eastern Transylvania—Harghita and Covasna. But Magyars are almost 24 percent of Transylvania's population. Ethnic differences were sometimes aggravated by religious and social differences, and in general, Romanian governments tended to follow assimilationist policies and to exclude Magyars from public life.

Having lost Transylvania to the newly created state of Romania in 1918, Hungary reoccupied the northern part of the province during the Second World War, only to lose it again to Romania after the defeat of the Axis powers in 1945. Following his accession to power in 1953, Gheorghe Gheorghiu-Dej repressed Magyars, dissolved the Magyar Autonomous Region established under the constitution of 1952 and removed Magyars from official posts. Romanians from Moldavia and Wallachia were settled in Transylvania. The trend continued under Nicolae Ceaușescu. His program of "systematization" led to the destruction of Magyar *and* Romanian enclaves in Transylvania as part of the process of creating a socialist mass culture, but Magyar minorities construed systematization as an attack on *their* identity and culture.

Even before the end of the cold war, the treatment of Magyars had strained relations between Budapest and Bucharest, and Hungary first placed the issue of minorities on the OSCE agenda in 1985. The friction between Romania and Hungary did not end with Ceaușescu's replacement as president by Ion Iliescu in 1989, for more liberal policies were slow to materialize.[37] At the CSCE Geneva meeting in 1991, Hungary crossed swords with Romania for imposing Romanian on minorities, restricting the use of Hungarian and defining Romania as a nation-state in its constitution.[38] Confronted with mounting dissatisfaction in the face of economic problems, Iliescu joined forces with the ultranationalist *Romania Mare*[39] and *Vatra Romaneasca* organizations and manipulated ethnic feeling to win elections. But this strategy had its limitations, and Iliescu was defeated in the elections of 1996 by a liberal coalition led by Emil Constantinescu, who polled the majority of Magyar votes.

Hungary's raising of the issue of Magyar minorities at regional and international fora did not go down well with Romania.[40] Iliescu resented what he saw as Hungarian intrusion into Romania's sovereignty. Much of the argument between them centered around the question of individual and collective rights. Hungary wanted collective rights to be codified in law on the grounds that provisions governing rights of individuals were insufficient to ensure the preservation of the ethnic identity of minorities. Hungary also wanted minorities to be given proportional representation at all levels of administration. Iliescu, no great democrat at home, stuck to individual rights, pointing out that the *International Covenant on Civil and Political Rights* conferred rights on individuals, not on groups or collectives. The issue of individual versus collective rights remained a bone of contention between Hungary and Romania.

The election of Gyula Horn as Hungary's president in 1994 introduced a shift in Budapest's tactics. Horn pointedly stated that he was prime minister of 10.4 million Magyars—that is, only of those who were living in Hungary[41]—and he took the view that minorities issues should not be raised at international meetings, as they exacerbated tension in bilateral ties.[42] Budapest gave no encouragement to parties calling for autonomy in Romania. No Magyar political party demanded a redrawing of borders between Hungary and neighboring countries, but to begin with Hungary refused to include an assurance on borders in any bilateral treaty with Romania. Horn regarded it as "unacceptable" for Hungary to demand that the Hungarian Democratic Union of Romania should participate in official talks between the two countries or that any reconciliation with Romania should require their permission.[43] The rights of Magyar minorities would be better served by soothing fears of neighbors. Meanwhile, the United States dangled the carrot and stick of NATO membership for Hungary and Romania if they sorted out their differences over minorities. The stage was set for a historic reconciliation, and the result, in September 1996, was the Hungarian-Romanian Treaty of Understanding, Cooperation and Good Neighborliness,[44] which affirmed the inviolability of the borders of the two countries as established after the defeat of the Habsburg Empire in 1918. This was the main Romanian demand. Hungary was mainly concerned about "kin" minorities and was satisfied by the Treaty's provisions on minorities, which were inspired by the *Copenhagen Document*, the UN *Declaration on Minorities* and *Recommendation 1201* of the Council of Europe. The Annex to the Treaty noted that *Recommendation 1201* did not refer to collective rights or impose any obligation on Hungary and Romania to grant "territorial autonomy based on ethnic criteria."[45] The Treaty stated that safeguards for minorities were within the ambit of international protection of human rights and would contribute to the strengthening of democracy in both countries and their integration into Europe.[46] Romania and Hungary made a commitment to enforce the provisions of the CE *Framework Convention for National Minorities*, "if more favourable provisions concerning the rights of persons belonging to national minorities do not exist in their domestic legislation to respect the cultural and historical heritage of minorities, to grant them the rights to education in their mother tongue and to participate in local or national political institutions through elected representatives." Minorities, for their part, would respect the national legislation and rights of other communities. An intergovernmental committee of experts would monitor the enforcement of the Treaty.[47]

At the time of the signing of the Treaty, Romania was still ruled by Iliescu, so it is doubtful that reconciliation was facilitated by a strong commitment to democracy on his part. A readiness on the part of the Romanian and Hungarian governments to bury old enmities and their desire to join "Europe" made them amenable to pressure from the West and eventually made possible the reduction of tension over minorities. Relations between the two countries have improved since the signing of the Treaty. Hungary has been invited to join NATO and the EU and favors membership for Romania so that it will not be isolated from Magyar minorities there.[48] Romanian educational and local administrative laws give minorities the right to use their mother tongues in education, courts and public administration. *All* ethnic differences will not vanish, but stability may be forged over time.[49] The extent to which this stability will ease Romania's transition to democracy is uncertain, but respect for existing borders will make war unlikely.

The issue of Russian minorities in Ukraine and Kazakhstan will take the argument further.

RUSSIAN MINORITIES IN COUNTRIES NEIGHBORING RUSSIA

Russians in Kazakhstan

Surrounded by Russia, Ukraine, Kyrgyzstan, Uzbekistan and China, Kazakhstan is landlocked. Kazakhstan was ceded to the Tsarist empire in 1731 and reorganized as a Union Republic by Stalin in 1936. Most Russians settled there in the 1920s and 1930s in the northern and eastern *oblasts*, including Pavlodar, Ust-Kamenogorst, Uralsk and Petropavlodar, where they are the dominant community. A country of minorities, Kazakhstan is the only CIS state in which the titular nationality, comprising less than 40 percent of the population, is in a minority, but it is the largest minority. Russians are 37.7 percent, and Slavic groups together make up 44 percent of the population. Today the majority of them regard northeastern Kazakhstan as part of Russia. This perception of Kazakhstan's status has been shared by Russian writers such as Alexandr Solzhenitsyn and right-wing politicians like Vladimir Zhirinovsky, both of whom have called on occasion for a redrawing of the Russo-Kazakh border.[50] An ethnic definition of the "nation" of Kazakhstan most certainly would antagonize its minorities as well as Moscow, yet Kazakhstan's ability to forge a territorial nationalism is doubtful, given that its Russian minorities want to remain under Moscow's wing, and some Russian political luminaries have invoked "history" to legitimize an ethnic Russian homeland.

Anti-Russian riots occurred in Almaty in 1986 but did not imply anti-Soviet sentiment, and Kazakhstan was never secessionist. Kazakhstan's call for sovereignty in October 1990 underlines the enigmas inherent in the terms "sovereignty" and "independence" in the Soviet and post-Soviet contexts. For President Nursultan Nazarbaev sovereignty implied a renegotiation of the powers between Moscow and the Union Republics rather than secession. Kazakhstan was the last Union Republic to issue a declaration of independence, and it did so with great reluctance on 16 December 1991, four days after the Russian *duma* had voted to annul the 1922 Treaty establishing the Soviet Union.

Kazakhstan's handling of ethnic variety has to be seen against the background of Nazarbaev's efforts to build new political structures.[51] Since independence, Nazarbaev's top priorities have been to preserve his country's territorial integrity and to maintain "order." He has tried to do this, partly by building a highly centralized state and by increasing Almaty's control over the Russian-majority *oblasts*. International pressure and the *zeitgeist* of the post–cold war age partly account for the fact that Kazakhstan's constitution defines it as a democracy. But there are few signs of a civic culture. Neither Nazarbaev nor Russian politicians in Kazakhstan display real democratic inclinations. Political coalitions and parties have revolved around ethnic identities. Russian political parties have narrow political agendas and seek to forge a Russian territorial identity. However, they are not well organized and have received little political help from Moscow. This coincidence of domestic discontent and Moscow's calculated indifference has reduced their potential to foment ethnic unrest and to threaten the international boundaries of Kazakhstan.

The government's authoritarian tendencies and the ethnic outlook of the Russian political parties simultaneously reflect and perpetuate an absence of consensus among all communities. One opportunity to build consensus did present itself after the elections of 1994. Voting in the elections followed ethnic lines, but many independent non-Kazakh candidates won seats in parliament, creating the basis for interethnic parliamentary coalitions and resistance to central control. This parliament forced Nazarbaev to change official personnel, including the prime minister. Nazarbaev reacted by dismissing the parliament in 1995, thus doing away with the one institution that could have facilitated the forging of interethnic alliances. A referendum was held on 29 April to cancel the presidential elections and to extend Nazarbaev's term in office until 2001. In August 1995 another referendum was called, this time on a new constitution. There were reports of electoral malpractice, but the complaints were ignored and the government pushed ahead with a constitution which enhanced the powers of the president while whittling down those of parliament. In December, Nazarbaev issued a decree which gave him near absolute powers. Evidently he is reluctant to champion democratization and interethnic coalitions if they appear to challenge his authority: this was demonstrated yet again by the electoral malpractices that attended the campaign and organization of the presidential elections in January 1999.

Two strands are discernible in Nazarbaev's stance toward Russian minorities. At the domestic level, since Kazakhstan's independence in 1991, a policy of nativization or *korennizatsiia*, has been taking place, and Russians have been weeded out of or excluded from official positions. Yet any attempt to forge a Kazakh cultural nation, as opposed to a territorial nation, flounders on the rock of domestic and geopolitical reality. Since independence, it has been virtually impossible for the Kazakh establishment to dispense with Russia or Russians in crucial military and economic areas. Militarily, the establishment of all-Kazakh armed forces seems out of question. The army is dominated by officers of Slavic origin, while the ranks are mixed. Morale in the army is low; desertion and evasion of draft are common. It is hardly surprising that Kazakhstan signed the Tashkent Agreement in 1993, and in January 1995 military cooperation was expanded to include plans for the unification of the armed forces of Russia and Kazakhstan.

Kazakhstan's landlocked position also makes it vulnerable to political and economic pressure from Russia. It can only export its oil through Russian pipelines. Russia more or less imposed itself as a partner in a Kazakh-Omani deal to build a pipeline to the Tengiz oilfield. Kazakhstan joined an Economic Union in July 1993 to coordinate its fiscal, monetary, banking and customs policies with Russia's. This agreement, in effect, recreated the rouble zone. Seeing little prospect of escaping Russia's embrace, Nazarbaev proposed a Eurasian Union in March 1994 with a single currency, parliament and citizenship and with Russian as its primary language. Ukraine's opposition to the idea effectively rendered it a nonstarter. Nazarbaev has been the greatest proponent of CIS integration, and his political vision encompasses cooperation and coexistence with Russia.

It is hard to say whether political and economic accord with Russia has helped to bridge the ethnic gap in Kazakhstan. It is more likely that the link with Russia helps to preserve Kazakhstan's territorial integrity, despite the existence of ethnic division. This is partly because Kazakhstan is in no position to instigate a conflict with Russia, partly because Yeltsin's government, despite some bluster, has shown little appetite for territorial aggrandizement. Russia does not need to embark on such a course, since it can at any time bring Kazakhstan to heel by flexing its political and economic muscles. The existence of discontented Russians in Kazakhstan is one of the many factors that gives Moscow leverage over Almaty. The ball is in Moscow's court; the onus, as it were, for the absence of conflict rests on Russia.

Russians in Ukraine

History has been the warehouse of Ukraine's post-communist ethnic problems. In the ninth century the territory of present-day Ukraine comprised the kingdom of Kievan Rus, from which Ukrainians, Belorussians and Russians trace their origins. Ukraine was throughout its history a region coveted by different states, including the Polish-Lithuanian Commonwealth, the Habsburg and Romanov empires, and the Soviet Union. In the eighteenth century the province of Galicia was incorporated into the Habsburg empire; Volhynia was transferred to the Tsarist empire. This political division coincided with and exacerbated the religious divide between Ukrainians belonging to the Uniate Catholic and Ukrainian Orthodox churches. Following the collapse of the Habsburg empire in 1918, parts of territories claimed by Ukrainian nationalists were lost to three newly created states: Galicia to Poland, Bukovina to Romania and Transcarpathia to Czechoslovakia. Eastern Ukraine became a battlefield in the Russian civil war and was eventually taken over by the Bolsheviks. During and after the Second World War, Stalin annexed eastern Galicia, northern Bukovina, Bessarabia and Transcarpathia and brought together most Ukrainians within a single political entity. In 1954 Nikita Khrushchev transferred the Crimea to Ukraine. Following the disintegration of the Soviet Union, the boundaries of the Ukraine Soviet Socialist Republic, redrawn by war and by administrative fiat, became the borders of independent Ukraine.

Historical ties and proximity to Russia, as well as the presence of a sizeable Russian minority, all underline the significance of the Russo-Ukrainian relationship for ethnic stability in Ukraine. Ukrainians are almost 73 percent of Ukraine's population; Russians 22.1 percent and other minorities, including Magyars and Romanian, 5.2 percent. Some 12 percent of Ukrainians regard Russian as their mother tongue, so ethnic and linguistic divisions are not aligned. Regional divisions are more significant than ethnic or linguistic ones. Not surprisingly, Ukrainians are divided over their identity even as they search for political stability.[52] Ukraine's attempts to forge a territorial nationalism are rooted in its troubled history under different masters, and its post-Soviet leaders have stressed its multinational character. Indeed the appeal of Ukrainian ethnonationalism is limited by historical, ethnic and linguistic factors. Attempts to take the sting out of minorities issues have been twofold: at the domestic level, by defining Ukraine as a democracy and by liberal citizenship laws, and at the diplomatic level, by treaties with neighboring countries. The 1990 Ukrainian Declaration of Sovereignty and the 1992 Law on National Minorities affirmed respect for the national rights of all peoples and guarantees to all nationalities of the right to free national and cultural development. The Citizenship Law of 1991 granted citizenship to anyone resident in Ukraine at the time. The need for good relations with neighboring countries also shaped Ukraine's stance toward its minorities. Ukraine signed good neighbor treaties with Hungary (1991), Slovakia and Poland (1992), Moldova (1993) and Romania and Russia (1997). The spirit of accommodation has probably been inspired, not merely by democratic proclivities or institutions, which are in a state of gestation, but by geopolitical reality: Ukraine cannot afford to antagonize its neighbors, especially Russia.

Like all CIS countries, Ukraine has to define its identity and the content of its nationhood. The conflict between executive and legislature—economic modernization, corruption and democratization—are part of the process of building a new state. The consolidation of democracy is a long haul, but as in Russia, the prevalence of general dissatisfaction with economic conditions and disappointment with the caliber of national politicians does not necessarily imply that authoritarian solutions have much popular appeal.[53] Indeed President Leonid Kuchma won the November 1999 presidential elections on a strong anti-communist platform.⁵⁴ Nor does it imply a desire to rejoin other former Soviet republics in a political arrangement. Most Ukrainians reject the idea of restrictions on freedom of speech and association in the name of the state. A threat by the armed forces to democratization seems unlikely, as the army is dependent on the civilian authority and is not involved in politics.⁵⁵ There also seems to be a general acceptance of the rules of democracy by most political parties. The parties which have tried to undermine attempts to forge a civic society and have not accepted democratic norms are extreme nationalist organizations like the Ukrainian National Assembly and the Ukrainian National Self-Defense League, but they have been marginalized because of their inability to muster substantial popular support.⁵⁶ Multiparty elections, then, have kept intolerant nationalists at bay.

Amicable ties with Russia are Ukraine's top foreign policy priority, not least because an acrimonious relationship could trigger ethnic unrest and challenges to Ukraine's territorial integrity.⁵⁷ In 1993 Ukraine became the first CIS state to join the Partnership for Peace, proposing a number of security initiatives in Central Europe and the Black Sea. Of the former Soviet republics, Ukraine is the only potential military counterpoise to Russia because of the size of its armed forces, which, after Russia's, are the second largest in Europe. In practice, however, Ukraine cannot sustain its armed forces economically. Ukraine's economy has lagged behind that of Russia, and, time and again, economic hardships have led Russian minorities to view Russia as the greener pasture. On the whole, however, regional divisions are of greater import than ethnic divisions,⁵⁸ and the threat of secession has reared its head mainly in Crimea.⁵⁹

Sixty-eight percent of Crimea's population is Russian, twenty-five percent Ukrainian. In theory that means Crimea could break away on the basis of a Russian vote. In 1991 only 54 percent of Crimea's population voted for Ukraine's independence, compared with the national figure of 90 percent. As in the former Soviet Union and post–communist Russia the real meaning of demands for "independence" and "sovereignty" in Crimea has always been open to interpretation. Was the declaration of independence in May 1992 by the Crimean Supreme Council merely a bargaining chip for more powers to Simferopol? In 1994 Yuri Meshkov won a landslide victory in the Crimean elections on the platform of independence, but his spokesman clarified that "there is no question of redrawing Ukraine's borders. Crimea cannot survive without Ukraine but relations must be built on equal terms." Meshkov's aides said that Crimea "only wants economic independence and not Ukraine's collapse." Meanwhile the Russian bloc was far from being a monolithic whole, and it was not long before it splintered. In September 1994 the Crimean parliament, dominated by Russian deputies, tried to strip Meshkov of his presidential powers.

The fluidity of Russian sentiment in Crimea created a challenge for the legitimacy of Ukraine's frontiers. In August 1991, just days after the failure of the coup, Yeltsin's spokesman asserted Russia's right to revise its borders with Ukraine. The challenge was reinforced in January 1992 by the Russian parliament's questioning of the transfer of Crimea to Ukraine in 1954. Barely a month after Russia and Ukraine had founded the CIS, Crimea had been placed on the Russo-Ukrainian diplomatic agenda.[60] The chances were that Russia was juggling with several balls in the air. It used the status of Sebastopol and the division of the Black Sea Fleet as bargaining counters to extract political concessions from Ukraine. Its tacit diplomatic threats hung over Ukraine's territorial integrity like a sword of Damocles—and nowhere more so than in Crimea. At the same time, however, Russia, along with all CIS states, was committed to the inviolability of borders as they stood at the time of the dissolution of the USSR in December 1991. Russia stood by its international obligations.

Regardless of what Crimea's Russian leaders meant by "independence," it is unlikely that Crimea could ever break away from Ukraine without Moscow's support. On the one hand, Russian politicians, in or out of office, claimed off and on that Crimea and Sebastopol belong to Russia. On the other hand, even as Meshkov won elections on the platform of "independence" (whatever that meant), Ivan Rybkin, speaker of the *duma* in May 1994, said that "the peoples of the [Crimean] peninsula have the right to self-determination, but within the framework of Ukraine and on the basis of the principles of the CSCE." The CSCE, for its part, consistently supported Ukraine's sovereignty and territorial integrity. Meanwhile, Russia, in view of its own involvement in Chechnya, could not establish a dangerous precedent by endorsing any Crimean demands for independence. Nor could it unleash "a new Chechen war" by calling for the reunification of Sebastopol with Russia.

In March 1995 President Leonid Kuchma exploited the disunity within the Russian bloc in the Crimean parliament. Seizing the initiative, he abolished Crimea's presidency and annulled its constitution. In April he brought the region directly under Kiev's control. Russia did nothing on the grounds that Crimea was an internal affair of Ukraine. In May 1997, the Treaty of Friendship and Cooperation laid the dispute to rest, stating that Russia and Ukraine would respect each other's territorial integrity and confirming "the immutability of the border existing between them."[61] Moscow's attitude toward any separatist movement has always been a major factor in defusing or exacerbating ethnic tensions; the stability of Crimea and Ukraine has hinged, to a considerable extent, on the inclinations of the holder of power in the Kremlin.

Russians in Estonia and Latvia

More than any other part of the former USSR, the Baltic countries are determined to be "Western" and "European," and they have invoked their short-lived success as democracies between the two world wars[62] not only as evidence of their democratic credentials but also to disassociate themselves from their Soviet past. When they regained their sovereign status in 1991, the problem of citizenship for Russians who had settled especially in Estonia and Latvia after the Soviet conquest of 1940[63] put a question mark over their democratic intentions, for it focussed attention on what proportion of their populations would participate in the democratic process. The dilemma faced by Balts and Russians had its roots in the period that Estonia and Latvia were occupied by the Soviets.

In 1990 the call by Lithuania, Estonia and Latvia for the restitution of their statehood rather than "independence" was intended to underline the continuity of their sovereignty after 1920.[64] But restoration of independence could not bring back the world that existed before their annexation by the USSR in 1940, if only because half a century of Soviet rule had changed their demography. Hundreds of thousands of Estonians and Latvians were deported after the Soviet occupation; many lost their lives in the war. They were replaced mostly by Russians, many of whom belonged to the Soviet military, intelligence and political establishments, and were regarded by the Balts as "occupiers" and "colonists." Lithuania's demography changed the least: Lithuanians were 89.2 percent of the population in 1923 and 79.5 percent in 1989. But Estonians made up 88.8 percent of their country's population in 1934, Russians 8.2 percent. In 1989 the figures were 61.5 percent and 30.3 percent respectively, and almost 27 percent of Estonia's population was of foreign origin—one of the highest proportions in Europe. In Latvia the titular nationality comprised 75.5 percent, and Russians 10.6 percent in 1939. By 1989 Russians made up 34 percent of the population, while Latvians had been reduced to 52 percent. Of Latvia's seven cities, Latvians were a small majority only in Jelgava, where they comprised 51.2 percent of the population. This radical demographic alteration aroused great resentment on the part of Balts against Russians and created the post–cold war "ethnic problem" of international proportions, notably in Estonia and Latvia. But in contrast to Nagorno-Karabakh and Abkhazia, which also saw ethnic deportations in the Soviet era, this demographic shift did not spark inter-ethnic or inter-state wars between Estonia, Latvia and Russia.

All three Baltic republics sustained their claims to independence because the majority of their populations voted for it.[65] After independence, the task of defining the nation raised the question of whether their Russian minorities should be given citizenship. Lithuania, which does not share a frontier with Russia and where the titular nationality remained a substantial majority under Soviet rule, gave citizenship to all those who were residents in 1989. But Estonians and Latvians, with sharply reduced majorities and with Russia on their eastern borders, were fearful of "Russian expansion" in more ways than one and were inclined to define the "nation" in a manner that excluded most Russians from citizenship. Estonia and Latvia were ready to grant citizenship to Russians or the descendants of Russians who had been living there before the Soviet annexation, but "post-1940" Russians, who had moved there after the Soviet occupation and who constituted the vast majority, had to apply for citizenship on the grounds that they had settled in Estonia and Latvia after their legitimate governments had been dislodged by the Soviets. These Russians suddenly found themselves noncitizens, having to fulfil several criteria in order to acquire citizenship. "Post-1940" Russians rejoined that they had been living in the USSR as Soviet citizens enjoying equal status with Estonians and Latvians and had not regarded themselves as aliens.

Citizenship laws introduced in Estonia after independence disenfranchised most Russians. These laws included the reinstatement in 1991 of the Estonian Citizenship Law of 1938, which confirmed citizenship for all those who had been born in Estonia up to June 1940 and their descendants. Consequently, most Russians, who had settled there after the Soviet annexation, could not participate in the elections of 1993. The Law on Aliens (1993) required all noncitizens to apply for residence permits and to decide which citizenship they wanted: this only institutionalised ethnic division. A new Citizenship Law, introduced in 1995, required noncitizens to have at least five years of residence in Estonia. These laws were inspired partly by ethnic nationalisms and partly by an animus against anything "Russian," which to most Balts was synonymous with "Soviet." The Latvian Citizenship Law of 1994 had a similar effect. Conditions for citizenship included at least five years of residence in the country, and Latvia would allow 2000 "post–1940" Russians to be naturalized every year. Other criteria for citizenship included a minimal knowledge of Estonian and Latvian and of the history and constitutions of the two countries and the swearing of an oath of loyalty. The language qualification was in accordance with the practice of most states, but Russians, who as Soviet citizens had not found it necessary to learn Estonian or Latvian, were disconcerted by them.

Estonian and Latvian citizenship laws reflected a contradiction between the logic of the nation-state and that of democracy[66] and stirred up an international flurry. Moscow's indignation at Estonian and Latvian citizenship legislation set off diplomatic alarm bells throughout Europe. Moscow rattled the saber and declared its intention to "defend" the human rights of Russian minorities. In July 1993, Andrei Kozyrev, then Russian Foreign Minister, accused Estonia of apartheid and called for the partition of Estonia. Russians in the city of Narva held a referendum in which the majority of voters favored autonomy, but the referendum was deemed invalid by the Estonian government. Fearful of another "Yugoslavia," regional European organizations, including the Council of Europe and the CSCE/OSCE, put pressure on Estonia and Latvia to amend their citizenship laws so that their political institutions would represent the plurality of their societies.[67] Subsequently, UN and CSCE/OSCE missions found no evidence of human rights abuses or systematic persecution of Russian minorities, and in December 1996 the UN General Assembly removed consideration of the situation of Russian speakers in Estonia and Latvia from its agenda.[68] But Russians still came up against layers of red tape, and a trend toward an integral nationalism was noticeable in both countries.[69]

In May 1998 the Latvian *Saiema* (parliament) voted to abolish naturalization quotas and to naturalize children of "noncitizens" and stateless persons born in Latvia since 1991 without their having passed a language test. This was endorsed by Latvians in a referendum held in October 1998. The State Language Law of 9 December 1999, confirming Latvian as the official language but giving minorities the right to use their own languages, was deemed by the HCNM and the EU presidency as being conducive to the integration of minorities in Latvia and in accordance with Latvia's international commitments.[70]

Democracy remains to be consolidated in Estonia and Latvia, but to date, ethnic divisions have not shown signs of overturning democracy. Democratization, in turn, has not led to a hardening of ethnic identities and interests. Since 1994 voting in Estonian elections has cut across ethnic fault lines. In Latvia, when no single party has won a majority, coalitions have been formed successfully, even resulting in the exclusion of extreme nationalist parties from the government. For example, in 1995 five Latvian parties, For Fatherland and Freedom, Latvia's Way, the Latvian Independence Movement, the Agrarian Union and the Latvian Unity Party, coalesced to keep the populist right-wing National Movement for Latvia out of the government.[71] And Estonian and Latvian leaders have had some success in building bridges with ethnic Russian organizations.

Perhaps it would be naïve to say that Estonia and Latvia have safeguarded the rights of Russian speakers out of generosity; it is more likely that a pragmatic desire to keep domestic peace has induced them to come to terms with the facts of their ethnically diverse societies and to carry on with the process of reconciliation and accommodation. This may be partly because the democratic inclinations of all Baltic countries and their "European" and "Western" orientation make them susceptible to international pressure: Latvia clearly hopes that its latest amendments to citizenship laws will enhance its eligibility for EU membership.[72]

Furthermore, Estonia and Latvia cannot disregard their geography and history. Neither is capable of taking on a Russian military challenge single-handed; their armed forces comprise between 10,000 to 20,000 men, and the West is reluctant to make any commitment to them in the teeth of a Russian security doctrine that gives priority to Russian minorities in the "near abroad." At one point Russia linked the question of citizenship rights with troop withdrawals but pulled its forces out of Latvia and Estonia. Meanwhile, it is preoccupied with its own domestic imbroglios and is unlikely to resort to force to settle *international* disputes: it is more probable that commerce, rather than strategic considerations, will govern its relations with the Baltic countries.

International influence has helped to ease the tension between the logic of the nation-state and democracy; it has moderated the nationalist zeal of Estonia and Latvia and reined Russia in. This is partly because the desire of Estonia and Latvia to join the EU and of Russia to engage with Europe through the Partnership and Cooperation Agreement with the EU and through membership of the Council of Europe have given West European countries some leverage over these states.[73] The inference is that the international community will be able to influence those countries which are willing to be influenced or are unable to resist international pressure—here, again, the ideology and nature of states will have a bearing on their external orientation. Last but certainly not least, the acceptance of international borders as they stood in 1991, or at least the disinclination of the Baltic countries and Russia to change them by force, will also go a long way toward the prevention of war. This, combined with the liberalization of citizenship laws, is likely to contribute to the strengthening of democracy in Estonia and Latvia.

Russia

Some are critical of Yeltsin for giving greater priority to economic reform than to the introduction of democratic institutions.[74] Economic reform has caused hardship to some but has opened a window of opportunity to others. This is probably one reason why Yeltsin received a popular mandate in the presidential elections of 1996. In both Russia and Ukraine the emphasis on a strong state tends to come from those who want an authoritarian form of governance, while opinion polls show that, whatever their economic problems, most Russians do not want a return to their Soviet past. This evidence questions the conventional wisdom that Russian history, culture and mindset would more or less rule out a successful transition to democracy. Moreover, Russian elections have been regarded by international observers as free, and their results have been accepted by all parties. Since 1991 political alliances between fair-weather friends have been a salient feature of the Russian political scene, illustrating the role of the possible in Russian politics.

Arguments about the "everlasting" authoritarian Russian tradition also have to be questioned in the face of Russian public opposition to the war in Chechnya between 1994 and 1996. Admittedly, this opposition in itself did not prompt the Kremlin to end the war, nor was it enough to ensure the consolidation of Russian democracy. Moscow's decision to embark on this war probably had much to do with the temporary ascendancy of illiberal forces, led in the Kremlin by Alexandr Korzhakov, and Yeltsin's susceptibility to their advice is hard to explain.[75] Yet one unintended result of the war (surely from the government's viewpoint) is the deep demoralization and disarray in the armed forces to an extent that would make it very difficult for any future leader to rule by the sword. If the fragility of democracy raises the specter of Russia's being recast in the authoritarian mould by a Lebed or Zyuganov—or even Vladimir Putin—the Russian army's rout in Chechnya between 1994 and 1996 and its inability to win a decisive victory in the second Chechya war between 1999 and 2000 reduced the chances of such a pessimistic scenario materializing. Chechnya—and in 1999 Dagestan—have also been the exceptions to Russian attempts to forge a new state without armed conflict. For the most part, predictions that Russia would splinter or lapse into innumerable ethnic wars have yet to be vindicated.

Admittedly, many Autonomous Republics declared "independence" in 1991, but this was not the whole story.[76] In most Autonomous Republics no ethnic group comprises a majority. Forty-two percent or just under half of ethnic Russians live in the Autonomous Republics, and a majority or a large minority in many of them. Ethnicity and territory, then, are not congruent in most Autonomous Republics. In Bashkhortostan, for example, the titular nationality comprises 21.9 percent; Russians, 39.3 percent. In Mordvinia the Mordvinians form 12.5 percent; Russians, 40 percent of the population. The Komi are 23.3 percent; Russians, 57.7 percent of the population in the Komi Autonomous Republic. Only in Chuvash, Tuva (64 percent) and Chechnya (55 percent) are the titular groups majorities; in the Komi-Permyak *oblast* the Komi comprise 59.7 percent of the population. What this amounts to is that most demands for sovereignty emanate from republics in which Russians comprise the majority or, at least, the largest ethnic group. Demands for more power were not tantamount to independence. Siberia and the Far East harbored greater fears of territorial claims by China and Japan than of "control" by Moscow.

Moreover, declarations of independence and sovereignty in the Soviet Union and Russia should be interpreted with some caution,[77] not least because the Soviet constitution granted Union Republics sovereignty in name, which was effectively nullified by the constitutional supremacy of the Communist Party. Between August and October 1990, declarations of sovereignty were made by the Komi, Tatar, Udmurt and Chuvash Autonmous Republics, but these republics merely sought the upgrading of their status to that of Union Republics. This fuzziness of interpretation prevailed after 1991.[78] In 1992, nineteen out of twenty-one Autonomous Republics, including most of those which had called for independence, signed the Federal Treaty, which defined them as sovereign republics. Since then Moscow has entered into a series of treaties, all with different definitions of the status of Autonomous Republics. The terms used to describe their rank have varied and, to a considerable extent, reflect their leverage with the center. For instance, the treaty with Bashkhortostan described it as a "sovereign state in the Russian Federation," with Kabardino-Balkaria as "a state within the Russian Federation," while Udmurtiya was termed "a full subject of the Russian Federation." The republics which did not sign the Treaty were Tatarstan and Chechnya. Meanwhile, some regional leaders made declarations of independence one day, only to withdraw them the next.

The 1993 Russian constitution ignored the Federal Treaty and accorded more or less equal treatment to republics and regions. Moscow also negotiated treaties with the regions, effectively raising their status.[79] Talk of "sovereignty" did not mean demands for separate armed forces, foreign policies or currencies. Moscow's contribution to republican and regional budgets also gives it some clout over them, but the greater the economic riches of a republic, the more it is likely to tug at Moscow's apron strings. By bestowing economic largesse on the most demanding and recalcitrant republics—which also happen to be the richest republics—Yeltsin all but did away with their main grievance against the center. The tactics paid off. In the 1996 presidential elections Yeltsin triumphed over Gennadi Zyuganov in fourteen out of the twenty-one republics, including Kabardino-Balkaria, Tatarstan and Bashkhortostan. However, in governor's elections in November 1996 many incumbents who were Yeltsin's appointees were unseated. Most newly elected governors were not beholden to Moscow, and scrimmages over control of resources, such as the controversy between Moscow and Vladimir Nazdratenko, the governor of Primorski Krai,[80] are likely to recur.

Tatarstan was never secessionist, and a combination of demography, geopolitics and political leadership might go some way to explaining why.[81] Tatars comprise 48 percent of the republic's population, Russians 42 percent. Less than one-third of some 5.5 million Tatars live in Tatarstan; the rest are dispersed throughout Russia. Kazan could hardly call for any brand of autonomy on ethnic grounds; indeed Mintimier Shamiev, the President of Tatarstan, studiously avoided couching demands for "independence" in ethnic terms.

Tatarstan's demand for the status of a Union Republic in 1990 met with a rebuff from Gorbachev. In August 1991 Shamiev supported the coup, but soon after its failure he negotiated with Moscow for a new rank for Tatarstan within the Russian Federation. Tatarstan's refusal in March 1992 to sign the Federal Treaty and a vote from 82 percent of the population in support of its "sovereignty" should be seen in this light. The size of the vote indicates that many Russians living in Tatarstan endorsed their republic's "sovereignty." Subsequently, Zhirinovsky's strong showing in the Russian elections of December 1993—and the poor performance of reformist parties—also enhanced Kazan's anxiety to reach accommodation with Moscow. The Treaty between Russia and Tatarstan in March 1994 made no reference to the latter's sovereignty but referred to Tatarstan as "a state united with Russia."

Moscow's ability to subsidize Tatarstan's economy was a lever with which it could control Kazan. In 1992 Kazan paid Moscow 93 billion roubles in taxes but received 386 million roubles in economic largesse. More generally, the Soviet legacy has left Tatarstan economically dependent on Russia, since many goods manufactured in the republic are produced out of raw materials from other parts of Russia. And while Tatarstan is a major oil producer, it has no oil refining facilities and can only send out its oil through Russian pipelines. The summer of 1999 found Shamiev engaged in finding political allies for elections to the state *duma*.[82] With the exception of Chechnya and Dagestan, the post-Soviet Russian state has been put together by agreement.

The 1994 war in Chechnya long will provoke debate about whether Dzhokar Dudaev really wanted complete independence or whether he merely pitched his demands too high.[83] The accord signed between Moscow and Chechen rebels in 1996 turned out to be a mere truce,[84] but the hue and cry raised by communists and extreme nationalists against it suggested that Yeltsin did not at that time consider force a feasible option for holding the Russian Federation together. The 1999 war in Chechnya may have changed that.[85] Meanwhile, the tussle between Moscow and Autonomous Republics and Regions over the control of resources and approaches to economic change will go on. Regional leaders have urged the center to continue subsidies to their producers. Taxation remains the subject of negotiation between Moscow and republican and regional capitals, which have had little scope for determining their own tax base and tax rates, but they have had opportunities to withold taxes from the center. Negotiations between the Kremlin and some regional leaders on the division of fiscal powers[86] points less to disintegration than to an incomplete process of political transformation and to the absence, in a weak state, of established rules or conventions for conducting the business of government. The year 1999 saw alliances made and unmade between political parties as they prepared to contest parliamentary elections in December. Following his election as president in March 2000, Putin is finding that keeping strong-willed regional and republican leaders under the Kremlin's thumb is easier said than done,[87] but this does not amount to the breakup of Russia.

SUMMING UP

The tacit optimism of international organizations that ethnic diversity may not lead to war seems to be borne out by the experience of Magyar and Russian minorities in countries neighboring Hungary and Russia respectively. The fashionable and somewhat escapist equation of ethnic identity and interests with division and conflict needs to be questioned,[88] for the evidence is that neither ethnicity nor divisions between ethnic groups are, in themselves, a sufficient condition for conflict. The national identities of former Soviet republics and of Hungary, Romania and Slovakia are inchoate and in flux, but in the majority of cases their post–communist nationalisms have not ignited conflagrations.

Nor are ethnic wars the consequence of "irrational" hatreds. War is rational; countries and groups go to war because they think they will benefit from it. "Economic rationale" does not necessarily persuade countries to refrain from war; if it did, then Georgia and Azerbaijan, like Serbia and Croatia, would have steered clear of armed conflict. But Georgia and Azerbaijan—like Russia—fought wars to preserve their territorial integrity; Serbia and Croatia, to acquire more territory. A discussion of ethnic conflict therefore needs to take into account not merely the religious, cultural, linguistic or political differences between the warring parties, but why they find it profitable to wage war. If Russia and most of its neighbors have not embarked on wars between themselves it is probably because none of them deems it to be in their interests.

Russia at one point evidently thought it worthwhile to use force against the Chechens, but the reverses suffered by the Russian army in Chechnya and Moscow's subsequent peace initiatives, its use of OSCE mediation and its holding of elections to restore confidence in its democratic intentions in Chechnya suggest that Yeltsin came around to the view that Russia might have been better off without war. But in 1999 a Wahabi insurrection in Dagestan, aided and abetted by Chechen separatists, dragged Russia into another war, the outcome of which is at present uncertain. It is too early to assess the impact of this ongoing war on the course of democratization in Russia. On the whole, since 1991 politicians interested in economic reform and democracy have usually been at the helm, and the chances are that they will remain there, albeit not without a struggle. For the moment, "nationalism" is not a significant political issue in

Russia;[89] even Lebed, a self-styled fighter for Russia's soul and a leading contender for the Kremlin in 1996, tried to win popular support on the "nonethnic" platform of anticorruption, order and economic betterment. In the 1999 elections Zhirinovsky's electoral fortunes sank to an all-time low.

Meanwhile, Russia has not instigated conflict with its neighbors. Much has been made about its desire to maintain its control over the CIS as the reason for military intervention in Georgia, and it has undoubtedly manipulated force to serve its own ends. Two points may be made here. Russia helped Abkhaz forces to defeat the Georgian army in September 1992 and to secure *de facto* independence. Russia's interest appears to have been to increase its influence over Tbilisi and put pressure on Georgia to join the CIS. But Russia has used its influence to preserve borders, not to annex territory. Indeed the most consistent strain in its policy has been to put pressure on the Abkhaz to remain within Georgia. Similarly, it has not supported the claims of the Trans-Dniestr leadership for independence but has used the issue of troop withdrawals to retain a military presence in Moldova.[90]

Indeed all Baltic and most CIS countries have committed themselves to accepting the internal boundaries of the Union Republics as the international frontiers of the post–communist states. As members of the OSCE, they have also committed themselves to refrain from changing borders by force of arms. So far all have stood by their international obligations. This may well be the single most important reason why the boundaries of post-Soviet states have been stable since 1991.

More broadly, the successor states to the Soviet Union are now engaged in a long, drawn out process of state building, which they have only recently begun. What is unprecedented is that most of them have not embarked on internal or external war to consolidate their power. This sets them apart from most Western states, including the United Kingdom, France and the United States, which were forged through war and conquest but are all now synonymous with democracy.

Also, the contrast between most post–communist states and the USSR from which they emerged could hardly be greater. In the name of ideology the Bolsheviks waged civil war for four years, crushed revolts in Central Asia well into the thirties and annexed Estonia, Latvia and Lithuania, western Ukraine and Moldova during the Second World War. The frontiers of the USSR as they stood in 1991 were carved out through war over a period lasting almost a quarter of a century.

After the end of the cold war, the borders of most states in the former communist bloc did not change through war. The majority of the new states renounced any idea of territorial expansion, and minorities in most of them are not secessionist. International organizations have played a role in helping majority and minority communities within states to cohabitate amicably. Many governments have sought and welcomed mediation by the OSCE, whose intervention helped to defuse tension between Moscow, Tallinn and Riga and persuaded Estonia and Latvia to amend citizenship laws to accommodate their "post–1940" Russian-speaking populations. The OSCE has also advised the Ukrainian government on framing language laws to mollify Russian minorities and to make political arrangements that will give the Crimea autonomy within a democratic Ukraine. In all these cases international intervention reduced ethnic tension.

Whether the absence of war will assure the success of democratization is an open question: Kazakhstan and Belarus demonstrate that the nature of the political leadership, and what Boutros-Ghali referred to as "the will of the people," may be crucial in steering a country toward democracy. At the same time peace can create an environment more favorable to democratization.

Democratization in itself does not cause or prevent war. War has broken out when assimilationist or discriminatory policies have provoked nationalists into trying to change borders through secession or territorial aggrandizement, or both. There has been no danger of war where minorities have not challenged the moral and political authority of the preponderant nation to rule over the territory it claims—as borne out by Romania, Slovakia, Estonia and Latvia.

The democratic orientation of states may not adequately explain why nationalism does not result in war: the more important factor in averting war may be the renunciation of territorial claims. Kazakhstan, Slovakia and Romania agreed to adhere to their existing international boundaries at a time when their respective political leaderships were far from liberal. Nationalism and ethnic diversity neither necessarily spell war nor stand in the way of democratization. Most postcommunist countries have shown that conflict can be avoided by conciliation of minorities by governments and respect for international boundaries by states, even weak states with insecure identities, and that ethnic variety is manageable. The international advocacy of democracy to maintain ethnic equilibrium and enhance international security is, then, quite well founded and will probably continue to influence post-communist states well into the twenty-first century.

NOTES

1. Cf. chapter 1.

2. For example, Edward D. Mansfield and Jack Snyder wrote that "Democratization typically creates a syndrome of weak central authority, unstable domestic coalitions, and high-energy mass politics.... Political leaders ... often use appeals to nationalism to stay astride their unmanageable political coalitions." Mansfield and Snyder, "Democratization and War," *Foreign Affairs*, vol. 74, no. 3 (May/June 1995): 88.

3. Rabushka and Shepsle, *Politics in Plural Societies: A Theory of Democratic Instability*; Donald L. Horowitz, "Democracy in Divided Societies," in Diamond and Plattner, eds., *Nationalism, Ethnic Conflict and Democracy*, pp. 35–55.

4. Neil Melvin, *Russians Beyond Russia: The Politics of National Identity* (London Royal Institute of International Affairs, 1995); Vladimir Shlapentokh, Munir Sendich, and Emil Payin, eds., *The New Russian Diaspora: Russian Minorities in the Former Soviet Republics* (Armonk, N.Y.: M. E. Sharpe, 1994); Roman Szporluk, "The Fall of the Tsarist Empire and the USSR: The Russian Question and Imperial Overextension,"

in Karen Dawisha and Bruce Parrott, eds., *The End of Empire? The Transformation of the USSR in Comparative Perspective* (Armonk, N.Y.: M. E. Sharpe, 1997), pp. 65–93.

5. Jyrki Iivonen, "Expansionism and the Russian Imperial Tradition," in Tuomas Forsberg, ed., *Contested Territory: Border Disputes at the Edge of the Former Soviet Empire*, (Aldershot: Edward Elgar, 1995), p. 79; Pavel K. Baev, "Old and New Border Problems in Russia's Security Policy," in ibid., p. 92.

6. Zbigniew Brzezinski, "Post-Communist Transitions," *Foreign Affairs*, vol. 89, no. 5 (September/October 1989): 1–25; Peter Reddaway, "Russia on the Brink?" *New York Review of Books*, 28 January 1993, pp. 30–35; Jessica Stern, "Moscow Meltdown," *International Security*, vol. 18, no. 4 (spring 1994): 40; Mathew Evangelista, "Historical Legacies and the Politics of Intervention in the Former Soviet Union," in Michael E. Brown, ed., *The International Dimensions of Internal Conflict* (Cambridge, Mass.: M.I.T. Press, 1996), pp. 107–40.

7. Russia is divided into twenty-one Autonomous Republics, fifty-two *Oblasts* (autonomous regions), including the city *oblasts* of Moscow and St. Petersburg, and the Jewish autonomous *oblast*, six *krais*, or provinces, and ten *okrugs*, or districts.

8. Michael McFaul, "A Precarious Peace: Domestic Policies in the Making of Russian Foreign Policy," *International Security*, vol. 22, no. 3 (winter 1997/98): 5–35.

9. To give just a few references see the essays in Michael Brown et al., *Nationalism and Ethnic Conflict* (Cambridge, Mass.: M.I.T., 1997); Branka Magaš, *The Destruction of Yugoslavia: Tracing the Break-Up 1980–91* (London: Verso, 1993); W. Raymond Duncan and G. Paul Holman Jr., eds., *Ethnic Nationalism and Regional Conflict in the Former Soviet Union and Yugoslavia* (Boulder, Colo.: Westview, 1994).

10. Melvin, *Russians Beyond Russia*, pp. 76–77.

11. All these countries go against the assertion of Mansfield and Snyder that democratizing countries going through "a rocky transition" become "more aggressive and war-prone." "Democratization and War," p. 79.

12. Stephen van Evera writes that war is likely to result if a nationalist movement seeks sovereign statehood, if it denies the right of other national groups to independence, if it does not treat its minorities equitably and if it seeks to incorporate its national diaspora by territorial expansion. More than one of these conditions was present in the case of Serbia, Croatia and Georgia. Stephen van Evera, "Hypotheses on Nationalism and the Causes of War," in Charles Kupchan, ed., *Nationalism and Nationalities in the New Europe* (Ithaca: Cornell University Press/Council on Foreign Relations, 1995), especially pp. 138ff.

13. Neil MacFarlane, "Democratization, Nationalism and Regional Security in the Southern Caucasus," *Government and Opposition*, vol. 32, no. 3 (summer 1997): pp. 399ff.

14. Glenny, *The Fall of Yugoslavia*, pp. 148–49; Donia and Fine, *Bosnia and Hercegovina*, p. 248; Laura Silber and Allan Little, *The Death of Yugoslavia* (London: Penguin/BBC Books, 1995), pp. 143–44.

15. See for example the essays in S. Frederick Starr, ed., *The Legacy of History in Russia and the New States of Eurasia* (Armonk, N.Y.: M. E. Sharpe, 1994).

16. Daniel Tarschys, then Secretary-General of the Council of Europe, said that Georgia's accession "brings us one step closer to realising the original vision of our founding fathers—uniting the whole of Europe into one family of democratic nations." Statement of 27 April 1999 <http://stars.coe.fr/act.compress/cp99/>.

17. Andrew Wilson, "Ukraine between Eurasia and the West," in Seamus Dunn and

T. G. Fraser, eds., *Europe and Ethnicity: The First World War and Contemporary Ethnic Conflict* (London: Routledge, 1996), pp. 110–37.

18. Linz and Stepan, *Problems of Democratic Consolidation*, pp. 370–86.

19. Juan J. Linz and Alfred Stepan, "Toward Consolidated Democracies," *Journal of Democracy*, vol. 7, no. 2 (April 1996): 15.

20. For example, Ralf Dahrendorf, *Reflections on the Revolution in Europe* (London: Chatto and Windus, 1990); J. F. Brown, *Hopes and Shadows: Eastern Europe after Communism* (Harlow: Longman, 1994), pp. 7–9.

21. Mark Webber, *The International Politics of Russia and the Successor States* (Manchester: Manchester University Press, 1996); John F. R. Wright, Suzanne Goldenberg, and Richard Schofield, eds., *Transcaucasian Boundaries* (London: U.C.L. Press, 1996).

22. *Moscow News*, 29 February to 5 March 1992, cited in Mark Webber, *CIS Integraton Trends: Russia and the Former Soviet South* (London: Royal Institute of International Affairs, 1997), pp. 22–23.

23. Rebecca Ann Haynes, "Hungarian National Identity: Definition and Redefinition," in Latawski, ed., *Contemporary Nationalism in East Central Europe*, pp. 87–104.

24. Magyars are 2.5 percent of the population in the Austrian Burgenland; 0.4 percent in Slovenia and 0.5 percent in Croatia.

25. BBC/*SWB*, EE 2510, C3-C5, 16 January 1996.

26. Edith Oltay, "Minorities as Stumbling Block in Relations with Neighbors," RFE/RL *Research Report*, vol. 1, no. 19 (8 May 1992): 28, 27.

27. *The Rebirth of Democracy: 12 Constitutions of Central and Eastern Europe*, 2nd ed. (Strasbourg: Council of Europe, 1996), p. 158.

28. Articles 5 and 6(1) of the 1990 version of the Hungarian constitution, in *The Rebirth of Democracy*, p. 158.

29. Edith Oltay, "Minorities as Stumbling Block in Relations with Neighbors," pp. 26–33. See also Kinga Gál, *Bilateral Agreements in Central and Eastern Europe: A New Inter-State Framework for Minority Protection?* Working Paper #4 (Flemsburg, Germany: European Centre for Minority Issues, 1999).

30. I have used Slovak place names.

31. Judy Batt, *The New Slovakia: National Identity, Political Integration and the Return to Europe* (London: Royal Institution of International Affairs Discussion Paper, 1996), pp. 3, 7. See also Sharon Wolchik, "Democratization and Political Participation in Slovakia," in Karen Dawisha and Bruce Parrott, eds., *The Consolidation of Democracy in East-Central Europe* (Cambridge: Cambridge University Press, 1997), pp. 197–244.

32. Article 3(1).

33. Article 12(6, 7, 8).

34. Article 15(1, 2 a,b,c,d).

35. Sharon Fisher, "Ethnic Hungarians Back Themselves Into a Corner," *Transition*, vol. 1, no. 24 (29 December 1995): 58–63.

36. Anatol Lieven, "The Focus Is Now on Accession to the EU and NATO," *Financial Times Supplement on Hungary*, 9 December 1997, p. iii.

37. Thomas Carothers, "Romania: The Political Background," in International Institute for Democracy and Electoral Assistance, *Democracy in Romania: Assessment Mission Report* (Stockholm: International Institute for Democracy and Electoral Assistance, 1997), pp. 1–10.

38. Vojtech Mastny, *The Helsinki Process and the Reintegration of Europe 1986–1991: Analysis and Documentation* (London: Pinter, 1992), pp. 177–79.

39. *Romania Mare* (Greater Romania) had a strong following in Moldavia and Wallachia. It attacked a variety of people, including Gypsies, Jews, Magyars, intellectuals and advocates of market reform. It seeks the restoration of dictatorship and reunification with Bessarabia. *Vatra Romaneasca* (Romanian Cradle) wants Transylvania to be a Romanian-majority area and champions the unity of the Romanian state and nation. It is critical of the values of the emerging middle class and espouses peasant populism. In the 1997 elections *Vatra Romaneasca* polled less than 5 percent of the vote, so it could not be represented in parliament.

40. Edith Oltay, "Minority Rights Still an Issue in Hungarian-Romanian Relations," RFE/RL *Research Report*, vol. 1, no. 12 (20 March 1992): pp. 16–20.

41. Michael Shafir, "A Possible Light at the End of the Tunnel," *Transition*, vol. 2, no. 19 (20 September 1996): 29. See also Matyas Szabo, " 'Historic Reconciliation' Awakens Old Disputes," in ibid., vol. 2, no. 5 (8 March 1996): 46–50.

42. BBC/*SWB*/EE/2510, C5, 16 January 1996.

43. BBC/*SWB*/EE/2510, C4, 16 January 1996.

44. 36 I.L.M. 340(1997).

45. Ibid., 353.

46. 36 I.L.M. 343(1997).

47. Article 15, in ibid., 348–53; and Maria Amor Martin Estébanez, "Inter-Ethnic Relations and the Protection of Minorities," in International Institute for Democracy and Electoral Assistance, *Democracy in Romania*, pp. 123–43.

48. Lieven, "The Focus Is Now on Accession to the EU and NATO," p. iii.

49. Tom Gallagher, "Conflicts Between East European States and Minorities in an Age of Democracy," *Democratization*, vol. 5, no. 3 (autumn 1998): 214.

50. FBIS *Daily Report: Central Eurasia*, April 1993; *Komsomolskaya Pravda*, 18 September 1990 and *Izvestia*, 4 May 1994.

51. Ian Bremmer, "Nazarbaev and the North: State-Building and Ethnic Relations in Kazakhstan," *Ethnic and Racial Studies*, vol. 17, no. 4 (July 1994): 619–35; Martha Brill Olcott, *Central Asia's New States: Independence, Foreign Policy and Regional Security* (Washington, D.C.: United States Institute of Peace, 1996); Bruce Pannier, "A Step Back for Democracy," *Transition*, vol. 1, no. 11 (30 June 1995): 62–66.

52. Andrew Wilson, *Ukrainian Nationalism in the 1990s: A Minority Faith* (Cambridge: Cambridge University Press, 1996): and Resler, "Dilemmas of Democratization: Safeguarding Minorities in Russia, Ukraine and Lithuania," especially pp. 97–98.

53. Charles R. Wise and Trevor L. Brown, "The Consolidation of Democracy in Ukraine," *Democratization*, vol. 5, no. 1 (spring 1998): 116–37.

54. Though not without restricting the access of his opponents to the media.

55. Ustina Markus, "No Longer as Mighty," *Transition*, vol. 1, no. 13 (28 July 1995): 24–29.

56. Bohdan Nahaylo, "Ukraine," REF/RL *Research Report*, vol. 3, no. 16 (22 April 1994): 42–49.

57. Tor Bukkvoll, *Ukraine and European Security* (London: Pinter /Royal Institute of International Affairs, 1997).

58. Roman Solchanyk, "The Politics of State-Building: Centre-Periphery Relations in Post-Soviet Ukraine," *Europe-Asia Studies*, vol. 46, no. 1 (January 1994): 47–68.

59. Roman Solchanyk, "Crimea: Between Ukraine and Russia," in Maria Drohobycky, ed., *Crimea: Dynamics, Challenges and Prospects* (Lanham, Md.: Rowman and Littlefield, 1995), p. 3; Wilson, "Ukraine between Eurasia and the West," pp. 107–31.

60. Solchanyk, "Crimea between Ukraine and Russia," p. 6.

61. BBC/*SWB*/SU/2934/S1/1-S1/11, 2 June 1997. See also James Sherr, "Russia-Ukraine *Rapprochement*? The Black Sea Fleet Accords," *Survival*, vol. 38, no. 3 (autumn 1997): 33–50.

62. In Lithuania democracy lasted until 1926; in Estonia and Latvia, until 1932.

63. Russians who settled in Estonia and Latvia after 1940 have been characterized in several ways. Rein Taagepera uses the term "colonists" in Rein Taagepera *Estonia: Return to Independence* (Boulder, Colo.: Westview, 1993), pp. 218–21. Andrejs Pantelejevs, head of the Latvian Supreme Council, referred to "post–1940" Russians as "immigrants," "migrants," "occupiers" and "integrated Russians." Cited in Richard Krickus, "Latvia's 'Russian Question,' " RFE/RL *Research Report*, vol. 2, no. 18 (30 April 1993): 31–33. The HCNM refers to them as "non-citizens" in his correspondence with the Foreign Ministers of Estonia and Latvia, 9 March 1994 and 23 May 1997, Refs 3005/94/L and 376/97/L respectively. In his letter to the Latvian Foreign Minister on 10 December 1993, Ref 1463/93/L, he refers to the "non-Latvian minority" and "non-citizens." The PACE resolution no. 1117, dated 30 January 1997, on the *Honouring of Obligations and Commitments by Estonia*, refers to the "non-historic Russian-speaking minority."

64. Cf. chapter 3.

65. Ibid.

66. Linz and Stepan, *Problems of Democratic Transition*, pp. 401–33.

67. See especially HCNM to Estonian and Latvian Foreign Ministers, 6 April 1993, Refs 206/93/L/Rev and 238/93/L/Rev respectively; HCNM to Estonian President, 1 July 1993; comments by Estonian Foreign Ministry (undated, but probably around mid-April 1993); Latvian Foreign Minister to HCNM, 18 April 1993, CSCE communication no. 124, 23 April 1993; Russian comments on HCNM's recommendation, 26 April 1993, CSCE communication no. 125/Add/1; HCNM to Latvian Foreign Minister, 10 December 1993, Ref 1463/93/L and reply from Latvian Foreign Minister, 25 January 1994, CSCE communication no. 8; 31 January 1994; HCNM to Latvian Foreign Minister, 23 May 1997, Ref. 376/97/L, and reply, 11 September 1997, HCNM GAL/L1/97.

68. UNGA decision A/51/421, 12 December 1996. I owe this reference to Mr. Björn Lyrvall. See also UNGA resolutions 47/115, 16 December 1992, and 48/155, 20 December 1993, on the situation of human rights in Estonia and Latvia; annex to letter from Russia's Permanent Representative to UN Secretary-General, 20 March 1996, and annex to letter from Estonia's Permanent Representative to UN Secretary-General, 12 April 1996, UNGA resolutions A/51/81 and A/51/114 respectively.

69. The HCNM opposes assimilationist or discriminatory policies by states but advises minorities to integrate into the society in which they live by, among other things, learning the local language and fulfilling their obligations to the state of which they are citizens. HCNM, Warsaw report, 12 November 1997.

70. Statement by HCNM, 9 December 1999, and Statement by EU Presidency on the Latvian State Law on Language, 9 December 1999. I owe these references to Ms. Dace Treija.

71. For a fuller discussion of this point see Andrejs Plakans, "Democratization and Political Participation in Post-Communist Societies: The Case of Latvia," in Dawisha and Parrott, eds., *The Consolidation of Democracy in East-Central Europe*, pp. 245–89.

72. BBC/*SWB*, SU/3353, E1–2, 9 October 1998.

73. See chapter 4 above.

74. Linz and Stepan, *Problems of Democratic Transition*, pp. 390–400.

75. Michael McFaul, "A Precarious Peace: Domestic Politics in the Making of Russian Foreign Policy," pp. 28–29, and John Dunlop, "The 'Party of War' and Russian Imperial Nationalism," *Problems of Post-Communism*, vol. 43, no. 2 (March/April 1996): 29–34.

76. See the discussion in my "On the Absence of War," *The World Today*, vol. 54, nos. 8/9 (August/September 1998): 236–39; Gail W. Lapidus, "Asymmetrical Federalism and State Breakdown in Russia," *Post-Soviet Affairs*, vol. 15, no. 1 (January/March 1999): 75, and Dmitry Gorenburg, "Regional Separatism in Russia: Ethnic Mobilisation or Power Grab?" *Europe-Asia Studies*, vol. 51, no. 2 (March 1999): 245–74.

77. Cf. chapter 3 above.

78. The following account is based on James Hughes, "Moscow's Bilateral Treaties Add to Confusion," *Transition*, vol. 1, no. 13 (20 September 1996): 39–43; Robert W. Orttung and Olga Paretskaya, "Presidential Election Demonstrates Rural-Urban Divide," in ibid., pp. 33–38; Daniel Treisman, "Russia's 'Ethnic Revival': The Separatist Activism of Regional Leaders in a Post-Communist Order," *World Politics*, vol. 49, no. 2 (January 1997): 212–49; Gail W. Lapidus and Edward W. Walker, "Nationalism, Regionalism and Federalism: Center-Periphery Relations in Post-Communist Russia," in Gail W. Lapidus, ed., *The New Russia: Troubled Transformation* (Boulder, Colo.: Westview, 1995), pp. 79ff.; and Tamara Resler, "Dilemmas of Democratization," pp. 95–96.

79. Lapidus, "Asymmetrical Federalism," p. 77.

80. *Russian Regional Report*, vol. 2, no. 22 (19 June 1997).

81. Elizabeth Teague, "Russia and Tatarstan Sign Power-Sharing Treaty," RFE/RL *Research Report*, vol. 3, no. 14 (8 April 1994): 19–27.

82. *Russian Regional Report*, vol. 4, no. 23 (17 June 1999), and vol. 4, no. 26 (8 July 1999).

83. The decision to wage war against Chechnya represented the temporary ascendancy of illiberal forces in the Kremlin, led by Alexandr Korzhakov, but in the end liberal sections of the foreign policy elite, interested in peace and knowing that Russia could only enter into partnership with Europe if it made a commitment to democratic norms, won out. McFaul, "A Precarious Peace," pp. 28–29.

84. BBC/*SWB*, SU/2918, 14 May 1997, B/6-B/9/9 and BBC/*SWB*/SU/2919, 15 May 1997, B1-B11.

85. RFE/RL *Newsline*, 16 November 1999.

86. *Russian Regional Report*, vol. 4, no. 13 (21 April 1999), vol. 4, no. 18 (12 May 1999), vol. 4, no. 21 (3 June 1999).

87. Philip Hanson, "The Center versus the Periphery in Russian Economic Policy," RFE/RL *Research Report*, vol. 3, no. 17 (29 April 1994): 23–28; and *Russian Regional Report*, vol. 4, no. 25 (1 July 1999), vol. 5, no. 28 (19 July 2000), vol. 5, no. 30 (2 August 2000), vol. 5 no. 31 (30 August 2000), vol. 5, no. 45 (6 December 2000), vol. 5, no. 46 (13 December 2000), vol. 5, no. 47 (20 December 2000).

88. Malcolm, *Bosnia: A Short History*, pp. 2–3; James Mayall and Mark Simpson, "Ethnicity is Not Enough: Reflections on Protracted Secessionism in the Third World," *International Journal of Comparative Sociology*, vol. 38, nos. 1–2 (1992): 5–25; Van Evera, "Hypotheses on Nationalism and the Causes of War," pp. 136–57.

89. Anatol Lieven, "The Weakness of Russian Nationalism," *Survival*, vol. 41, no. 2 (summer 1999): 53–70.

90. Sherman W. Garnett and Rachel Lebenson, "Ukraine Joins the Fray: Will Peace Come to Trans-Dniestria?" *Problems of Post-Communism*, vol. 45, no. 6 (November/December 1998): 22–32.

Conclusions

MANAGING ETHNIC DIVERSITY THROUGH DEMOCRACY: THE QUESTIONS

What was the significance of international recommendations in favor of handling ethnic diversity through democratic governance, and how could the management of ethnically mixed populations through democracy enhance regional security? What lessons did countries with weak democratic traditions, such as India and Spain, in handling ethnically mixed populations through democratic rule have for post-communist countries? How did the international community apply the democratic principle to secessionist movements in the former Yugoslavia and USSR? Does international engagement in elections assure successful transitions to democracy? And if democracy draws international attention to the way in which states treat their citizens, can the tension between the sovereignty of states and their international obligations be eased? Last, but certainly not least, the emphasis on democracy also implies that nationalism does not necessarily cause war and that nations do not have to be bound by their past enmities but can build a more amicable and secure future by observing democratic norms. Has the experience of post-communist countries justified this optimism?

DEMOCRACY VERSUS THE NATION-STATE

International instruments since 1990 assume that democracy can only be created within the sovereign state and that states will anchor international society. The advocacy of democracy by the international community to handle ethnically diverse populations is biased against the idea of the nation-state. International instruments do not spell this out, but it is hard to read any other inference in their recommendation that democracy should be the means of reconciling ethnically mixed peoples. Democracy assumes the primacy of the individual, the rule of law, freedom of thought, belief, speech and association. The intellectual and political pluralism inherent in democracy goes against the intolerant assimilationist and discriminatory logic of the nation-state, with its inbuilt assumptions that there can be no political and intellectual differences within and between communities and that different communities cannot coexist in one country. Indeed the acceptance of linguistic, cultural and religious diversity is the cornerstone of all international proposals on managing ethnic variety through democracy.

At the end of the twentieth century the antithetical ideals of the nation-state and democracy seemed to be running in parallel, and the international community, reacting to new situations as they arose, was inconsistent in its responses to the crises created by the tension between these ideals. This was only natural. No two situations are alike: history does not necessarily repeat itself, and international policy-makers had to craft new norms, on the hoof, to handle the many dilemmas that followed in the wake of the disintegration of the former Yugoslavia and Soviet Union in 1991.[1]

If the collapse of the former Soviet Union signaled the triumph of the democratic principle, the wars in the former Yugoslavia were fought to achieve nation-states, the very opposite of democracy. In 1991, invoking "history," Serbia and Croatia waged war against each other and against Bosnia with the intention of uniting all Serbs and Croats in "Greater" Serbia and "Greater" Croatia respectively. They had to be content with something less, for neither succeeded in hiving off the Serbian and Croatian majority areas of Bosnia. But in 1995 Croatia defined its nationhood by expelling some 200,000 Serbs from their historic homeland in the Krajina. Four years later Serbia's attempt to retain Kosovo—without Albanians—and the vengeance wreaked by the KLA and its supporters against Kosovar Serbs following Serbia's military débâcle echo the same intolerance, the same belief that unwanted minorities can literally be driven into history, that the political nation should be an indivisible ethnic nation—or made into one—by denying, ironing out or physically removing any perceived obstacles and consigning them to the history books. Attempts to carve out ethnically pure states also display a lack of intellectual and political pluralism. Meanwhile, multiethnic Bosnia's post–cold war borders, like previous borders, have been drawn by international agreement. Its nascent democracy was legitimized in the first instance by international instruments, including the UN Charter and *Universal Declaration of Human Rights*, the Genocide Convention, the *European Convention on Human Rights*, the International Covenants on Political and Civil Rights and on Economic, Social and Cultural Rights, and then by flawed elections. Whether the ideal of the nation-state or democracy will ultimately win out in Bosnia and Kosovo remains uncertain.

NATO's announcement in April 1999 that it was fighting for democracy, human rights and the rule of law in Kosovo echoed the *leitmotif* of international officials since the end of the cold war and raised yet again the question of whether the international and domestic dimensions of democratization could be reconciled. The question was more easily asked than answered. Moreover, NATO's assertion that it was waging war against the repressive government of Milošević but not the people of Serbia only highlighted one of many political dilemmas faced by international officials—that the people of Serbia had elected him three times in succession and were bewildered and angered by NATO's bombing of their country. NATO's intervention in Kosovo only served to underline the most important aspect of democracy—the domestic one. The difficulties encountered by IFOR in Bosnia and the Kosovo Force in Kosovo suggest that outside military intervention is not the ideal solution to wars fought between hostile nations seeking either to preserve control over existing states or to create new ones. In such circumstances international intervention cannot guarantee a successful transition to democracy.

This takes us back to the main reason why the international community advocated democracy as the best method for accommodating ethnic diversity in the early nineties—namely that ethnic wars usually have internal roots and that timely domestic treatment is most likely to avert international conflicts.

BUILDING DEMOCRACY: CONCEPTUAL AND POLITICAL PROBLEMS

In building democracy many conceptual and practical problems must be grappled with. Not least of these is the conflict between individual and group rights, which lies at the heart of any debate on minority and human rights and democracy. Nationalism is a collective sentiment which may connote either the collective identity and interests of a single ethnic group or embrace the identities, interests and ideals of different communities. Indeed the national identity of democratic countries, including India and Spain, is a collective assertion of the identities of individual ethnic groups. International instruments have stressed that identification with a national minority lies in the realm of individual choice. This is justified. In the end democracy is about individuals; given that every individual is unique, democracy is in one sense about the expression and articulation of that uniqueness. Democracy implies acceptance of intellectual and political pluralism within groups and the opportunity for individuals to develop their identity, culture and language. Democratic institutions are more conducive to protecting human rights because they give space for all communities and individuals to articulate and reconcile their differences through mediating institutions. Again, the inference is that managing ethnic diversity through democratic political structures is against the concept of the nation-state.

International instruments since 1990 have affirmed that national minorities, as groups, have the right to preserve their identities and to give stronger expression to those identities. The anticipation is that differences between ethnic groups will remain and that the development of their identities, languages and cultures should be encouraged. It is envisaged that strong states, encompassing diverse identities and interests, will be based on the consensus of their multi-ethnic populations. At the same time minorities have obligations to the states of which they are citizens, and the protection and encouragement of minority or regional languages should not be at the expense of the official language and the need to learn it. Territorial autonomy is not considered necessary: the OSCE High Commissioner on National Minorities is inclined to think that the provision of adequate facilities to develop culture, identity and language can keep the grievances of minorities at bay. At the same time international officials stress that minorities should integrate into the society in which they live and should seek solutions to their problems within the countries in which they reside. The emphasis is on integrating diversity.[2] The politically and intellectually pluralist nation is the imagined community of the future—a veritable ethnic mosaic made up of many colors, not a straitjacket in which the distinctive identity of different communities has been ironed out beyond recognition.

THE DEMOCRATIC MULTIETHNIC STATE AND INTERNATIONAL SECURITY

How can management of ethnically mixed populations through democracy enhance international security? There are no sure-fire answers; democracy is first and foremost about the politics of uncertainty and choice; it is the art of the possible.

Several problems must be faced. For example, it is impossible for every nation to have its own state, if only because in most countries ethnic communities are interspersed. In many countries the presence of minorities was decided through war, conquest and international treaties rather than by choice. The frontiers drawn by international statesmen often divided ethnic nations, so that the ethnic and political nations were frequently incongruent. Consequently, the ethnic nation, straddling international borders, could threaten the survival of the multi-ethnic state, and it was partly to prevent this from happening that international officials recommended democracy as the desirable method of accommodating ethnic variety.

The contribution made by nationalism to the collapse of authoritarian states, whether of the imperial or nonimperial variety, and the wars that accompanied this collapse in the former Yugoslavia and Soviet Union revealed that authoritarian states had no answers to the problem of handling ethnic diversity and preventing conflict. Attempts to carry out the logic of the nation-state in the former Yugoslavia since 1991 only confirm that exclusivist nationalism is a destabilizing force precisely because it has no room for reconciliation and dialogue, which are the hallmarks of democracy.

Moreover, as illustrated in many countries in and outside Europe since the end of the Second World War, irredentism, border disputes or external intervention may exacerbate communal tensions. Minorities are often concentrated around international frontiers, so minority problems have usually come to the fore when international borders have been redrawn. If borders are to be preserved without the use of force it is quite natural that governments should be advised to treat their minorities equitably, for it is assimilationist and discriminatory policies that are likely to stir discontent and provoke secessionist claims. Serbia, Croatia and Georgia under Gamsakhurdia illustrate this amply. If stable international borders create the framework within which democracy may be built, brick by brick, democratic institutions and practices will in turn accommodate minorities, enhance ethnic stability within states, discourage separatism and so facilitate amicable relations between countries. Democracy as a means of forging ethnic harmony cannot be separated from the idea of democracy as an end in itself. Ends and means, then, are inextricably intertwined.

The UN *Declaration on Minorities, Recommendation 1201* of the Council of Europe and the Council of Europe *Framework Convention for National Minorities* advise that minorities should have the right to have links with their "kin" in neighboring countries, but this can only be possible if there is no fear of irredentism. The old concern about irredentism existed precisely because it could destabilize countries. In post–cold war Europe cross-border links are possible and are regarded as a right, as harbingers of peace, but they entail the renunciation by countries of territorial claims. This is the context in which international instruments such as the Council of Europe *Framework Convention for National Minorities* and the *European Charter for Regional or Minority Languages* recommend cooperation between regional or local authorities in territories where the same language is used.

The desire of the international community for stable borders stems from the fact that democracy stands a better chance of taking off where countries are not quarreling over borders. This coincidence is important. A borderless Europe entails uncontested state borders; transfrontier ties between "kin" ethnic groups in neighboring countries can only be forged if borders are secure and the sovereignty of governments over their territories is uncontested. A Europe in which countries or ethnic groups need to redefine their identities, interests or sovereignty by war cannot be borderless. Stable borders and democracy could each strengthen the other, and this in turn would enhance regional and international security.

MANAGING ETHNIC DIVERSITY THROUGH DEMOCRACY: THE POSTWAR EXPERIENCES OF INDIA, SRI LANKA AND SPAIN

The international preference for democracy as the means of maintaining ethnic equilibrium goes against much historical precedent and conventional wisdom but is not without foundation. Ethnic conflicts have domestic causes, so it is reasonable to assume that domestic remedies will prevent conflict. International officials also assume that culture is not necessarily a barrier to democracy—a point confirmed by the experiences of post–1945 India and Spain, which, without strong democratic traditions, managed their ethnically mixed populations and built consensus through democratic political arrangements. These countries showed that consensus was achieved precisely where democratic principles had been put into practice—and this consensus was forged as democratization proceeded apace. Especially in India and Spain, regional, religious or linguistic identities and interests have cut across the broader national identity, and coalitions between national and regional parties have frequently been formed at the center. This has given regional parties a sense of inclusion in the political system.

Moreover, extreme nationalist parties have not won electoral majorities. Electoral failure in their chosen constituencies induced such parties to resort to extreme nationalist propaganda, to mastermind communal violence and to disrupt the democratic process. India also showed that conflict was exacerbated precisely when the center tried to take more power to itself. Such conflict has dented but not destroyed India's democratic architecture. In general, the ability of India and Spain to make democratic political arrangements in diverse and difficult political and cultural circumstances suggests that democracy can accommodate ethnic variety in very different environments and that ethnic divisions do not necessarily block the development of democracy and lead to war. This offers hope for the management of ethnic diversity through democratic governance in many post-communist countries.

Sri Lanka, on the other hand, showed what could go wrong in a democracy. Because there was no national party embracing both Tamils and Sinhalese, political and ethnic affiliations inevitably became aligned. Sinhalese parties displayed a penchant for passing legislation which put Tamils at a disadvantage in educational and political institutions. They also identified the Sri Lankan state with Buddhism, the religion of the Sinhalese majority, and built a highly centralized administration, which gave the Tamil-dominated districts in the northeast very little autonomy. The result, in the eighties, was civil war. Sri Lanka did exactly the opposite of what post–cold war international instruments have advocated: it restricted political pluralism and the development of multiple centers of power, while the state openly sided with the majority community and discriminated against the minority group. Sri Lanka's experience reveals that the international emphasis on political and intellectual pluralism and on multiple centers of power, which facilitate the expression of diverse identities and interests as the way of building and preserving domestic and regional stability, is correct. The extent to which these principles will be implemented in the former communist bloc remains to be seen.

Conclusions

RECONCILING THE INTERNATIONAL AND DOMESTIC DIMENSIONS OF DEMOCRACY: SELF-DETERMINATION AND THE WILL OF THE PEOPLE

While the international community is clear on what it means by democracy, it is unclear how the democratic principle should be applied. The ambiguity of the term "self-determination" poses the first dilemma. Self-determination, as an embodiment of the will of the people, implies democracy, but this interpretation has created problems of implementation in both the international and domestic spheres. As a human right, self-determination comes into conflict with international law when it leads to calls for secession. It then threatens the territorial integrity of states and international stability.

The international community has never recognized a breakaway nation just because a majority of the inhabitants of a territory voted for independence. Since 1991, except in the case of Czechoslovakia, state collapse through war or domestic implosion has been the trigger: necessity the mother of diplomatic recognition. Soon after the collapse of the coup of 1991, the Russian Federation led the way to the recognition of Estonia, Latvia and Lithuania; EC countries and the United States followed suit. Other former Soviet republics were recognized after the EC had announced its terms on 16 December 1991. Recognition was made conditional on their commitment to democracy and provision of guarantees for the rights of minorities. Whether these commitments have been fulfilled is questionable. The EC evoked the democratic principle to justify recognition of new states, glossing over its inability to shape events on the ground and its tacit acceptance of them. New states were asked to give assurances of equitable treatment for minorities—whether or how they would implement them was not spelled out. Croatia was recognized although it failed to meet the EC's conditions for recognition. In contrast, Macedonia had complied with the conditions, but recognition was delayed because of Greek objections. Moreover, with Serb minorities in Croatia and Bosnia in open revolt against their incorporation into independent Croatia and Bosnia, the two seceding governments were hardly in control over their territories yet received recognition.

The international response to calls for independence by Kosovo and Chechnya echoed responses to similar demands by Slovenia, Croatia, Estonia, Lithuania, Latvia and Georgia between 1990 and 1991. Western countries first affirmed their support for the territorial status quo. In Chechnya and Kosovo, despite massive human rights abuses by the Russian and Serbian armies respectively, the initial reaction of Western countries was to refrain from doing anything that might savor support for secession. Atrocities by the Russian army were condemned, but Western governments had no wish to see Russia disintegrate. They were also loath to take any action that might embarrass Yeltsin's government, which was regarded as a democratizing force. Meanwhile, violence by Chechen separatists did little to endear their cause to Western officials. Western reactions to human rights abuses by the Russian army in the 1999 war in Chechnya echoed those between 1994 and 1996. Criticism of human rights violations was accompanied by expressions of support for Russia's territorial integrity.

To begin with, human rights violations by the Serbian army aroused much criticism. Military action against Serbia was considered, but the West was reluctant to embark on it, not least because it might appear to be giving the green light to Albanian separatists for the dismemberment of Serbia. Then NATO favored autonomy within Serbia guaranteed by an international force.[3] Most recently, following Koštunica's election as President in October 2000, NATO hinted at some form of cooperation with Belgrade to check extremists.[4]

DOES "THE PEOPLE'S CHOICE" GUARANTEE DEMOCRACY?

At another level self-determination, like democracy, symbolizes the wishes of the people, but what if they elect illiberal rulers like Tudjman, Gamsakhurdia and Milošević, who identify with the majority and then proceed to discriminate against minorities? This created new regional and international problems after 1990. The problem for international officials seeking to foster the idea that the "people"—regardless of communal affiliation—represent the whole population inhabiting a territory is that the majority community has sometimes voted for protagonists of the nation-state. *Est-ce que c'est que le premièr pas qui coute?* For illiberal nationalist leaders of multiethnic countries, "our state" has been synonymous with "my nation": they have identified territory with ethnicity and tried to forge a nation through measures ranging from assimilation, discrimination and forced transfers of population to genocide. But such measures are not democratic and, when combined with calls for independence by leaders identifying with the majority community, only arouse fears of minorities for their very survival in a new sovereign state. It is this fear that induces minorities to resist incorporation. Illiberal leaders have also tended to be irredentist: Tudjman and Milošević, seeking to create "Greater" Croatia and Serbia respectively, aided and abetted separatist violence by "kin" minorities in Bosnia, while Sali Berisha, seeking to create a "Greater Albania," encouraged Albanian separatism in Kosovo, Serbia and Croatia demonstrate that deviation from democratic norms and abuses of individual, minority and human rights often go together.

However, the first step toward democracy may not necessarily be the last. The electoral triumph of illiberal nationalists in Serbia and Croatia was a prelude to extremes of violence, but the pattern was not replicated in all post–communist countries. Indeed, even in Croatia liberal forces led by Ivica Račan triumphed in the December 1999 elections—their first victory since Croatia's independence. In Serbia, October 2000 saw the electoral defeat of the seemingly invincible Milošević by the more moderate Koštunica. Two months later, in December 2000, democratic parties won a resounding victory in the parliamentary elections, raising hopes of a new era of liberal politics in Serbia. Post-Soviet Russia and Ukraine have seen the marginalization of bigoted nationalists in elections. In Estonia, Latvia, Hungary, Ukraine and Moldova, free and fair elections have generally seen the rout of intransigent nationalists. This is particularly noticeable in Moldova, which saw its legitimacy challenged through force of arms by its Russian and Gagauz minorities at the time of independence.

In Romania and Slovakia elections have enabled voters to change their political alignments in a peaceful way. Iliescu and Mečiar were replaced by the more liberal Constantinescu (1996) and Dzurinda (1998), who both included representatives from Magyar political parties in their governments. Here democratization proved to be an antidote to ethnic nationalism and conflict. Whether Iliescu's re-election in December 2000 will slow down the pace of democratization in Romania is an open question; what is clear is that it represented a defeat for extreme nationalist forces led by Corneliu Vadim Tudor.

International officials are aware that domestic factors are the prime movers behind successful transitions to democracy. Elections are a prerequisite for democracy, but the international community cannot influence the choices made by voters. Would a popular vote for illiberal rulers frustrate Western plans to build stability through democratic principles? Human rights and democracy cannot be imposed by international fiat. The will of the people, that very linchpin of democracy, can make it hard to reconcile the domestic and international dimensions of democracy. Nevertheless, democracy can only be created through the ballot box. Even illiberal leaders gain legitimacy through elections—which is probably why they try to rig them.

DEMOCRACY AND THE SOVEREIGNTY OF STATES: ARE THEY SET ON A COLLISION COURSE?

Democracy and human rights attract international attention to the ways in which states treat their citizens. Human rights are intended to ensure that the needs of individuals who make up states are not ignored. In the age of globalization and the Internet some take the view that the sovereignty of states is an obsolete concept. This glosses over the fact that international society is premised on the sovereignty of states. States, not individuals, are subjects of international law, and it is the hope of international policy-makers that democracy and human rights will promote international and regional security by enhancing domestic stability and so strengthening states.

Indeed this is precisely why former communist states have welcomed democracy assistance from the EU, the Council of Europe and the OSCE on political and economic reform. Moreover, countries such as Hungary have sought the framing of international norms on minorities issues, and the OSCE has brokered peace settlements to end the wars in Abkhazia and Chechnya. At another level, entry into the Council of Europe is dependent on aspiring states fulfilling the Council's norms on human rights and democracy and incorporation of them into their domestic legislation. Reasons of state are thus not always at odds with international obligations.

Nevertheless the tension between the emphasis on democracy and human rights and the sovereignty of states remains, and nowhere is it more evident than on the issues of minority rights and self-determination. These two issues highlight the dilemmas at the heart of any debate on democracy and human rights. Self-determination is a human right, but can it be reconciled with the principle of the territorial integrity of states? Since the First World War most states that have splintered have done so along ethnic lines. The majority of conflicts since 1945 have occurred within states; many were fuelled by the discontent of minorities. The wars in Croatia, Bosnia, Kosovo, Nagorno-Karabakh and Chechnya showed, not for the first time, the gap between the rhetoric of self-determination and democracy on the international stage and its translation into practice in the domestic arena. This is largely because ethnic division has not always been conducive to reconciling demands for self-determination and democracy with the territorial integrity of countries.

Not surprisingly post–cold war international instruments have attempted to address minority problems which also reflect the intellectual and political dilemmas experienced by democracies, in particular the conflict between individual and group rights. The UN *Declaration on Minorities* and the Council of Europe *Framework Convention for National Minorities* suggest the accommodation of ethnic identities and interests within a democratic framework based on the rule of law; they also assert that individuals may choose whether they wish to be identified with a group. The implication—rightly—is that a nationalism that does not allow for political and intellectual pluralism within groups is not democratic. The need to find ways to reconcile individual and group rights is important, as discontented minorities are potentially secessionist. If democracy underlines individual rights and separatism collective rights, only the fair exercise of individual rights will dissuade minorities from demanding the collective right to secede.

However, international and regional organizations can merely offer guidelines and attempt to influence, for no international machinery exists to ensure the implementation of measures for the protection of minorities. Whether such organizations manage to steer states into the accommodation of minorities through democratic institutions may depend on factors as varied as the ideological orientation of individual states and their geopolitical circumstances, or simply *raisons d'état*. Varied experiences suggest that democratic principles in themselves may be insufficient to persuade states to accommodate minorities and honor their obligations on human rights. For example, pressure by European regional organizations played a part in persuading Estonia and Latvia to amend their citizenship laws in favor of their Russian-speaking populations. However, international pressure did not lead Serbia and Croatia to comply with international norms in dealing with their Albanian and Serb minorities respectively.

SOVEREIGNTY, DEMOCRACY AND THE IMPLEMENTATION OF MINORITY RIGHTS

Only after 1991 did minorities issues feature prominently on the international agenda. This was probably because the ethnic conflicts that had accompanied the breakup of the USSR and Yugoslavia became wars between some of the new states and threatened European security. Until then the international community was generally silent on the treatment of minorities and more concerned with the preservation of the territorial integrity of those countries. The political implications of Serb minorities in Bosnia and Croatia boycotting referendums for the independence of those two national republics and holding their own to create separate states attracted little attention or debate. In January 1992 the Badinter Commission advised the accommodation of Serb minorities in these seceding entities through autonomous political structures and guarantees for individual and minority rights. Similarly, the vote of Kosovar Albanians for independence in 1991 was ignored by international policy-makers who expected the Albanians to remain within Serbia.

In general the international community remains opposed to changing borders by force and favors solutions to minorities problems within the framework of existing states. As the OSCE High Commissioner on National Minorities puts it: "secession is not helpful."[5] The UN has no mechanism to enforce its *Declaration on Minorities*. Existing UN bodies such as the Human Rights Committee, the Committee on Economic, Social and Cultural Rights and the Committee for the Elimination of Racial Discrimination, keep an eye on the treatment of minorities. The Optional Protocol to the International Convention on Cultural and Political Rights (1976) provided a quasi-judicial mechanism to look into alleged abuses of minority rights, but its decisions have no legal force.

The desire of most post-communist countries to join the Council of Europe has given it some leverage in persuading aspiring states to make a commitment to democracy and to ratify international conventions on human rights. But there is no consistency in applying the yardstick. Countries like Estonia and Latvia, either out of pragmatism or their democratic political orientation, have been amenable to international influence. Latvia's admission to the Council of Europe was delayed because of its tardiness in conferring citizenship on Russian speakers who had settled there after the Soviet invasion of 1940. But Croatia was admitted to the Council *after* its government had rigged elections, muzzled the media, imposed restrictions on freedom of association and expelled Serb minorities from their ancestral homelands in Western Slavonia and the Krajina in 1995. Consideration of Russia's application for membership was interrupted on account of the human rights abuses committed by its army in Chechnya, but Russia's military reverses made it responsive to OSCE mediation to end the war. The Council of Europe's terms were eventually accepted, and Russia was admitted in 1996. Council officials argue that dialogue rather than pariah status is the best way of persuading governments to adhere to international standards on minority rights.

The OSCE has several instruments to monitor and promote the implementation of minority rights. The most important of these is the High Commissioner on National Minorities who has contributed to the defusing of tensions over minorities issues in many post-communist countries. His mandate is to provide early warning of potential conflicts and to promote early resolution of any ethnic friction that threatens domestic stability and good relations between OSCE member-states. Through diplomacy he works for compromises that will be acceptable to both states and nationalists. To earn the confidence of the opposing sides he must be seen to be impartial. He has made it plain that he acts through states and that he is not acting on behalf of minorities. His impartiality and the confidentiality maintained by him in negotiations have made his mediation acceptable to both states and nationalists. But the success of diplomacy ultimately rests on the readiness of governments—and nationalists—to implement his recommendations. For example, Romania, Slovakia, Ukraine and Estonia have not used the argument of sovereignty to back off from their international obligations. Many states have asked for the drafting of new international norms on minority rights and have sought international mediation on minorities issues. They have done so precisely because they were not encouraging irredentism and did not wish to use transfers of populations, assimilation or discrimination as "solutions" to their minorities problems; they have accepted the diversity of their populations and are willing to retain it within their existing borders through democratic governance.

Initially—in 1994—Russia used the argument of sovereignty to counter criticism of human rights abuses by its army in Chechnya, but a military fiasco induced the Kremlin to accept mediation by the OSCE. With the support of the EU and the Council of Europe, the HCNM helped to broker a peace settlement based on democratic principles between the Russian government and Chechen rebels in 1996. First, both sides were urged to negotiate, to engage in dialogue. Second, the Russian government was persuaded to conduct free and fair elections in Chechnya, partly in order to demonstrate its own intention to govern democratically, partly to give the people of Chechnya the opportunity to choose their regional rulers in the belief that free and fair elections would create confidence in Moscow's intentions and thus facilitate negotiations. Third, the HCNM encouraged discussions between Moscow and the elected Chechen government over a real division of powers between Moscow and Grozny based on the idea of political pluralism and multiple centers of power in a democracy.[6]

These negotiations helped to end the war. That both Chechen leaders and the Russian government accepted outside mediation and that the OSCE was able to bring about a settlement suggest that dialogue did play a significant role in containing conflict and forging domestic stability. Whatever the constraints on the OSCE, the Russian government had a real need for peace in Chechnya. Moscow found a meeting ground with European regional organizations on the

Conclusions

principle of the territorial integrity of states and the accommodation of Russia's ethnically diverse populations through democracy. Russia's acceptance of OSCE mediation showed, not for the first time, that sovereignty is not always a barrier to outside mediation in settling ethnic disputes. So far, "post–1999 Chechnya" has told a different story, with Russia advising the international community to stay out of its domestic quarrels and, seemingly inspired by the calculation that "all's fair in war," determined to fight to the finish. But Vladimir Putin is likely to find, as Boris Yeltsin did, that one can do anything at the point of the sword except sit on it.

In Kosovo, the illiberal inclinations and intransigence of both the Milošević leadership and the KLA made it unlikely that democratic principles could be applied to maintain stability in Kosovo. Milošević was hostile to outside mediation, while his discriminatory and repressive policies against Kosovar Albanians made any democratic solution a remote prospect.

The Rambouillet proposals of February 1999 provided for protection of human rights at the local level under international supervision and withdrawal of Serb military and police forces from Kosovo. In effect that would have greatly reduced, if not done away with, Belgrade's control over Kosovo. Kosovo's future political status would be ascertained by the will of the people after three years, in effect implying that an international protectorate could be the prelude to its independence from Serbia.

This raises crucial questions about Western aims in Kosovo. Western officials stressed democratic solutions, but what did this mean? Was the West's main aim to preserve the territorial integrity of Serbia while having greater autonomy for Kosovo? If so, could the future of Kosovo be separated from political developments in Serbia? Was enough attention paid to the domestic dimensions of building democracy?

Moreover, are states with democratic inclinations more likely to comply with international norms? There is no single answer. It is arguable that Yeltsin's government accepted OSCE mediation in 1996 because it lost the war in Chechnya. But the turn of the century saw Moscow disinclined to accept outside mediation in "1999 Chechen war," presumably because it reckoned that Russian forces would win out in the long run. Meanwhile, the democratic inclinations of Estonia and Latvia, their desire to join Europe and to develop a national identity based on democracy have all played a part in their amenability to international influence on the issue of citizenship for their "post–1940" Russian-speaking populations. Slovakia and Romania were governed by Mečiar and Iliescu respectively at the time of the signing of the treaties with Hungary in 1995 and 1996. Both played the ethnic card; neither had any pronounced liberal inclinations. The wish to be part of "Europe" was a factor in their decision to renounce territorial claims and promise equitable treatment to their Magyar minorities. It is noteworthy that, since 1996, in both Romania and Slovakia the accession to power of more liberal political parties has seen coalitions with Magyar political parties: inclusion was the norm. There appeared to be a connection between political liberalism and a willingness to accommodate minorities and to coalesce with Magyar parties where there was broad agreement on objectives. Will Iliescu's return to power in December 2000 see a more uncompromising attitude toward Magyar minorities? At the start of 2001 one can only speculate.

HAS THE ABSENCE OF WAR IMPLIED SUCCESSFUL TRANSITIONS TO DEMOCRACY?

Ethnic division is not the only factor involved in a country's success or failure in making the transition to democracy. Belarus is a good example of a country with no significant ethnic tensions but making little progress towards democracy. Ethnic conflict has not occurred in Kazakhstan, but Nazarbaev makes no secret of his authoritarian tendencies. He has continually rigged elections, and, anticipating the emergence of a parliamentary consensus that could challenge his political supremacy, he dissolved parliament in 1994.

With democracy unfolding by fits and starts in other nonwarring countries, including Ukraine, Estonia, Slovakia and Romania, the time needed for consolidation cannot be estimated. Constitutional wrangles are commonplace in many post-communist countries but are being sorted out through dialogue between parliament and the executive, not by force. Elections—the starting point of the democratic process—have been held in most of these countries, and election results accepted by all parties. Political alignments have also changed through the ballot box. This was of significance in Romania and Slovakia, where liberal leaders like Constantinescu and Dzurinda built coalitions with Magyar parties, thus broadening the area of consensus. In Ukraine extreme nationalists have been marginalized politically. In Estonia and Latvia voting has cut across ethnic lines; citizenship legislation was amended in Latvia in 1998 to enfranchise more "post–1940" Russians. In nonwarring countries political alignments have shifted in elections, and intolerant nationalists have not fared well. In Latvia moderate political parties combined to keep the populist right-wing party out of the government in 1995. All this, combined with the commitments of Estonia, Latvia and Russia not to change borders by force, should contribute to the consolidation of democracy. In general the absence of war in much of post-communist Europe is quite remarkable, given that there were said to be at least 300 contested borders in the former communist bloc at the beginning of the nineties and that more than 8,000 miles of new borders have been drawn in Europe since the end of the cold war. That most of these borders were drawn without war—combined with the absence of secessionist demands in many countries—increases the chances of democracy taking off in much of the former communist bloc.

THE TWENTY-FIRST CENTURY: CAN DEMOCRACY TRIUMPH OVER THE NATION-STATE?

The last decade of the twentieth century saw attempts to create the nation-state as well as democracy in the former communist bloc. The nationalisms of many post-communist countries were inspired by the desire to be democratic, and most countries tried to accommodate ethnically diverse populations and to build consensus through democracy. However, impressions of the nation-state probably stand out. The excesses of nationalist bigotry and the failure even to conceive of ethnic coexistence were seemingly beyond the imagination of protagonists of the nation-state as minorities in the Krajina and Kosovo were forced to flee their homelands. Ethnic massacres and expulsions made instant news; their images were recorded for posterity by television cameras, in contrast to the slower, less dramatic progress of democracy reported in the more run-of-the-mill home pages of the Council of Europe, OSCE and UN on the Internet.

The gap between advice and reality, counseling and implementation is wide. The ejection of minorities from the Krajina and Kosovo have seen the most conspicuous attempts since 1945 to redraw the political and ethnic map of Europe by force. And yet, however great the impact of wars fought to create nation-states in the former Yugoslavia in *fin de siècle* Europe, it is not the whole story. The majority of post-communist governments renounced territorial claims on neighboring countries. Most nonwarring countries also tried, while continuing to democratize, to forge new politically pluralist nations without war and through democratic practices. The chances are that they will succeed, although it is impossible to fix a time limit for the consolidation of democracy. On the whole, nation-building in most post-communist countries has not involved war; the successor states to the former Yugoslavia are the exception rather than the rule in that they have tried to forge their nations through violent conflict. And even as some political leaders seem to find it easier to preserve their states through repression and war, these wars only prove that the international preference for building international and regional stability through democratic means is well founded.

There are at least three reasons for concern. Since 1991 the wars in the former Yugoslavia show that the nation-state has not withered away, and it remains one of the main threats to peace in Europe.[7] On a different level, it is impossible to predict a date by which democracy will have been made strong and secure throughout post-communist Europe. Moreover, European regional organizations, which have tried to set democratic standards, have not applied them with any uniformity.

Yet there is a silver lining. Many countries are forging consensus through democracy, which is innate in their nationalism, if only because they wish to disassociate themselves from their communist past. In the former communist bloc the attempt to forge new states through democratic processes and institutions is unprecedented, not least because history shows that most states have been built through war and conquest. In contrast, the majority of these countries have blazed a trail by trying to consolidate statehood without war, and ethnic division has not always been an obstacle to democracy. Whether the absence of war will make for successful transitions to democracy remains to be seen, but perhaps there is room for qualified optimism.

NOTES

1. The HCNM takes the view that the political will or at least the foresight is lacking when it comes to preventing conflicts. "I find this ironic, for in our Internet and media-driven world of rapid communications there is no shortage of information. But attention spans are short, and sometimes longer term trends are not properly analysed. As a result, warning signs are often overlooked. Decision-makers at the highest levels are often unable—or simply fail—to draw the logical conclusions from the facts. In many cases, they are so preoccupied with the crisis of the day that they do not think about the potential crises of tomorrow." HCNM, London address, 9 July 1999.

2. HCNM, London address, 9 July 1999.

3. Will the short-term tactic of using the KLA to defeat the Serbian army eventually lead to the defeat of NATO's long-term objective of preserving the territorial integrity of Serbia? The KLA, after all, stands for the independence of Kosovo from Serbia.

4. RFE/RL *Newsline*, 22 December 2000.

5. HCNM, Warsaw report, 12 November 1997.

6. See BBC/*SWB*, SU2919/B1-B10, 15 May 1997. The European Parliament thought that "the course of negotiations chosen by the Russian Federation and Tatarstan can be utilised in the context of other zones of potential conflict between the centre and the regions in Russia." Resolution A4–0134/95/rev., 15 June 1995, *Official Journal of the European Communities*, vol. 38.

7. HCNM, London address, 9 July 1999, Jacques Paul Klein, "Stopping the Whirlwind," *The World Today*, vol. 55, no. 6 (June 1999): 7.

Selected Bibliography

(Note. I have included in this bibliography only those works that I have found most helpful. Unless stated otherwise, official documents are listed chronologically.)

PRIMARY SOURCES: OFFICIAL DOCUMENTS

Council of Europe

European Convention for the Protection of Human Rights and Fundamental Freedoms (1950).
European Charter for Regional or Minority Languages (1992).
Vienna Declaration (1993).
Parliamentary Assembly Recommendation 1201 on an Additional Protocol on the Rights of National Minorities to the European Convention on Human Rights (1993).
Communication from the Committee of Ministers 7316 Interim Report on the Rights of Minorities (1995).
Framework Convention for the Protection of National Minorities (1995).
Parliamentary Assembly Report 7228 on the Protection of the Rights of National Minorities (1995).
Parliamentary Assembly Recommendation 1255 on the Protection of the Rights of National Minorities (1995).
Parliamentary Assembly Recommendation 1285 (1996).
Parliamentary Assembly Recommendation 1300 (1996).
Parliamentary Assembly Order 513 (1996).
The Rebirth of Democracy: 12 Constitutions of Central and Eastern Europe. 2nd ed. Strasbourg: Council of Europe, 1996.

Implementation by Croatia of Its Commitments in the Framework of Accession to the Council of Europe. Parliamentary Assembly of the Council of Europe doc. 7569, 27 May 1996.
Recommendation 34 (1997) on the Draft European Charter of Regional Self-Government.
Recommendation 1345 (1997).
Assistance with the Development and Consolidation of Democratic Security, Cooperation and Assistance Programmes with Countries of Central and Eastern Europe, Annual Report 1996. Council of Europe document SG/INF(97)1.
Honouring of Obligations and Commitments by Estonia. Parliamentary Assembly of the Council of Europe. Resolution 1117, 30 January 1997.
Recommendation 1353 (1998).
Activities for the Development and Consolidation of Democratic Stability (ADACS), Synopses of Activities—1997 Russian Federation, Council of Europe Document SG/INF(98)Iadd/Russia, 14 April 1998, Division for Pan-European Co-operation Programmes, Directorate of Political Affairs.
Activities for the Development and Consolidation of Democratic Stability, Joint Programmes between the European Commission (PHARE and TACIS) and the Council of Europe, Council of Europe, Information Document ADACS/JP(98)1.
Honouring of Obligations and Commitments by the Russian Federation. Parliamentary Assembly of the Council of Europe Information Department, doc. 8127, 2 June 1998.
Report on Chechnya. Parliamentary Assembly of the Council of Europe doc. 8585, 3 November 1999.
Final Declaration of Conference on the Parliamentary Contribution to the Implementation of the Stability Pact for South-Eastern Europe: Sofia, 25–26 November 1999.
Conflict in Chechnya—Implementation by Russia of Recommendation 1444 (2000). Parliamentary Assembly of the Council of Europe, doc. 8697, 4 April 2000.
Conflict in Chechnya. Parliamentary Assembly of the Council of Europe, doc. 8705, 5 April 2000.
Recommendation 1456, Conflict in the Chechen Republic—Implementation by the Russian Federation of Recommendation 1444 (2000). Parliamentary Assembly of the Council of Europe. 6 April 2000.

European Community/European Union

European Community Declaration on the Guidelines for the Recognition of New States in Eastern Europe and in the Soviet Union, 16 December 1991.
Agreement on Partnership and Cooperation Establishing a Partnership Between the European Communities and Their Member States and the Russian Federation 1994.
Bulletin of the European Union.
Official Journal of the European Communities.
European Commission, *Tacis Annual Report 1994*, Com(95)349 final, Brussels 18.7.95.
European Commission, *The Tacis Programme Annual Report 1995*, Com(96)345 final, Brussels 18.7.1996.
European Commission, *The Tacis Programme Annual Report 1996*, Com(97)400 final, Brussels 25.07.97.

European Commission, *The Tacis Programme Annual Report 1997*, Com(98)416 final, Brussels 03.07.98.
2217th Council meeting. General Affairs. 15 November 1999, PRES/99/344.
"Declaration on Chechnya." Speech by Chris Patten, European Parliament, Strasbourg, 17 November 1999, SPEECH/99/166.
2232nd Council meeting. General Affairs. 6/7 December 1999, PRES/99/390.
Statement by EU Presidency on the Latvian State Law on Language, 9 December 1999.
European Council, *Presidency Conclusions*, Helsinki, 10 and 11 December 1999, DOC/99/16. 13 December 1999.
2239th Council meeting. General Affairs. 24 January 2000, PRES/00/10.
2243rd Council meeting. General Affairs. 14/15 February 2000, PRES/00/32.

CSCE/OSCE

OSCE *Newsletter*.
OSCE/ODIHR *Bulletin*.
Helsinki Final Act (1975).
Vienna Document (1989).
Copenhagen Document (1990).
Charter of Paris for a New Europe (1990).
Report of the CSCE Meeting of Experts on the Peaceful Settlement of Disputes (1991).
Meeting of Experts on National Minorities, Geneva Report (1991).
Moscow Document (1991).
Prague Document on Further Development of CSCE Institutions and Structures (1992).
Vienna Document (1992).
Budapest Declaration of the CSCE Parliamentary Assembly (1992).
Report of the CSCE Rapporteur Mission to Yugoslavia (1992).
Report of the Second CSCE Mission to Nagorno-Karabakh (1992).
Report of the CSCE Rapporteur Mission to the Republic of Georgia (1992).
Report of the CSCE Mission to Bosnia-Herzegovina (1992).
Report of the Mission to Croatia Established Under the Human Dimension Mechanism (1992).
CSCE and the New Europe—Our Security is Indivisible: Decisions of the Rome Council (1993).
Budapest Document 1994: Towards a Genuine Partnership in a New Era.
Lisbon Document (1996).
OSCE Annual Report 1996.
OSCE Secretary General, Annual Report on OSCE Activities 1997.
Updated Consolidated Text on OSCE Mechanisms and Procedures. OSCE Ref. SEC.GAL/92/98, 3 November 1998.
Culture and Conflict Prevention, Rapporteur's Report, Joint OSCE-CE Conference, Bergen, 21 May 1999; CIO.GAL/55/99, 3 June 1999.
Review of the Implementation of All OSCE Principles and Commitments: Human Dimension. Report of the Rapporteurs. Ref.RC(99)JOUR/10, 1 October 1999.
Charter for European Security (1999).
Istanbul Summit Declaration (1999).

OSCE High Commissioner on National Minorities (HCNM)

HCNM to Foreign Minister of Latvia, 6 April 1993, Ref. 238/93/L/Rev.
HCNM to Foreign Minister of Estonia, 6 April 1993, Ref. 206/93/L/Rev.
HCNM to President of Estonia, 1 July 1993, in CSCE. Communication no. 124, 23 April 1993.
HCNM to Foreign Minister of Latvia, 10 December 1993, Ref. 1463/93/L, and Foreign Minister of Latvia to HCNM, 25 January 1994, CSCE. Communication no. 8, 31 January 1994.
HCNM to Foreign Minister of Estonia, 9 March 1994, Ref. 3005/94/L.
HCNM to Foreign Minister of Latvia, 23 May 1997, Ref. 376/97/L, HCNM. GAL/1/97, 11 September 1997.
HCNM's Address to CSCE Human Dimension Seminar. "Case Studies on National Minority Issues: Positive Results." Warsaw, 23 May 1993.
Report of Mr Max van der Stoel, OSCE High Commissioner on National Minorities, 12 November 1997, to the OSCE Implementation Meeting on Human Dimension Issues, Warsaw, 12–28 November 1997.
Early Warning and Early Action: Preventing Inter-Ethnic Conflict, Speech by High Commissioner on National Minorities at the Royal Institute of International Affairs, London, on 9 July 1999, HCNM.GAL/5/99, 20 August 1999.

Material Related to OSCE/HCNM

The Oslo Recommendations Regarding the Linguistic Rights of National Minorities & Explanatory Note. The Hague: The Foundation on Inter-Ethnic Relations, February 1998.
The Lund Recommendations on the Effective Participation of National Minorities in Public Life & Explanatory Note. The Hague: The Foundation on Inter-Ethnic Relations, June 1999.

OSCE Office for Democratic Institutions and Human Rights (ODIHR)

Elections in the OSCE Region. ODIHR Background Material for the Review Conference. Warsaw, 1 October 1996. REF.RM/1/96Add.1, 11 October 1996.
Bosnia and Herzegovina Municipal Elections, 13–14 September 1997. ODIHR.GAL/22/97, 13 November 1997.
Republic of Serbia Parliamentary and Presidential Elections on September 21 and October 5, 1997. ODIHR.GAL/10/97, 24 October 1997.
Republic of Serbia Rerun of the Presidential Election December 7 and December 21, 1997. ODIHR.GAL/2/98, 10 February 1998.
Republic of Moldova Parliamentary Elections, 22 March 1998.
Republic of Ukraine Parliamentary Elections, 29 March 1998. ODIHR.GAL/31/98, 2 July 1998.
Republic of Armenia Presidential Election, March 16 and March 30, 1998. ODIHR Final Report. Ref. GAL/15/98, 16 April 1998.

Selected Bibliography 151

Bosnia and Herzegovina Elections 1998, 12–13 September 1998. ODIHR.GAL/52/98, 30 October 1998.
Presidential Election in the Republic of Azerbaijan, 11 October 1998. ODIHR.GAL/55/98, 11 November 1998.
Republic of Kazakstan (sic) Presidential Election, 10 January 1999. ODIHR.GAL/7/99, 8 February 1999.
Republic of Georgia Presidential Election, 9 April 2000, Final Report. ODIHR.GAL/34/00, 13 June 2000.

North Atlantic Treaty Organization (NATO)

Statement on Kosovo, 23 April 1999. Press Communiqué S-1(99)62.
NATO Parliamentary Assembly Warsaw Plenary Declaration on Kosovo, 31 May 2000. AS.182. SA(99)1 rev.1.
Speech by NATO Secretary-General Janvier Solana, 21 June 1999.

United Nations

Charter of the United Nations (1945).
The International Protection of Minorities Under the League of Nations. E/CN.4/Sub.2/6 (1947).
Universal Declaration of Human Rights (1948).
Convention on the Prevention and Punishment of the Crime of Genocide (1948).
Definition and Classification of Minorities. E/CN.4/Sub.2/83 (1949).
Draft Resolution on the Definition of Minorities. E/CN.4/Sub.2/107 (1950).
Definition and Classification of Minorities. E/CN.4/Sub.2/107 (1950).
Treaties and International Instruments Concerning the Protection of Minorities. E/CN.4/Sub.2/133 (1951).
Convention Against Discrimination in Education (1960).
International Convention on the Elimination of All Forms of Racial Discrimination (1965).
International Covenant on Civil and Political Rights (1966).
International Covenant on Economic, Social and Cultural Rights (1966).
Special Study on Racial Discrimination in the Political, Economic, Social and Cultural Spheres. E/CN.4/Sub.2/307/Res.1 (1971).
Declaration on Race and Racial Prejudice (1978).
Convention on the Rights of the Child (1989).
Declaration on the Rights of Persons Belonging to National or Ethnic, Religious and Linguistic Minorities (1992).
The United Nations and Human Rights. New York: United Nations, 1995.
Boutros-Ghali, Boutros. *An Agenda for Peace.* 2nd ed. New York: United Nations, 1995.
United Nations Commission on Human Rights. Resolution on Promotion of Democracy. E/CN.4/RES/1999/57, 27 April 1999.
Effective Promotion of the Declaration on the Rights of Persons Belonging to National or Ethnic, Religious and Linguistic Minorities. A/RES/54/162, 23 February 2000.
Promoting and Consolidating Democracy. E/CN.4/RES/2000/47, 25 April 2000.

Rights of Persons Belonging to National or Ethnic, Religious and Linguistic Minorities. E/CN.4/RES/2000/52, 25 April 2000.

Commentary to the Declaration on the Rights of Persons Belonging to National or Ethnic, Religious and Linguistic Minorities. Working Paper Submitted by Asbjørn Eide. E/CN.4/Sub.2/AC.5/2000/WP.1, 27 April 2000.

United Nations General Assembly: Special Reports

United Nations General Assembly. 50th session. *Support by the United Nations System of the Efforts of Governments to Promote and Consolidate New or Restored Democracies. Report of the Secretary-General.* Doc. A/50/332, 7 August 1995.

United Nations General Assembly. 51st session. *Support by the United Nations System of the Efforts of Governments to Promote and Consolidate New or Restored Democracies. Report of the Secretary-General.* Doc. A/51/761, 20 December 1996.

United Nations General Assembly. 52nd session. *Support by the United Nations System of the Efforts of Governments to Promote and Consolidate New or Restored Democracies. Report of the Secretary-General.* Doc. A/52/513, 21 October 1997.

United Nations General Assembly. 53rd session. *Support by the United Nations System of the Efforts of Governments to Promote and Consolidate New or Restored Democracies. Report of the Secretary-General.* Doc. A/53/554, 29 October 1998.

United Nations General Assembly. 55th session. *Support by the United Nations System of the Efforts of Governments to Promote and Consolidate New or Restored Democracies. Report of the Secretary-General.* Doc. A/55/189, 13 October 2000.

United Nations General Assembly Resolutions and Decisions

15th session. Resolution 1514 (XV), 14 December 1960.
15th session. Resolution 1541 (XV), 15 December 1960.
85th plenary meeting, A/RES/48/155, 20 December 1993.
52nd plenary meeting, 1995/31, 25 July 1995.
51st session, A/RES/51/91, 12 December 1996.
51/421, 12 December 1996.
51/422, 12 December 1996.
51/423, 12 December 1996.
52nd session, A/RES/52/123, 12 December 1997.

United Nations Security Council Resolutions

3205th meeting, S/RES/822, 30 April 1993.
3268th meeting, S/RES/858, 24 August 1993.
3313th meeting, S/RES/884, 12 November 1993.
3332nd meeting, S/RES/896, 31 January 1994.
3354th meeting, S/RES/906, 25 March 1994.
3488th meeting, S/RES/971, 12 January 1995.
3680th meeting, S/RES/1065, 12 July 1996.
3707th meeting, S/RES/1077, 22 October 1996.
3851st meeting, S/RES/1150, 30 January 1998.
3868th meeting, S/RES/1160, 31 March 1998.
3930th meeting, S/RES/1199, 23 September 1998.

3966th meeting, S/RES/1222, 15 January 1999.
3972nd meeting, S/RES/1225, 28 January 1999.
4011th meeting, S/RES/1244, 10 June 1999.
4023rd meeting, S/RES/1252, 15 July 1999.

Other UN Documents

Letter dated 6 May 1999 from the Permanent Representative of Germany to the United Nations Addressed to the Secretary-General, S/1999/516, 6 May 1999, with Annexes.

Letter dated 19 May 1999 from the Permanent Representative of Germany to the United Nations Addressed to the Secretary-General, S/1999/589, 20 May 1999, with Annexes.

Other Official Documents

General Framework Agreement for Peace in Bosnia and Herzegovina. Paris, 14 December 1995.

SECONDARY SOURCES: ARTICLES AND BOOKS

Acton, Lord. *Essays on Freedom and Power.* Boston: N.p., 1948.
Akashi, Yakushi. "The Limits of UN Diplomacy and the Future of Conflict Mediation." *Survival*, vol. 37, no. 4 (winter 1995): 83–98.
Alcock, Anthony. *The History of the South Tyrol Question.* London: Michael Joseph/Graduate Institute of International Studies, Geneva, 1970.
Allworth, Edward D. *The Modern Uzbeks.* Stanford: Hoover Institution Press, 1990.
Alstadt, Audrey L. *The Azerbaijani Turks: Power and Identity Under Russian Rule.* Stanford: Hoover Institution Press, 1992.
Anderson, Barbara, and Brian Silver. "Some Factors in the Linguistic and Ethnic Russification of Soviet Nationalities: Is Everyone Becoming Russian?" In Lubomyr Hajda and Mark Beissinger, eds., *The Nationalities Factor in Soviet Politics and Society.* Boulder, Colo.: Westview, 1990: 95–130.
Anderson, Benedict. *Imagined Communities: Reflections on the Origins and Spread of Nationalism.* London: Verso, 1983.
An-Na"im, Abdullahi Ahmed, ed. *Human Rights in Cross-Cultural Perspectives: A Quest for Consensus.* Philadelphia: University of Pennsylvania Press, 1992.
Ardy, Brian, and Jackie Gower. *Relations between Russia and the EU.* London: Royal Institute of International Affairs, 1996.
Arendt, Hannah. *The Origins of Totalitarianism.* London: Allen and Unwin, 1958.
Åslund, Anders. *Gorbachev's Struggle for Economic Reform.* 2nd ed. Ithaca: Cornell University Press, 1991.
Åslund, Anders, and Martha Brill Olcott, eds. *Russia after Communism.* Washington, D.C.: Carnegie Endowment for International Peace, 1999.
Aung San Suu Kyi. "Freedom, Development and Human Worth." *Journal of Democracy*, vol. 6, no. 2 (April 1995): 11–19.
Aves, Johnathan. *Post-Soviet Transcaucasia.* London: Royal Institute of International Affairs, 1993.

Baev, Pavel K. "Old and New Border Problems in Russia's Security Policy." In Tuomas Forsberg, ed., *Contested Territory: Border Disputes at the Edge of the Former Soviet Empire*. Aldershot: Edward Elgar, 1995: 86–103.

Bahry, Donna. "The Union Republics and Contradictions in Gorbachev's Economic Reform." *Soviet Economy*, vol. 7, no. 3 (July/September 1991): 215–55.

———. *Outside Moscow: Power, Politics and Budgetary Policy in the Soviet Republics*. New York: Columbia University Press, 1987.

Banac, Ivo. "The Fearful Asymmetry of War: The Causes and Consequences of Yugoslavia's Demise." *Daedalus*, vol. 121, no. 2 (spring 1992): 141–74.

———. *The National Question in Yugoslavia: Origins, History, Politics*. Ithaca: Cornell University Press, 1984.

Banerjee, Sumanta. " 'Hindutva'—Ideology and Social Psychology." *Economic and Political Weekly*, vol. 26, no. 3 (19 January 1991): 97–101.

Barnett, Michael. "Partners in Peace? The UN, Regional Organizations and Peacekeeping." *Review of International Studies*, vol. 21, no. 4 (October 1995): 411–34.

Barros, J. *The Aaland Islands Question: Its Settlement by the League of Nations*. New Haven: Yale University Press, 1968.

Bartley, Robert. "The Case for Optimism: The West Should Believe in Itself." *Foreign Affairs*, vol. 72, no. 4 (September/October 1993): 15–18.

Barzun, Jacques. "Is Democratic Theory For Export?" In Joel H. Rosenthal, ed., *Ethics and International Affairs: A Reader*. Washington, D.C.: Georgetown University Press, 1995: 39–57.

Batt, Judy. *The New Slovakia: National Identity, Political Integration and the Return to Europe*. London: Royal Institute of International Affairs Discussion Paper, 1996.

BBC Monitoring. "OSCE Refuses to Send Full Mission to Uzbek Elections." *Inside Central Asia*, no. 302 (22 November to 28 November 1999): 1–2.

British Broadcasting Corporation *Selected World Broadcasts*.

Bealey, Frank. "The Slovak Constitution." *Democratization*, vol. 2, no. 2 (summer 1995): 179–97.

Bebler, Anton. "Yugoslavia's Variety of Communist Federalism and Her Demise." *Communist and Post-Communist Studies*, vol. 26, no. 1 (March 1993): 72–86.

Beigbeder, Yves. *International Monitoring of Plebiscites, Referenda and National Elections: Self-Determination and Transition to Democracy*. Dordrecht: Martinus Nijhoff, 1994.

Bennett, Christopher. *Yugoslavia's Bloody Collapse: Causes, Course and Consequences*. London: Hurst, 1995.

Bennigsen, Alexandre, and S. Enders Wimbush. *Muslims of the Former Soviet Empire: A Guide*. Bloomington: Indiana University Press, 1986.

Bhargava, P. K. "Transfers From Centre to the States in India." *Asian Survey*, vol. 24, no. 6 (June 1984): 666–68.

Bildt, Carl. "Déjà vu in Kosovo." *Financial Times*, 9 June 1998.

———. "Extend the Brief on Bosnia." *Financial Times*, 2 August 1996.

———. "When Force is not Enough." *Financial Times*, 8 December 1995.

Birch, Anthony H. *Nationalism and National Integration*. London: Unwin Hyman, 1989.

Bociurkiw, Bohdan R. "Nationalities and Soviet Religious Policies." In Lubomyr Hajda and Mark Beissinger, eds., *The Nationalities Factor in Soviet Politics and Society*. Boulder, Colo.: Westview, 1990: 148–74.

Bogdanor, Vernon. "Forms of Autonomy and the Protection of Minorities." *Daedalus*, vol. 126, no. 2 (spring 1997): 65–87.

Bookman, Milica. "War and Peace: The Divergent Breakups of Yugoslavia and Czechoslovakia." *Journal of Peace Research*, vol. 31, no. 2 (1994): 175–87.

Bothe, Michael, Natalino Ronzitt, and Allan Rosas, eds. *The OSCE in the Maintenance of Peace and Security: Conflict Prevention, Crisis Management and Peaceful Settlement of Disputes*. The Hague: Kluwer Law International, 1997.

Bova, Russell. "Democracy and Liberty: The Cultural Connection." *Journal of Democracy*, vol. 8, no. 1 (January 1997): 112–26.

Brass, Paul. *The Politics of India Since Independence*. Cambridge: Cambridge University Press, 1990.

———. "The Punjab Crisis and the Unity of India." In Atul Kohli, ed., *India's Democracy: An Analysis of Changing State-Society Relations*. Princeton: Princeton University Press, 1988: 169–213.

Brassloff, Audrey. "Spain: The State of the Autonomies." In Murray Forsyth, ed., *Federalism and Nationalism*. Leicester: Leicester University Press, 1989: 24–50.

Bremmer, Ian. "Nazarbaev and the North: State-Building and Ethnic Relations in Kazakhstan." *Ethnic and Racial Studies*, vol. 17, no. 4 (July 1994): 619–35.

Bremmer, Ian, and Ray Taras, eds. *New States, New Politics: Building the Post-Soviet Nations*. Cambridge: Cambridge University Press, 1997.

———. *Nations and Politics in the Soviet Successor States*. Cambridge: Cambridge University Press, 1993.

Breuilly, John. *Nationalism and the State*. 2nd ed. Manchester: Manchester University Press, 1993.

Brzezinski, Zbigniew. "Post-Communist Transitions." *Foreign Affairs*, vol. 89, no. 5 (September/October 1989): 1–25.

Brölman, Catherine, René Leféber, and Marjoleine Zieck, eds. *Peoples and Minorities in International Law*. Dordrecht: Martinus Nijhoff, 1993.

Brown, J. F. *Hopes and Shadows: Eastern Europe after Communism*. Harlow: Longman, 1994.

Brown, Michael E., ed. *The International Dimensions of Internal Conflict*. Cambridge, Mass.: M.I.T. Press, 1996.

Brown, Michael E., Sean Lynn-Jones, and Steven E. Miller, eds. *Debating the Democratic Peace*. Cambridge, Mass.: M.I.T. Press, 1996.

Brown, Michael, J. R. Coté, R. Owen, Sean Lynn-Jones, and Steven Miller, eds. *Nationalism and Ethnic Conflict*. Cambridge, Mass.: M.I.T. Press, 1997.

Brubaker, Rogers. "Nationhood and the National Question in the Soviet Union and Post-Soviet Eurasia: An Institutionalist Account." *Theory and Society*, vol. 23, no. 1 (February 1991):47–78.

Buchanan, Allen. *Secession: The Morality of Political Divorce from Fort Sumter to Lithuania and Quebec*. Boulder, Colo.: Westview, 1991.

Bukkvoll, Tor. *Ukraine and European Security*. London: Pinter/Royal Institute of International Affairs, 1997.

Bull, Hedley. *The Anarchical Society: A Study of Order in World Politics*. 2nd ed. Basingstoke: Macmillan, 1995.

Burg, Steven L. *War or Peace? Nationalism, Democracy and American Foreign Policy in Post-Communist Europe*. New York: Twentieth Century Fund Press, 1996.

———. "The International Community and the Yugoslav Crisis." In Milton Esman and

Shibley Telhami, eds., *International Organizations and Ethnic Conflict*. Ithaca: Cornell University Press, 1995: 235–71.

Burgess, Michael, and Alain-G. Gagnon, eds. *Comparative Federalism and Federation: Competing Traditions and Future Directions*. New York: Harvester Wheatsheaf, 1993.

Caplan, Richard. "Christopher Hill's Road Show." *The World Today*, vol. 55, no. 1 (January 1999): 13–14.

Caplan, Richard, and John Feffer, eds. *Europe's New Nationalism: States and Minorities in Conflict*. New York: Oxford University Press, 1996.

Capotorti, Francesco. *Study on the Rights of Persons Belonging to Ethnic, Religious and Linguistic Minorities*. New York: United Nations, 1991.

Carothers, Thomas. "Romania: The Political Background." In International Institute for Democracy and Electoral Assistance, *Democracy in Romania: Assessment Mission Report*. Stockholm: International Institute for Democracy and Electoral Assistance, 1997: 1–10.

———. "Democracy Assistance: The Question of Strategy." *Democratization*, vol. 4, no. 3 (autumn 1997): 109–32.

———. "Democracy without Illusions." *Foreign Affairs*, vol. 76, no. 1 (January/February 1997): 85–99.

———. "Democracy and Human Rights: Policy Allies or Rivals?" *Washington Quarterly*, vol. 17, no. 3 (summer 1994): 109–20.

Carpenter, Michael. "Slovakia and the Triumph of Nationalist Populism." *Communist and Post-Communist Studies*, vol. 30, no. 3 (June 1997): 205–20.

Carrère d'Encausse, Hélène. *The End of the Soviet Empire: The Triumph of the Nations*. New York: Basic Books, 1993.

———. *Decline of an Empire: The Soviet Socialist Republics in Revolt*. New York: Newsweek Books, 1979.

Cassese, Antonio. *Self-Determination of Peoples: A Legal Appraisal*. Cambridge: Cambridge University Press, 1995.

Chandler, David. "Democratization in Bosnia: The Limits of Civil Society Building Strategies." *Democratization*, vol. 5, no. 4 (winter 1998): 78–102.

Chigas, Diana, Elizabeth McClintock, and Christophe Kemp. "Preventive Diplomacy and the Organization for Security and Cooperation in Europe: Creating Incentives for Dialogue and Cooperation." In Abram Chayes and Antonia Chayes, eds., *Preventing Conflict in the Post-Communist World: Mobilizing International and Regional Organizations*. Washington, D.C.: Brookings Institution, 1996: 25–97.

Claude, Inis. *National Minorities: An International Problem*. Cambridge, Mass.: Harvard University Press, 1953.

Cobban, Alfred. *The Nation-State and National Self-Determination*. London: Collins, 1944.

Cohen, Leonard. "Embattled Democracy: Post-Communist Croatia in Transition." In Karen Dawisha and Bruce Parrott, eds., *Politics, Power and the Struggle for Democracy in South-East Europe*. Cambridge: Cambridge University Press, 1997: 69–121.

Connor, Walker. "Nation-Building or Nation-Destroying?" *World Politics*, vol. 24, no. 3 (April 1972): 39–55, reprinted in Walker Connor, *Ethno-Nationalism: The Quest for Understanding*. Princeton: Princeton University Press, 1994: 29–66.

———. "A Nation Is a Nation, Is a State, Is an Ethnic Group. Is a. . . ." *Ethnic and*

Racial Studies, vol. 1, no. 4 (July 1978), reprinted in Walker Connor, *Ethno-Nationalism: The Quest for Understanding*. Princeton: Princeton University Press, 1994: 89–117.

———. "Ethno-Nationalism and Political Instability: An Overview." In Hermann Giliomee and Jannie Gagiano, eds., *The Elusive Search for Peace: South Africa, Israel, Northern Ireland*. Cape Town: Oxford University Press, 1990: 9–32.

———. *The National Question in Marxist-Leninist Theory and Strategy*. Princeton: Princeton University Press, 1984.

Conquest, Robert. *The Last Empire: Nationality and the Soviet Future*. Stanford: Hoover Institution Press, 1986.

———. *Soviet Nationalities Policy in Practice*. London: The Bodley Head, 1967.

Conversi, Daniele. *The Basques, the Catalans and Spain: Alternative Routes to Nationalist Mobilization*. London: Hurst, 1997.

Cooper, Robert. "Integration and Disintegration." *Journal of Democracy*, vol. 10, no. 1 (January 1999): 8–21.

Crawford, Beverly. "Explaining Defection From International Cooperation: Germany's Unilateral Recognition of Croatia." *World Politics*, vol. 48, no. 4 (July 1996): 482–521.

Crawford, James. *Democracy in International Law*. Cambridge: Cambridge University Press, 1993.

Critchlow, James. *Nationalism in Uzbekistan: A Soviet Republic's Road to Sovereignty*. Boulder, Colo.: Westview, 1991.

Crowther, William. "The Politics of Democratization in Post-Communist Moldova." In Karen Dawisha and Bruce Parrott, eds., *Democratic Changes and Authoritarian Reactions in Russia, Ukraine, Belarus and Moldova*. Cambridge: Cambridge University Press, 1997: 282–329.

Daalder, Ivo H., and Michael B. G. Froman. "Dayton's Incomplete Peace." *Foreign Affairs*, vol. 78, no. 6 (November/December 1999): 106–13.

Dae Jung, Kim. "Is Culture Destiny? The Myth of Asia's Anti-Democratic Values." *Foreign Affairs*, vol. 73, no. 6 (November/December 1994): 189–94.

Dahl, Robert. *Democracy and Its Critics*. New Haven: Yale University Press, 1989.

Dahrendorf, Ralf. *Reflections on the Revolution in Europe*. London: Chatto and Windus, 1990.

Dawisha, Karen, and Bruce Parrott, eds. *The International Dimensions of Post-Communist Transitions in Russia and New States of Eurasia*. Armonk, N.Y.: M. E. Sharpe, 1997.

———. *The End of Empire? The Transformation of the USSR in Comparative Perspective*. Armonk, N.Y.: M. E. Sharpe, 1997.

———. *Conflict, Cleavage and Change in Central Asia and the Caucasus*. Cambridge: Cambridge University Press, 1997.

———. *Democratic Changes and Authoritarian Reactions in Russia, Ukraine, Belarus and Moldova*. Cambridge: Cambridge University Press, 1997.

———. *Politics, Power and the Struggle for Democracy in South-East Europe*. Cambridge: Cambridge University Press, 1997.

———. *The Consolidation of Democracy in East-Central Europe*. Cambridge: Cambridge University Press, 1997.

———. *Russia and the New States of Eurasia: The Politics of Upheaval*. Cambridge: Cambridge University Press, 1994.

Deletant, Denis. "The Role of '*Vatra Romaneasca*' in Transylvania." RFE/RL *Research Report*, vol. 2, no. 5 (1 February 1991): 28–37.

Deutsch, Karl. *Nationalism and Social Communication*. Cambridge, Mass.: M.I.T. Press, 1953.

Diamond, Larry. *Promoting Democracy in the 1990s: Actors and Instruments, Issues and Imperatives*. Washington, D.C.: Carnegie Commission on Preventing Deadly Conflict, 1995.

Diamond, Larry, and Marc Plattner, eds. *The Global Resurgence of Democracy*. Baltimore: Johns Hopkins University Press, 1996.

———. *Nationalism, Ethnic Conflict and Democracy*. Baltimore: Johns Hopkins University Press, 1994.

Donia, Robert, and John Fine Jr. *Bosnia and Hercegovina: A Tradition Betrayed*. London: Hurst, 1994.

Donnelly, Jack. "Human Rights: Old Scepticisms, New Standards." *International Affairs*, vol. 74, no. 1 (January 1998): 1–23.

———. "State Sovereignty and International Intervention: The Case of Human Rights." In Gene Lyons and Michael Mastanduno, eds., *Beyond Westphalia? State Sovereignty and International Intervention*. Baltimore: Johns Hopkins University Press, 1995: 115–46.

Doyle, Michael. "Kant, Liberal Legacies and Foreign Affairs." In Michael E. Brown, Sean Lynn-Jones, and Steven Miller, eds., *Debating the Democratic Peace*. Cambridge, Mass.: M.I.T. Press, 1996: 3–57.

———. *Empires*. Ithaca: Cornell University Press, 1986.

Dreifelds, Juris. *Latvia in Transition*. Cambridge: Cambridge University Press, 1996.

Dunay, Pál. "Nationalism and Ethnic Conflicts in Eastern Europe: Imposed, Induced or (Simply Reemerged?" In István Pogany, ed., *Human Rights in Eastern Europe*. Aldershot: Edward Elgar, 1995: 17–45.

Duncan, W. Raymond, and G. Paul Holman Jr., eds. *Ethnic Nationalism and Regional Conflict in the Former Soviet Union and Yugoslavia*. Boulder, Colo.: Westview, 1994.

Dunlop, John. "The 'Party of War' and Russian Imperial Nationalism." *Problems of Post-Communism*, vol. 43, no. 2 (March/April 1996): 29–34.

———. "Zhirinovsky's World." *Journal of Democracy*, vol. 5, no. 2 (April 1994): 27–32.

———. *The Rise of Russia and the Fall of the Soviet Empire*. Princeton: Princeton University Press, 1993.

———. *The Faces of Contemporary Russian Nationalism*. Princeton: Princeton University Press, 1983.

Dunn, John. "Conclusion." In John Dunn, ed., *Democracy: The Unfinished Journey, 508 B.C. to A.D. 1993*. Oxford: Oxford University Press, 1992: 239–66.

Economides, Spyros, and Paul Taylor. "Former Yugoslavia." In James Mayall, ed., *The New Interventionism: United Nations Experience in Cambodia, Former Yugoslavia and Somalia*. Cambridge: Cambridge University Press, 1996: 59–93.

Elman, Miriam F., ed. *Paths to Peace: Is Democracy the Answer?* Cambridge, Mass.: M.I.T. Press, 1997.

Engman, Max. "Finns and Swedes in Finland." In Sven Tägil, ed., *Ethnicity and Nation-Building in the Nordic World*. London: Hurst, 1995: 179–216.

Estébanez, Maria Amor Martin. "Inter-Ethnic Relations and the Protection of Minorities."

In International Institute for Democracy and Electoral Assistance, *Democracy in Romania: Assessment Mission Report*. Stockholm: International Institute for Democracy and Electoral Assistance, 1997: 123–43.

———. "The Protection of National or Ethnic, Religious and Linguistic Minorities." In Nanette A. Neuwahl and Allan Rosas, eds., *The European Union and Human Rights*. The Hague: Martinus Nijhoff, 1995: 133–63.

Evangelista, Matthew. "Historical Legacies and the Politics of Intervention in the Former Soviet Union." In Michael E. Brown, ed., *The International Dimensions of Internal Conflict*. Cambridge, Mass.: M.I.T. Press, 1996: 107–40.

Fairbanks, Charles, Jr. "The Federalization of the State." *Journal of Democracy*, vol. 10, no. 2 (April 1999): 47–53.

Falk, Richard. "Toward Obsolescence: Sovereignty in the Era of Globalization." *Harvard International Review*, vol. 17, no. 3 (summer 1995):34ff.

Fane, Daria. "Moldova: Breaking Loose From Moscow." In Ian Bremmer and Ray Taras, eds., *Nations and Politics in the Soviet Successor States*. Cambridge: Cambridge University Press, 1993: 121–53.

Fawn, Rick, and James Mayall. "Recognition, Self-Determination and Secession in Post–Cold War International Society." In Rick Fawn and Jeremy Larkins, eds., *International Society after the Cold War: Anarchy and Order Reconsidered*. Basingstoke: Macmillan, 1996: 193–219.

Foreign Broadcast Information Service, Daily Report, Eastern Europe.

Foreign Broadcast Information Service, [Daily Bulletin]. Soviet Union.

Final Report: Evaluation of the Phare and Tacis Democracy Programme, 1992–1997.

Financial Times.

Fisher, Sharon. "Ethnic Hungarians Back Themselves Into a Corner." *Transition*, vol. 1, no. 24 (29 December 1995): 58–63.

Forsythe, David P. *Human Rights in the New Europe: Problems and Progress*. Lincoln: University of Nebraska Press, 1994.

Forum. Strasbourg: Council of Europe.

Fowler, Michael Ross, and Julie Marie Bunck. "What Constitutes the Sovereign State?" *Review of International Studies*, vol. 22, no. 4 (October 1996): 381–404.

Franck, Thomas. "The Emerging Right to Democratic Governance." *American Journal of International Law*, vol. 86, no. 1 (January 1992): 46–91.

Friedrich, Carl, and Zbigniew Brzezinski. *Totalitarian Dictatorship and Autocracy*. 2nd ed. Cambridge, Mass.: Harvard University Press, 1965.

Fukuyama, Francis. "The End of History?" *National Interest*, no. 16 (summer 1989): 3–18.

Fuller, Elizabeth. "Caucasus: Karabakh—A Quasi-Independent State—South Ossetia's Status Unclear." RFE/RL *Report*, July 1998.

———. *Azerbaijan at the Crossroads*. London: Royal Institute of International Affairs and RFE/RL Research Institute, 1994.

Gál, Kinga. *Bilateral Agreements in Central and Eastern Europe: A New Inter-State Framework for Minority Protection?* Working Paper #4. Flemsburg, Germany: European Centre for Minority Issues, 1999.

Gallagher, Tom. "Conflicts Between East European States and Minorities in an Age of Democracy." *Democratization*, vol. 5, no. 3 (autumn 1998): 200–223.

Ganguly, Sumit. *The Crisis in Kashmir*. Cambridge: Cambridge University Press, 1997.

———. "Explaining the Kashmir Insurgency: Political Mobilization and Institutional Decay." *International Security*, vol. 21, no. 2 (fall 1996): 76–107.
———. *The Origins of War in South Asia: Indo-Pakistani Conflicts since 1947*. Boulder, Colo.: Westview, 1986.
Garnett, Sherman W., and Rachel Lebenson. "Ukraine Joins the Fray: Will Peace Come to Trans-Dniestria?" *Problems of Post-Communism*, vol. 45, no. 6 (November/December 1998): 22–32.
Geistlinger, Michael, and Axel Kirch. *Estonia: A New Framework for the Estonian Majority and the Russian Minority*. Wien: Braumüller, 1995.
Gellner, Ernest. *Nations and Nationalism*. Oxford: Blackwell, 1993.
———. "Homeland of the Unrevolution." *Daedalus*, vol. 122, no. 3 (summer 1993): 141–53.
Gitelman, Zvi. "Development and Ethnicity in the Soviet Union." In Alexander Motyl, ed., *The Post-Soviet Nations: Perspectives on the Demise of the USSR*. New York: Columbia University Press, 1992: 220–39.
Gleason, Gregory. *Federalism and Nationalism: The Struggle for Republican Rights in the USSR*. Boulder, Colo.: Westview, 1990.
Glenny, Misha. *The Balkans 1804–1999: Nationalism, War and the Great Powers*. London: Granta Books, 1999.
———. *The Fall of Yugoslavia: The Third Balkan War*. London: Penguin Books, 1992.
Goble, Paul. "When Communists Win Elections." RFE/RL Endnote, 6 April 1998.
Goldman, Marshall. *What Went Wrong With Perestroika*. New York: W. W. Norton, 1991.
Goldwin, Robert A., Art Kaufman, and William A. Schambra, eds. *Forging Unity Out of Diversity: The Approaches of Eight Nations*. Washington, D.C.: American Enterprise Institute for Public Policy Research, 1989.
Gorenburg, Dmitry. "Regional Separatism in Russia: Ethnic Mobilization or Power Grab?" *Europe-Asia Studies*, vol. 51, no. 2 (March 1999): 245–74.
Graham, Bruce D. *Hindu Nationalism and Indian Politics*. Cambridge: Cambridge University Press, 1991.
Gurr, Ted Robert. *Minorities at Risk: A Global View of Ethnopolitical Conflicts*. Washington, D.C.: United States Institute of Peace, 1993.
Haass, Richard. "What to Do with American Primacy." *Foreign Affairs*, vol. 78, no. 5 (September/October 1999): 37–49.
Hadenius, Axel. *Democracy and Development*. Cambridge: Cambridge University Press, 1992.
Hajda, Lubomyr, and Mark Beissinger, eds. *The Nationalities Factor in Soviet Politics and Society*. Boulder, Colo.: Westview, 1990.
Halperin, Morton, and David Scheffer, with Particia Small. *Self-Determination in the New World Order*. Washington, D.C.: Carnegie Endowment for International Peace, 1992.
Hannum, Hurst. *Autonomy, Sovereignty and Self-Determination: The Accommodation of Conflicting Rights*. Rev. ed. Philadelphia: University of Pennsylvania Press, 1996.
Hanson, Philip, "The Center versus the Periphery in Russian Economic Policy." *RFE/RL Research Report*, vol. 3, no. 17 (29 April 1994): 23–28.
Haqqi, S.A.H., and A. P. Sharma. "Centre-State Relations: A Study of Structural Processual Determinants." In K. Bombwall, ed., *National Power and State Autonomy*. Meerut, India: Meenakshi Prakashan, 1964: 42–47.

Selected Bibliography 161

Hassner, Perre. "Huntington's Clash: I." *The National Interest*, no. 46 (winter 1996/97): 63–69.

Hayden, Robert. "The Partition of Bosnia and Herzogovina, 1990–1993." RFE/RL *Research Report*, vol. 2, no. 22 (28 May 1993): 1–14.

———. "Constitutional Nationalism in the Formerly Yugoslav Republics." *Slavic Review*, vol. 51, no. 4 (winter 1992): 654–73.

Haynes, Rebecca Ann. "Hungarian National Identity: Definition and Redefinition." In Paul Latawski, ed., *Contemporary Nationalism in East Central Europe*. Basingstoke: Macmillan, 1995: 87–104.

Heraclides, Alexis. *The Self-Determination of Minorities in International Politics*. London: Frank Cass, 1991.

Higgins, Rosalyn. "Responding to Individual Needs: Human Rights." *Problems and Process: International Law and How We Use It*. Oxford: Clarendon Press, 1994: 95–110.

———. "The New United Nations and Former Yugoslavia." *International Affairs*, vol. 69, no. 3 (July 1993): 465–83.

Hillgruber, Christian. "The Admission of New States to the International Community." *European Journal of International Law*, vol. 9, no. 3 (1998): 491–509.

Hindus, Maurice. *House Without a Roof: Russia After Forty-Three Years of Revolution*. New York: Doubleday, 1961.

Hinsley, F. H. *Nationalism and the International System*. London: Hodder and Stoughton, 1973.

———. *Power and the Pursuit of Peace*. Cambridge: Cambridge University Press, 1963.

Hobsbawm, Eric. *Nations and Nationalism since 1780: Programme, Myth, Reality*. Cambridge: Cambridge University Press, 1990.

Horowitz, Donald L. "Democracy in Divided Societies." In Larry Diamond and Marc Plattner, eds., *Nationalism, Ethnic Conflict and Democracy*. Baltimore: Johns Hopkins University Press, 1994: 35–55.

———. "Making Moderation Pay: The Comparative Politics of Ethnic Conflict Management." In Joseph Montville, ed., *Conflict and Peacemaking in Multiethnic Societies*. Lexington, Mass.: Lexington Books, 1990:

———. *Ethnic Groups in Conflict*. Berkeley and Los Angeles: University of California Press, 1985.

Howard, Michael. *War and the Nation-State*. Oxford: Clarendon Press, 1978.

Hroch, Miroslav. "From National Movement to the Fully-Formed Nation: The Nation-Building Process in Europe." In Gopal Balakrishnan, ed., *Mapping the Nation*. London: Verso/New Left Review, 1996: 78–97.

Hughes, James. "Moscow's Bilateral Treaties Add to Confusion." *Transition*, vol. 1, no. 13 (20 September 1996): 39–43.

Huntington, Samuel P. "The Clash of Civilizations?" *Foreign Affairs*, vol. 72, no. 3 (summer 1993): 22–49.

———. "Democracy's Third Wave." *Journal of Democracy*, vol. 2, no. 2 (April 1991): 12–34.

———. "Political Development and Political Decay." In Claude E. Welch Jr., ed., *Political Modernization: A Reader in Comparative Political Change*. Belmont, Calif.: Wadsworth Publishing Co., 1967: 207–45.

Huntington, Samuel P., and Clement H. Moore. *Authoritarian Politics in Modern Society: The Dynamics of Established One-Party Systems*. New York: Basic Books, 1970.

Iivonen, Jyrki. "Expansionism and the Russian Imperial Tradition." In Tuomas Forsberg, ed., *Contested Territory: Border Disputes at the Edge of the Former Soviet Empire*. Aldershot: Edward Elgar, 1995: 62–85.

Independent Commission on International Humanitarian Issues. *Modern Wars: The Humanitarian Challenge: A Report for the Independent Commission on International Humanitarian Issues*. London: Zed, 1986.

Inder Singh, Anita. "Democracy as Conflict Prevention." *United Nations Chronicle*, vol. 37, no. 3 (2000): 14–15.

———. "The People's Choice." *The World Today*, vol. 55, nos. 8/9 (August/September 1999): 22–24.

———. "On the Absence of War." *The World Today*, vol. 54, nos. 8/9 (August/September 1998): 236–39.

———. "Where Does Kashmir End?" *Times Literary Supplement*, 7 November 1997, 31.

———. "Democracy and Ethnic Diversity: A New International Priority?" *The World Today*, vol. 52, no. 1 (January 1996): 20–22.

———. "Managing Ethnic Diversity Through Political Ideologies and Structures: The Soviet Experience in Comparative Perspective." *Nations and Nationalism*, vol. 1, part 2 (July 1995): 197–220.

———. "Is Ethnicity Enough?" *Times Literary Supplement*, 17 March 1995, 12.

———. "Forging a Multi-Ethnic Union: A Comparative Study of State Nationalism in India and the Soviet Union." *Journal of Area Studies*, no. 5 (autumn 1994): 190–204.

———. *Forging a Multi-Ethnic Union: The Case of India*. Working paper no. 17, Center for the Comparative Study of Development, Brown University (February 1992).

International Herald Tribune.

International Institute for Democracy and Electoral Assistance. *Democracy and Deep-Rooted Conflict: Options for Negotiators*. Stockholm: International Institute for Democracy and Electoral Assistance, 1998.

International Legal Materials.

Irvine, Jill A. "Ultranationalist Ideology and State-Building in Croatia, 1990–1996." *Problems of Post-Communism*, vol. 44, no. 4 (July/August 1997): 30–43.

Izvestia.

Jackson Preece, Jennifer. *National Minorities and the European Nation-States System*. Oxford: Clarendon Press, 1999.

Jackson, Robert H., and Alan James, eds. *States in a Changing World: A Contemporary Analysis*. Oxford: Clarendon Press, 1993.

Jakobson, Max. "Is Kosovo a Turning Point?" *International Herald Tribune*, 31 August 1999.

Janis, Mark. "Russia and the 'Legality' of Strasbourg Law." *European Journal of International Law*, vol. 8, no. 1 (1997): 93–99.

Jeffrey, Robin. *What's Happening to India? Punjab, Ethnic Conflict, Mrs. Gandhi's Death and the Test for Federalism*. Basingstoke: Macmillan, 1986.

Joffe, Joseph. "Rethinking the Nation-State." *Foreign Affairs*, vol. 78, no. 6 (November/December 1999): 122–27.

Jones, Stephen. "Georgia: The Trauma of Statehood." In Ian Bremmer and Ray Taras, eds., *New States, New Politics: Building the Post-Soviet Nations*. Cambridge: Cambridge University Press, 1997: 505–43.

Judah, Tim. "Kosovo's Road to War." *Survival*, vol. 41, no. 2 (summer 1999): 5–18.
———. *The Serbs: History, Myth and the Destruction of Yugoslavia*. New Haven: Yale University Press, 1997.
Kaiser, David. *Politics and War: European Conflict from Philip II to Hitler*. London: I. B. Tauris, 1990.
Kaldor, Mary, and Ivan Vejvoda. "Democratization in Central and East European Countries." *International Affairs*, vol. 73, no. 1 (January 1997): 59–82.
Kaplan, Robert. "Was Democracy Just a Moment?" *The Atlantic Monthly*, vol. 280, no. 6 (December 1997): 55ff.
Kappeler, Andreas. *Russland als Vielvölkerreich*. Munich: Verlag C. H. Beck, 1993.
Karklins, Rasma. *Ethnopolitics and Transition to Democracy: The Collapse of the USSR and Latvia*. Baltimore: Johns Hopkins University Press, 1994.
Kaufman, Chaim. "Possible and Impossible Solutions to Ethnic Civil Wars." *International Security*, vol. 20, no. 4 (spring 1996): 136–75.
Kaufman, Stuart J. "Spiralling to Ethnic War: Elites, Masses and Moscow in Moldova's Civil War." *International Security*, vol. 21, no. 2 (fall 1996): 108–38.
———. "An 'International' Theory of Inter-Ethnic War." *Review of International Studies*, vol. 22, no. 2 (April 1996): 144–71.
Kaviraj, Sudipto. "Crisis of the Nation-State in India." In John Dunn, ed., *Contemporary Crisis of the Nation-State?* Oxford: Blackwell, 1995: 115–29.
Keating, Michael. "Stateless Nation-Building: Quebec, Catalonia and Scotland in the Changing State System." *Nations and Nationalism*, vol. 3, part 4 (October 1997): 689–717.
———. *Nations against the State: The New Politics of Nationalism in Quebec, Catalonia and Scotland*. Basingstoke: Macmillan, 1996.
———. "Spain: Peripheral Nationalism and State Response." In John McGarry and Brendan O'Leary, eds., *The Politics of Ethnic Conflict Regulation*. London: Routledge, 1993: 204–25.
Kedourie, Elie. "A New International Disorder." In Hedley Bull and Adam Watson, eds., *The Expansion of International Society*. Oxford: Clarendon Press, 1984: 347–55.
———. *Nationalism*. 3rd ed. London: Hutchinson, 1960.
Kellas, James G. *The Politics of Nationalism and Ethnicity*. Basingstoke: Macmillan, 1991.
Khazanov, Anatoly M. "The Ethnic Problems of Contemporary Kazakhstan." *Central Asian Survey*, vol. 14, no. 2 (June 1995): 243–64.
Khilnani, Sunil. *The Idea of India*. London: Hamish Hamilton, 1997.
———. "India's Democratic Career." In John Dunn, ed., *Democracy: The Unfinished Journey, 508 B.C. to A.D. 1993*. Oxford: Oxford University Press, 1992: 189–205.
King, Charles, and Neil Melvin, eds. *Nations Abroad: Diaspora Politics and International Relations in the Former Soviet Union*. Boulder, Colo.: Westview, 1998.
Klein, Jacques Paul. "Reaping the Whirlwind." *The World Today*, vol. 55, no. 6 (June 1999): 7–9.
Kohli, Atul, ed. *India's Democracy: An Analysis of State-Society Relations*. Princeton: Princeton University Press, 1988.
Kohn, Hans. *The Idea of Nationalism*. New York: Macmillan, 1945.
Kolakowski, Leszek. *Main Currents of Marxism: Its Rise, Growth, and Dissolution. Vol. 2. The Golden Age*. Trans. P. S. Falla. Oxford: Oxford University Press, 1981.

———. *Main Currents of Marxism: Its Rise, Growth, and Dissolution. Vol. 3. The Breakdown.* Trans. P. S. Falla. Oxford: Oxford University Press, 1981.
Kolarz, Walter. *Religion in the Soviet Union.* London: Macmillan, 1961.
Kolstø, Pal, and Andrei Edemsky, with Natalya Kalashnikova. "The Dniestr Conflict: Between Irredentism and Separatism." *Europe-Asia Studies*, vol. 45, no. 6 (September 1993): 973–1000.
Korman, Sharon. *The Right of Conquest: The Forcible Annexation of Territory in International Law and Practice.* Oxford: Clarendon Press, 1996.
Kothari, Rajni. "The Crisis of the Moderate State and the Decline of Democracy." In James Manor, ed., *Transfer and Transformation: Political Institutions in the New Commonwealth.* Leicester: Leicester University Press, 1983: 29–46.
———. *Politics in India.* Delhi: Orient Longman, 1970.
Krech, Hans. *Der Russische Krieg in Tschetschenien (1994–1996): Ein Handbuch. M.I.T. einem Sicherheitskonzept zur Einbindung der Russischen Foderation in die NATO und die Europaische Union.* Berlin: Verlag Dr. Koster, 1997.
Krickus, Richard. "Latvia's 'Russian Question.' " *RFE/RL Research Report*, vol. 2, no. 18 (30 April 1993): 29–34.
Krushnelnycky, Askold. "Ukraine: Incumbent President Plays on Fears of a Communist Return." *RFE/RL Research Report*, 10 November 1999.
Kumar, Ravinder. *Essays in the Social History of Modern India.* Delhi: Oxford University Press, 1983.
Kux, Stephen. *Soviet Federalism: A Comparative Perspective.* New York: IEWS, 1990.
Kuzio, Taras. *Ukrainian Security Policy.* Westport, Conn.: Center for Strategic and International Studies/Praeger Washington Papers/167, 1995.
Kymlicka, Will. *Multicultural Citizenship: A Liberal Theory of Minority Rights.* Oxford: Clarendon Press, 1995.
Kymlicka, Will, ed. *The Rights of Minority Cultures.* Oxford: Oxford University Press, 1995.
Lambeth, Richard. "Russia's Wounded Military." *Foreign Affairs*, vol. 74, no. 2 (March 1995): 86–98.
Lapidoth, Ruth. *Autonomy: Flexible Solutions to Ethnic Conflicts.* Washington, D.C.: United States Institute of Peace Press, 1997.
Lapidus, Gail W. "Asymmetrical Federalism and State Breakdown in Russia." *Post-Soviet Affairs*, vol. 15, no. 1 (January/March 1999): 74–82.
———. "Contested Sovereignty: The Tragedy of Chechnya." *International Security*, vol. 23, no. 1 (summer 1998): 5–49.
Lapidus, Gail W., and Edward W. Walker. "Nationalism, Regionalism and Federalism: Center-Periphery Relations in Post-Communist Russia." In Gail W. Lapidus, ed., *The New Russia: Troubled Transformation.* Boulder, Colo.: Westview, 1995: 79–113.
Lapidus, Gail W., and Victor Zaslavsky, with Philip Goldman, eds. *From Union to Commonwealth: Nationalism and Separatism in the Soviet Republics.* Cambridge: Cambridge University Press, 1992.
La Ponce, J. *The Protection of Minorities.* Berkeley and Los Angeles: University of California Press, 1960.
Lapychak, Christina. "Showdown Yields Political Reform." *Transition*, vol. 1, no. 13 (28 July 1995): 3–5.

Lasota, Irena, "Sometimes Less is More." *Journal of Democracy*, vol. 10, no. 4 (October 1999): 125–28.

Layne, Christopher, "Kant or Cant? The Myth of the Democratic Peace." In Michael E. Brown, ed., *Debating the Democratic Peace*. Cambridge, Mass.: M.I.T. Press, 1996: 157–201.

Lenin, V. I. *Collected Works*, vol. 21, cited in Bernard Semmel, *Marxism and the Science of War*. Oxford: Oxford University Press, 1981: 164–67.

Lieven, Anatol. "The Weakness of Russian Nationalism." *Survival*, vol. 41, no. 2 (summer 1999): 53–70.

———. *Chechnya: Tombstone of Russian Power*. New Haven: Yale University Press, 1998.

———. "The Focus is Now on Accession to the EU and NATO." *Financial Times Supplement on Hungary*, 9 December 1997, p. iii.

———. *The Baltic Revolution: Estonia, Latvia, Lithuania and the Path to Independence*. New Haven: Yale University Press, 1993.

Lieven, Dominic. "The Russian Empire and the Soviet Union as Imperial Polities." *Journal of Contemporary History*, vol. 30, no. 4 (October 1995): 607–36.

———. "Empires, Russian and Other." In Marco Buttino, ed., *In a Collapsing Empire: Underdevelopment, Ethnic Conflicts and Nationalisms in the Soviet Union*. Milan: Feltrinelli Editore, 1993: 89–103.

Light, Margot. "Russia and Transcaucasia." In John Wright, Suzanne Goldberg, and Richard Schofield, eds., *Transcaucasian Boundaries*. London: U.C.L. Press, 1996: 35–53.

———. "Russian Statehood and Nationalism." *Oxford International Review* (summer 1994): 38–42.

Lijphart, Arend. *Democracy in Plural Societies: A Comparative Exploration*. New Haven: Yale University Press, 1977.

Linz, Juan J. "Spanish Democracy and the *Estado de las Autonomías*." In Robert A. Goldwin, Art Kaufman, and William A. Schambra, eds., *Forging Unity Out of Diversity: The Approaches of Eight Nations*. Washington, D.C.: American Enterprise Institute for Public Policy Research, 1989: 260–303.

Linz, Juan J., and Alfred Stepan. *Problems of Democratic Transition and Consolidation: Southern Europe, South America and Post-Communist Europe*. Baltimore: Johns Hopkins University Press, 1996.

———. "Toward Consolidated Democracies." *Journal of Democracy*, vol. 7, no. 2 (April 1996): 14–33.

———. "Political Identities and Electoral Sequences: Spain, the Soviet Union and Yugoslavia." *Daedalus*, vol. 121, no. 2 (spring 1992): 123–39.

Little, Richard. *Governing the Soviet Union*. London: Longman, 1989.

Low, D. A. *Eclipse of Empire*. Cambridge: Cambridge University Press, 1990.

Lund, Michael. *Preventing Violent Conflicts*. Washington, D.C.: United States Institute of Peace, 1996.

Lundestad, Geir, ed. *The Fall of the Great Powers: Peace, Stability and Legitimacy*. Oslo: Scandinavian University Press, 1994.

Lyons, Gene M., and Michael Mastanduno, eds. *Beyond Westphalia? State Sovereignty and International Intervention*. Baltimore: Johns Hopkins University Press, 1995.

Macartney, C. A. *National States and National Minorities*. London: Oxford University Press, 1934.

MacFarlane, Neil. "Democratization, Nationalism and Regional Security in the Southern Caucasus." *Government and Opposition*, vol. 32, no. 3 (summer 1997): 399–420.
Magaš, Branka. *The Destruction of Yugoslavia: Tracking the Break-Up 1980–91*. London: Verso, 1993.
Malcolm, Neil, and Alex Pravda. "Democratization and Russian Foreign Policy." *International Affairs*, vol. 72, no. 3 (July 1996): 537–52.
Malcolm, Noel. *Bosnia: A Short History*. Basingstoke: Macmillan, 1994.
Malik, Y. K. "The Akali Party and Sikh Militancy: Move for Greater Autonomy or Secession in Punjab." *Asian Survey*, vol. 26, no. 3 (March 1986): 345–62.
Malik, Y. K. and D. K. Vajpeyi "The Rise of Hindu Militancy: India's Secular Democracy at Risk." *Asian Survey*, vol. 29, no. 3 (March 1986): 308–25.
Manas, Jean. "The Council of Europe's Democracy Ideal and the Challenge of Ethno-National Strife." In Abram Chayes and Antonia Chayes, eds., *Preventing Conflict in the Post-Communist World: Mobilizing International and Regional Organizations*. Washington, D.C.: Brookings Institution, 1996: 99–144.
Mandelbaum, Michael. "A Perfect Failure." *Foreign Affairs*, vol. 78, no. 5 (September/October 1999): 2–8.
Mandelbaum, Michael, ed. *Diasporas: The New European Minorities and Conflict in Eastern Europe*. New York: Council on Foreign Relations, 2000.
———. *Post-Communism: Four Perspectives*. New York: Council on Foreign Relations, 1996.
———. *Central Asia and the World: Kazakhstan, Uzbekistan, Tajikistan, Kyrgyzstan and Turkmenistan*. New York: Council on Foreign Relations, 1994.
Manor, James. "India: The Misconceptions and the Reality." *The World Today*, vol. 47, no. 11 (November 1991): 193–96.
———. *The Expedient Utopian: Bandaranaike and Ceylon*. Cambridge: Cambridge University Press, 1989.
———. "The Dynamics of Political Integration and Disintegration." In A. Jeyaratnam Wilson and Denis Dalton, eds., *The States of South*. London: Hurst, 1982: 89–110.
Mansfield, Edward D., and Jack Snyder. "Democratization and War." *Foreign Affairs*, vol. 74, no. 3 (May/June 1995): 79–97.
Markus, Ustina. "No Longer as Mighty." *Transition*, vol. 1, no. 13 (28 July 1995): 24–29.
Mastny, Vojtech. *The Helsinki Process and the Reintegration of Europe 1986–1991: Analysis and Documentation*. London: Pinter, 1992.
Mayall, James. "Sovereignty, Nationalism and Self-Determination." *Political Studies*, vol. 47, no. 3 (September 1999): 474–502.
———. "Introduction." In James Mayall, ed., *The New Interventionism, 1991–1994: United Nations Experience in Cambodia, Former Yugoslavia and Somalia*. Cambridge: Cambridge University Press, 1996: 1–24.
———. "Ideological Sources of Conflict: The Principle of National Self-Determination, Religion and the Legitimacy of the State." In Trevor Taylor and Sato Seizaburo, eds., *Future Sources of Global Conflict*. London: Royal Institute of International Affairs and Institute for International Policy Studies, 1995: 7–23.
———. "Sovereignty and Self-Determination in the New Europe." In Hugh Miall, ed., *Minority Rights in Europe: Prospects for a Transnational Regime*. London: Royal Institute of International Affairs, 1994: 7–13.

———. "Non-Intervention, Self-Determination and the 'New World Order.'" *International Affairs*, vol. 67, no. 3 (July 1991): 421–29.
———. *Nationalism and International Society*. Cambridge: Cambridge University Press, 1990.
———. "1789 and the Liberal Theory of International Society." *Review of International Studies*, vol. 15, no. 4 (October 1989): 297–307.
Mayall, James, and Mark Simpson. "Ethnicity is Not Enough: Reflections on Protracted Secessionism in the Third World." *International Journal of Comparative Sociology*, vol. 33, nos. 1–2 (1992): 5–25.
McAuley, Alistair, ed. *Soviet Federalism: Nationalism and Economic Decentralization*. Leicester: Leicester University Press, 1991.
McFaul, Michael. "The Perils of a Protracted Transition." *Journal of Democracy*, vol. 10, no. 2 (April 1999): 4–18.
———. "A Precarious Peace: Domestic Politics in the Making of Russian Foreign Policy." *International Security*, vol. 22, no. 3 (winter 1997/98): 5–35.
———. "Revolutionary Ideas, State Interests and Russian Foreign Policy." In Vladimir Tismaneanu, ed., *Political Culture and Civil Society in Russia and the New States of Eurasia*. Armonk, N.Y.: M. E. Sharpe, 1995: 27–52.
———. "Eurasia Letter: Russian Politics After Chechnya." *Foreign Policy*, vol. 99 (summer 1995): 149–65.
Melvin, Neil. *Russians Beyond Russia: The Politics of National Identity*. London: Royal Institute of International Affairs, 1995.
Mihalisko, Kathleen. "Belarus: Retreat to Authoritarianism." In Karen Dawisha and Bruce Parrott, eds., *Democratic Changes and Authoritarian Reactions in Russia, Ukraine, Belarus and Moldova*. Cambridge: Cambridge University Press, 1997: 223–81.
Mill, John Stuart. *Considerations on Representative Sovereignty*. London: Longman, Green, Longman, Roberts and Green, 1865.
Millard, Frances. "Nationalism in Poland." In Paul Latawski, ed., *Contemporary Nationalism in East-Central Europe*. Basingstoke: Macmillan, 1995: 105–26.
Montville, Joseph, ed. *Conflict and Peacemaking in Multiethnic Societies*. Lexington, Mass.: Lexington Books, 1991.
Morris-Jones, W. H. *The Government and Politics of India*. 2nd ed. London: Hutchinson University Library, 1964.
Motyl, Alexandr, ed. *Thinking Theoretically About Soviet Nationalities: History and Comparison in the Study of the USSR*. New York: Columbia University Press, 1992.
———. *The Post-Soviet Nations: Perspectives on the Demise of the USSR*. New York: Columbia University Press, 1992.
Müllerson, Rein. *Human Rights Diplomacy*. London: Routledge, 1997.
———. *International Law, Rights and Politics: Developments in Eastern Europe and the CIS*. London: Routledge, 1994.
Musgrave, Thomas. *Self-Determination and National Minorities*. Oxford: Oxford University Press, 1997.
Myrdal, Gunnar. *Asian Drama: An Inquiry into the Poverty of Nations*. 3 vols. New York: Twentieth Century Fund, 1968.
Nezavisimaya Gazeta.

Nahaylo, Bohdan. "Ukraine." RFE/RL *Research Report*, vol. 3, no. 16 (22 April 1994): 42–49.
Napoli, Daniela. "The European Union's Foreign Policy and Human Rights." In Nanette A. Neuwahl and Allan Rosas, eds., *The European Union and Human Rights*. The Hague: Martinus Nijhoff, 1995: 297–312.
Nayar, B. R. *Minority Politics in the Punjab*. Princeton: Princeton University Press, 1966.
Neuberger, Benyamin. "National Self-Determination: Dilemmas of a Concept." *Nations and Nationalism*, vol. 1, part 3 (November 1995): 297–325.
New Statesman and Society. Issue entitled, "Eurogeddon? The Coming Conflagration in East-Central Europe," 19 June 1992.
Nimni, Ephraim. "Marx, Engels and the National Question." In Will Kymlicka, ed., *The Rights of Minority Cultures*. Oxford: Oxford University Press, 1995: 57–75.
Nordlinger, Eric. *Conflict Regulation in Divided Societies*. Cambridge, Mass.: Center for International Affairs, Harvard University, 1972.
Nove, Alec. "The Soviet Model and Underdeveloped Countries." In Claude E. Welch Jr., ed., *Political Modernization: A Reader in Comparative Political Change*. Belmont, Calif.: Wadsworth Publishing, 1972: 363–72.
O'Duffy, Brendan. "Containment or Regulation? The British Approach to Ethnic Conflict in Northern Ireland." In John McGarry and Brendan O'Leary, eds., *The Politics of Ethnic Conflict Regulation*. London: Routledge, 1993: 128–50.
Olcott, Martha Brill. *Central Asia's New States: Independence, Foreign Policy and Regional Security*. Washington, D.C.: United States Institute of Peace Press, 1996.
———. *The Kazakhs*. Stanford: Hoover Institution Press, 1987.
Oltay, Edith. "Minorities as Stumbling Block in Relations with Neighbors." RFE/RL *Research Report*, vol. 1, no. 19 (8 May 1992): 26–33.
———. "Minority Rights Still an Issue in Hungarian-Romanian Relations." RFE/RL *Research Report*, vol. 1, no. 12 (20 March 1992): 16–20.
Omrod, Jane. "The North Caucasus: Confederation in Conflict." In Ian Bremmer and Ray Taras, eds., *New States, New Politics: Building the Post-Soviet Nations*. Cambridge: Cambridge University Press, 1997: 96–107.
Orttung, Robert W., and Olga Paretskaya. "Presidential Election Demonstrates Rural-Urban Divide." *Transition*, vol. 1, no. 13 (20 September 1996): 33–38.
Pandey, Gyanendra. "Hindus and Others: The Militant Hindu Construction." *Economic and Political Weekly*, vol. 26, no. 52 (28 December 1991): 2997–3009.
Pannier, Bruce. "A Step Back for Democracy." *Transition*, vol. 1, no. 11 (30 June 1995): 62–66.
Park, Andrus. "Ethnicity and Independence: The Case of Estonia in Comparative Perspective." *Europe-Asia Studies*, vol. 46, no. 1 (January 1994): 69–87.
Parthasarathi, G., ed. *Letters to Chief Ministers, 1947–1964*. 5 vols. New Delhi: Oxford University Press Jawaharlal Nehru Memorial Fund, 1985–90.
Payin, Emil. "Separatism and Federalism in Contemporary Russia." In Heyward Isham, ed., *Remaking Russia: Voices From Within*. Armonk, N.Y.: M. E. Sharpe, 1995: 185–201.
Pearson, Raymond. "Hungary: A State Truncated, A Nation Dismembered." In Seamus Dunn and T. G. Fraser, eds., *Europe and Ethnicity: The First World War and Contemporary Ethnic Conflict*. London: Routledge, 1996: 88–109.
Peck, Connie. *Sustainable Peace: The Role of the UN and Regional Organizations in Preventing Conflict*. Lanham, Md.: Rowman and Littlefield, 1998.

Perry, Duncan M. "The Republic of Macedonia and the Odds for Survival." RFE/RL *Research Report*, vol. 1, no. 46 (20 November 1992): 12–19.

Petersen, Niels Helveg. "Vital Partnership: Russia in Europe." *Forum* (June 1996): 6–8.

Phadnis, Urmila. "Sri Lanka: Crises of Legitimacy and Integration." In Larry Diamond, Juan Linz, and Seymour Martin Lipset, eds., *Democracy in Developing Countries. Vol. 3, Asia*. Boulder, Colo.: Lynne Rienner Publishers, 1989: 143–85.

Pikhovshek, Viacheslav. "Will the Crimean Crisis Explode?" In Maria Drohobycky, ed., *Crimea: Dynamics, Challenges and Prospects*. Lanham, Md.: Rowman and Littlefield, 1995: 39–65.

Pinto, D. *From Assistance to Democracy to Democratic Security*. Strasbourg: Council of Europe, n.d.

Pipes, Richard. "Introduction." In Heyward Isham, ed., *Remaking Russia*. Armonk, N.Y.: M. E. Sharpe, 1995: 3–10.

———. *The Formation of the Soviet Union: Communism and Nationalism 1917–1923*. Rev. ed. Cambridge, Mass.: Harvard University Press, 1964.

Plakans, Andrejs. "Democratization and Political Participation in Post-Communist Societies: The Case of Latvia." In Karen Dawisha and Bruce Parrott, eds., *The Consolidation of Democracy in East-Central Europe*. Cambridge: Cambridge University Press, 1997: 245–89.

———. *The Latvians: A Short History*. Stanford: Hoover Institution Press, 1995.

Preston, Paul. *The Triumph of Democracy in Spain*. London: Routledge, 1990.

Pridham, Geoffrey, and Tatu Vanhanen, eds. *Democratization in Eastern Europe: Domestic and International Perspectives*. London: Routledge, 1994.

Pridham, Geoffrey, Eric Herring, and George Sanford, eds. *Building Democracy? The International Dimension of Democratization in Eastern Europe*. London: Leicester University Press, 1994.

Ra'anan, Uri, et al. *State and Nation in Multi-Ethnic Societies: The Breakup of Multinational States*. Manchester: Manchester University Press, 1991.

Rabushka, Alvin, and Kenneth Shepsle. *Politics in Plural Societies: A Theory of Democratic Instability*. Columbus, Ohio: Merrill, 1972.

Radio Free Europe/Radio Liberty *Newsline*.

Rady, Martin. "Self-Determination and the Dissolution of Yugoslavia." *Ethnic and Racial Studies*, vol. 19, no. 2 (April 1996): 379–90.

———. "Nationalism and Nationality in Romania." In Paul Latawski, ed., *Contemporary Nationalism in East-Central Europe*. Basingstoke: Macmillan, 1995: 127–42.

Rakowska-Harmstone, Teresa. "Islam and Nationalism: Central Asia and Kazakhstan under Soviet Rule." *Central Asian Survey*, vol. 2, no. 2 (September 1983): 129–53.

———. "The Dialectics of Nationalism in the USSR." *Problems of Communism*, vol. 23, no. 3 (May/June 1974): 1–22.

Ramet, Pedro. *Cross and Commissar: The Politics of Religion in Eastern Europe and the USSR*. Bloomington: Indiana University Press, 1987.

Reddaway, Peter. "Instability and Fragmentation." *Journal of Democracy*, vol. 5, no. 2 (April 1994): 13–19.

———. "Russia on the Brink?" *New York Review of Books*, 28 January 1993: 30–35.

Reilhac, Gilbert. "Democracy: Key to Peace in Bosnia." *Forum* (March 1996): 9–11.

Reisch, Alfred A. "Transcarpathia's Hungarian Minority and the Autonomy Issue." RFE/RL *Research Report*, vol. 1, no. 6 (7 February 1992): 17–23.

Resler, Tamara J. "Dilemmas of Democratization: Safeguarding Minorities in Russia, Ukraine and Lithuania." *Europe Asia Studies*, vol. 49, no. 1 (January 1997): 89–106.

Rich, Roland. "Recognition of States: The Collapse of Yugoslavia and the Soviet Union." *European Journal of International Law*, vol. 4, no. 1 (1993): 36–65.

Roberts, Adam. "NATO's 'Humanitarian War' over Kosovo." *Survival*, vol. 41, no. 3 (autumn 1999): 102–23.

———. "Communal Conflict as a Challenge to International Organization: The Case of Former Yugoslavia." *Review of International Studies*, vol. 21, no. 4 (October 1995): 389–410.

———. "Humanitarian War: Military Intervention and Human Rights." *International Affairs*, vol. 69, no. 3 (July 1993): 429–49.

Ronen, Dov. *The Quest for Self-Determination*. New Haven: Yale University Press, 1979.

Rudolph, Richard L., and David F. Good, eds. *Nationalism and Empire: The Habsburg Monarchy and the Soviet Union*. New York: St. Martin's Press, 1992.

Rumer, Boris. *Soviet Central Asia*. Boston: Unwin Hyman, 1989.

Rummel, Reinhardt. "The European Union's Politico-Diplomatic Contribution to the Prevention of Ethno-National Conflict." In Abram Chayes and Antonia Chayes, eds., *Preventing Conflict in the Post-Communist World: Mobilizing International and Regional Organizations*. Washington, D.C.: Brookings Institution, 1996: 197–235.

Rupesinghe, Kumar, Peter G. King, and Olga Vorkunova. *Ethnicity and Conflict in a Post-Communist World: The Soviet Union, Eastern Europe and China*. New York: St. Martin's Press and Oslo: International Peace Research Institute, 1992.

Samarasinghe, S.W.R. de A. "The Dynamics of Separatism: The Case of Sri Lanka." In Ralph E. Premdas, S.W.R. de A. Samarasinghe, and Alan B. Anderson, eds., *Secessionist Movements in Comparative Perspective*. London: Pinter, 1990: 48–70.

Sarkar, Sumit *Modern India 1885–1947*. Delhi: Macmillan, 1983.

Schedler, Andreas. "How Should We Study Democratic Consolidation?" *Democratization*, vol. 5, no. 4 (winter 1998): 1–19.

Schifter, Richard. "Is There a Democracy Gene?" *Washington Quarterly*, vol. 17, no. 3 (summer 1994): 121–27.

Schöpflin, George. "The Rise of Anti-Democratic Movements in Post-Communist Societies." In Hugh Miall, ed., *Redefining Europe: New Patterns of Conflict and Cooperation*. London: Royal Institute of International Affairs, Pinter, 1994.

———. "National Identity in the Soviet Union and East Central Europe." *Ethnic and Racial Studies*, vol. 14, no. 1 (January 1991): 3–14.

Schumann, Klaus. "The Role of the Council of Europe." In Hugh Miall, ed., *Minority Rights in Europe: The Scope for a Translational Regime*. London: Royal Institute of International Affairs, Pinter, 1994: 87–98.

Seton-Watson, Hugh. *Nations and States*. Boulder, Colo.: Westview, 1977.

Shafir, Michael. "A Possible Light at the End of the Tunnel." *Transition*, vol. 2, no. 19 (20 September 1996): 29–32.

Sharlet, Robert. "Russian Constitutional Crisis." *Post-Soviet Affairs*, vol. 9, no. 4 (October/December 1993): 314–36.

Sheehy, Ann. "Power Struggle in Checheno-Ingushetia." *RFE/RL Report on the USSR* (15 November 1991): 20–26.

Sherr, James. "Russia-Ukraine *Rapprochement*? The Black Sea Fleet Accords." *Survival*, vol. 38, no. 3 (autumn 1997): 33–50.
Shlapentokh, Vladimir, Munir Sendich, and Emil Payin, eds. *The New Russian Diaspora: Russian Minorities in the Former Soviet Republics*. Armonk, N.Y.: M. E. Sharpe, 1994.
Silber, Laura, and Allan Little. *The Death of Yugoslavia*. London: Penguin/BBC Books, 1995.
Simon, Gerhard. *Nationalism and Policy Toward the Nationalities in the Soviet Union: From Totalitarian Dictatorship to Post-Stalinist Society*. Trans. Karen Forster and Oswald Forster. Boulder, Colo.: Westview, 1991.
Simons, William B., ed. *The Constitutions of the Communist World*. Germantown, Md.: Aalphen aan den Rijn and Sijthoff and Noordhoff, 1980.
Sisk, Timothy. *Power Sharing and International Mediation in Ethnic Conflicts*. Washington, D.C.: United States Institute of Peace, 1996.
Slider, Darrell. "Democratization in Georgia." In Karen Dawisha and Bruce Parrott, eds., *Conflict, Cleavage and Change in Central Asia and the Caucasus*. Cambridge: Cambridge University Press, 1997: 156–98.
Smith, Anthony D. "The Nations of Europe after the Cold War." In Jack Hayward and Edward Page, eds., *Governing the New Europe*. Cambridge: Polity Press, 1995: 44–66.

———. *Nations and Nationalism in a Global Era*. Cambridge: Polity Press, 1995.

———. *National Identity*. London: Penguin Books, 1991.

Smith, Graham, ed. *Federalism: The Multiethnic Challenge*. London: Longman, 1995.
Solchanyk, Roman. "Crimea: Between Ukraine and Russia." In Maria Drohobycky, ed., *Crimea: Dynamics, Challenges and Prospects*. Lanham, Md.: Rowman and Littlefield, 1995: 3–13.

———. "The Politics of State-Building: Centre-Periphery Relations in Post-Soviet Ukraine." *Europe-Asia Studies*, vol. 46, no. 1 (January 1994): 47–68.

Splidsboel-Hansen. "The 1991 Chechen Revolution: The Response of Moscow." *Central Asian Survey*, vol. 13, no. 3 (September 1994): 395–407.
Stalin, J. V. *Works*. Moscow: Foreign Languages Publishing House, 1954.
Starovoitova, Galina. "Modern Russia and the Ghost of Weimar Germany." In Heyward Isham, ed., *Remaking Russia*. Armonk, N.Y.: M. E. Sharpe, 1995: 129–45.
Starr. S. Frederick, ed. *The Legacy of History in Russia and the New States of Eurasia*. Armonk, N.Y.: M. E. Sharpe, 1994.
Stepan, Alfred. "Federalism and Democracy." *Journal of Democracy*, vol. 10, no. 4 (October 1999): 19–34.

———. "Modern Multi-National Democracies: Transcending the Gellnerian Oxymoron." *Oxford International Review*, vol. 8, no. 2 (spring 1997): 19–29.

Stern, Jessica. "Moscow Meltdown." *International Security*, vol. 18, no. 4 (spring 1994): 40–65.
Suny, Ronald. "Transcaucasia: Cultural Cohesion and Ethnic Revival." In Lubomyr Hajda and Mark Beissinger, eds., *The Nationalities Factor in Soviet Politics and Society*. Boulder, Colo.: Westview, 1990: 228–52.

———. *The Making of the Georgian Nation*. Bloomington: Indiana University Press, 1988.

Szabo, Matyas. " 'Historic Reconciliation' Awakens Old Disputes." *Transition*, vol. 2, no. 5 (8 March 1996): 46–50.

Szporluk, Roman. "Nationalism after Communism." *Nations and Nationalism*, vol. 4, part 3 (July 1998): 301–20.
———. "The Fall of the Tsarist Empire and the USSR: The Russian Question and Imperial Overextension." In Karen Dawisha and Bruce Parrott, eds., *The End of Empire? The Transformation of the USSR in Comparative Perspective*. Armonk, N.Y.: M. E. Sharpe, 1997: 65–93.
———. "Reflections on Ukraine after 1994, Dilemmas of Nationhood." *The Harriman Review*, vol. 7, nos. 7–9 (March/May 1994): 1–9.
———. *Communism and Nationalism: Karl Marx versus Friedrich List*. New York: Oxford University Press, 1988.
Taagepera, Rein. *Estonia: Return to Independence*. Boulder, Colo.: Westview, 1993.
Tanner, Marcus. *Croatia: A Nation Forged in War*. New Haven: Yale University Press, 1997.
Tarschys, Daniel. "The Council of Europe and the Challenge of Enlargement." *The World Today*, vol. 51, no. 5 (May 1995): 62–64.
Taylor, David, and Malcolm Yapp, eds. *Political Identity in South Asia*. London: Curzon Press, 1979.
Teague, Elizabeth. "Russia and Tatarstan Sign Power-Sharing Treaty." RFE/RL *Research Report*, vol. 3, no. 14 (8 April 1994): 19–27.
———. "Center-Periphery Relations in the Russian Federation." In Roman Szporluk, ed., *National Identity and Ethnicity in Russia and the New States of Eurasia*. Armonk, N.Y.: M. E. Sharpe, 1994: 21–57.
The Unfinished Peace: Report of the International Commission on the Balkans. Washington, D.C.: Carnegie Endowment for International Peace, 1996.
Thornberry, Patrick. *International Law and the Rights of Minorities*. Oxford: Clarendon Press, 1991.
———. *Minorities and Human Rights Law*. London: Minority Rights Group, 1991.
———. "Self-Determination, Minorities, Human Rights: A Review of International Instruments." *International and Comparative Law Quarterly*, vol. 38, part 4 (October 1989): 867–89.
Tilly, Charles. "How Empires End." In Karen Barkey and Mark von Hagen, eds., *After Empire: Multi-Ethnic Societies and Nation-Building: The Soviet Union and the Russian, Ottoman, and Habsburg Empires*. Boulder, Colo.: Westview, 1997: 1–11.
Tolz, Vera, and Iain Elliot, eds. *The Demise of the USSR: From Communism to Independence*. Basingstoke: Macmillan, 1995.
Tomuschat, Christian, ed. *Modern Law of Self-Determination*. Dordrecht: Martinus Nijhoff, 1993.
Treisman, Daniel. "Russia's 'Ethnic Revival': The Separatist Activism of Regional Leaders in a Post-Communist Order." *World Politics*, vol. 49, no. 2 (January 1997): 212–49.
Tucker, Robert. *Stalin in Power: The Revolution from Above, 1928–1941*. New York: W. W. Norton, 1990.
Tully, Mark, and Satish Jacob. *Amritsar: Mrs. Gandhi's Last Battle*. London: Jonathan Cape, 1985.
Unger, Aryeh. *Constitutional Development in the USSR: A Guide to the Soviet Constitutions*. London: Methuen, 1981.
U.S. State Department. *Country Reports on Human Rights Practices for 1991*. Report

Selected Bibliography

Submitted to the Committee on Foreign Affairs, House of Representatives and the Committee on Foreign Relations. Washington, D.C.: U.S. Senate (February 1992).

Van Dyke, Vernon, "The Individual, the State and Ethnic Communities in Political Theory," *World Politics*, vol. 3, no. 3 (April 1977): 343–49, reprinted in Will Kymlicka, ed., *The Rights of Minority Cultures*. Oxford: Oxford University Press, 1995: 31–55.

Van Evera, Stephen. "Hypotheses on Nationalism and the Causes of War." In Charles Kupchan, ed., *Nationalism and Nationalities in the New Europe*. Ithaca, N.Y.: Cornell University Press/Council on Foreign Relations, 1995: 136–57.

Vickers, Miranda. *Between Serb and Albanian: A History of Kosovo*. London: Hurst, 1998.

Vickers, Miranda, and James Pettifer. *Albania: From Anarchy to a Balkan Identity*. London: Hurst, 1997.

Vincent, R. J. *Human Rights and International Relations*. Cambridge: Cambridge University Press, 1986.

Vogel, Heinrich. "Partnership with Russia: Some Lessons from Chechnya." *The World Today*, vol. 51, no. 4 (April 1995): 64–67.

Von Hagen, Mark. "The Russian Empire." In Karen Barkey and Mark von Hagen, eds., *After Empire: Multi-Ethnic Societies and Nation-Building: The Soviet Union and the Russian, Ottoman, and Habsburg Empires*. Boulder, Colo.: Westview, 1997: 58–72.

Von Hippel, Karin. "The Resurgence of Nationalism and Its International Implications." *Washington Quarterly*, vol. 17, no. 4 (autumn 1994): 185–200.

Wallace, Paul. "The Sikhs as a 'Minority' in a Sikh Majority State in India." *Asian Survey*, vol. 26, no. 3 (March 1986): 363–77.

Webber, Mark. *CIS Integration Trends: Russia and the Former Soviet South*. London: Royal Institute of International Affairs, 1997.

———. *The International Politics of Russia and the Successor States*. Manchester: Manchester University Press, 1996.

———. "Coping with Anarchy: Ethnic Conflict and International Organizations in the Former Soviet Union." *International Relations*, vol. 13, no. 1 (April 1996): 1–27.

Weller, Marc. "The Rambouillet Conference on Kosovo." *International Affairs*, vol. 75, no. 2 (April 1999): 211–51.

White, Stephen, Graeme Gill, and Darrell Slider. *The Politics of Transition: Shaping a Post-Soviet Future*. Cambridge: Cambridge University Press, 1993.

Whitehead, Laurence "Geography and Democratic Destiny." *Journal of Democracy*, vol. 10, no. 1 (January 1999): 74–79.

———. *The International Dimensions of Democratization: Europe and the Americas*. New York: Oxford University Press, 1996.

Wilber, Charles. *The Soviet Model and Underdeveloped Countries*. Chapel Hill: University of North Carolina Press, 1969.

Wilson, A. Jeyaratnam. *The Breakup of Sri Lanka: Tamil-Sinhalese Conflict*. London: Hurst, 1988.

Wilson, Andrew. "Ukraine between Eurasia and the West." In Seamus Dunn and T. G. Fraser, eds., *Europe and Ethnicity: The First World War and Contemporary Ethnic Conflict*. London: Routledge, 1996: 110–37.

———. *Ukrainian Nationalism in the 1990s: A Minority Faith*. Cambridge: Cambridge University Press, 1996.

Wilson, Heather A. *International Law and the Use of Force by National Liberation Movements*. Oxford: Clarendon Press, 1988.

Wise, Charles R., and Trevor L. Brown. "The Consolidation of Democracy in Ukraine." *Democratization*, vol. 5, no. 1 (spring 1998): 116–37.

Wolchik, Sharon. "Democratization and Political Participation in Slovakia." In Karen Dawisha and Bruce Parrott, eds., *The Consolidation of Democracy in East-Central Europe*. Cambridge: Cambridge University Press, 1997: 197–244.

Wright, John F. R., Suzanne Goldenberg, and Richard Schofield, eds. *Transcaucasian Boundaries*. London: U.C.L. Press, 1996.

Wyman, Mathew, Bill Miller, Stephen White, and Paul Heywood. "The Russian Elections of December 1993." *Electoral Studies*, vol. 13, no. 3 (September 1994): 254–71.

Yevtoukh, Volodymyr. "The Dynamics of Interethnic Relations in Crimea." In Maria Drohobycky, ed., *Crimea: Dynamics, Challenges and Prospects*. Lanham, Md.: Rowman and Littlefield, 1995: 69–85.

Zaslavsky, Victor. "Nationalism and Democratic Transition in Post-Communist Societies." *Daedalus*, vol. 121, no. 2 (spring 1992): 97–121.

Zimmerman, Warren. *Origins of a Catastrophe*. New York: Times Books, 1996.

Index

Abkhaz, 6, 9, 58–60, 97, 99, 101, 103–4. *See also* Georgia
Acton, Lord, 61–62
Åland Islands, 11
Albania, 80, 81
Antall, József, 104–6
Armenia, 9, 52, 60–62, 63; elections in, 87–88; independence of, 61, 63, 64. *See also* Nagorno-Karabakh
Authoritarian states: cannot forge consensus, 7–9; and ethnic diversity, 16
Azerbaijan, 9, 52, 60–62, 64, 69, 89, 99. *See also* Nagorno-Karabakh

Badinter Commission, 53, 55, 57, 141
Belarus, 87, 144
Berisha, Sali, 80, 103, 138
Borders, international: acceptance of, 101, 103, 104, 118–19, 123, 124, 135, 144, 145
Bosnia, elections in, 55, 84, 86; Dayton/Paris Agreement and, 76, 85–86; ethnic division in, 55, 57, 64, 65, 140; Milošević-Tudjman understanding on, 101

Boutros-Ghali, Boutros, vii, xviii-xix, 18, 52, 56, 69, 124

Carlos, King Juan, 42
Ceaușescu, Nicolae, 9, 108
Chechnya, xxii-xxiii, 18, 71, 72, 77–79, 89, 90, 91, 119, 122, 137, 138, 140, 141, 142–43
Commonwealth of Independent States (CIS), 60, 63–64, 98, 101, 102, 103–4, 123
Conference on Security and Cooperation in Europe (CSCE). *See* Organization for Security and Cooperation in Europe (OSCE) and Conference on Security and Cooperation in Europe (CSCE)
Constantinescu, Emil, 99, 108, 144
Council of Europe (CE), xv, 1, 71–74; and *Council of Europe Framework Convention for the Protection of National Minorities* (1995), xix, xx, 3, 13, 18–19, 73, 90, 107, 109, 135, 140; and *European Charter for Regional or Minority Languages,* 6, 19–20, 73, 90, 135; and *European Convention for the Protection of Human Rights* (1950),

12, 15, 72, 85; and *Recommendation 1201* (1995), 107, 109, 135
Crimea. *See* Russia; Ukraine
Croatia: elections in, 87; recognition of, 54, 65–66; Serb minorities in, 54–55, 72–76, 97, 99, 135, 140, 141
Csurka, István, 98
Culture, and democracy, 27–28

Dayton/Paris Agreement (1995). *See* Bosnia
Democracy: conceptual and political problems, xviii-xix, 1–6, 14–20, 133–34; conflict prevention and, xv-xvi, 3–4, 69–70, 134–36; consensus and, 94, 111–13; culture and, 27–28; ethnic diversity and, xxii, 1–6, 15, 36–37, 45–47, 131, 134, 144; human rights and, xv-xvii, 15–19, 85–86, 138, 139; international community and, xviii-xix, 1–18 *passim*, 70–71, 131, 145; not defined in international law, xviii; pluralist nation and, 5; the political majority and, 15, 134; reconciling international and domestic dimensions of, xxii-xxiii, 19–20, 69–77, 84–91; self-determination and, 14–15, 55–57, 58, 137; sovereignty and, 19–20, 70–71, 79–84, 139–44; versus the nation-state, 3–5, 131, 132, 134, 140, 144–45; weak liberal traditions and, xxii, 71–72, 159–63. *See also* Democratizaton; Nationalism; Sovereignty
Democratization, xviii-xix, 84–90, 99–100, 102–3, 122–24, 138–39, 143–45
Diplomatic recognition: democratic principles and, xxii, 52–58, 61, 62, 64–66, 131, 137
Dzurinda, Mikuláš, 106, 107, 144

Elections, international involvement in, 84; in post-communist Europe, xxii, 84–90, 102–3, 138–39, 144
Estonia: CE and, 117–18; elections in, 87, 144; EU and, 117–18; Russia and, 117–19; Russian minorities in, 115–19, 140; UN and, 117
Ethnic conflict, not inevitable, xix-xx, 6

European Community (EC), and breakup of Yugoslavia and USSR, 51, 54, 55, 58, 64–66, 137. *See also* European Union (EU)
European Union (EU): and Chechnya, 77–79, 90, 142; and democratization, 71, 84; and Estonia, 117; and Kosovo, 81; and Latvia, 117; and minorities, 19; and Stability Pact, 165
Extreme nationalism, failure of, 98–99, 103, 118, 136, 139, 144

Franco, General Francisco, 28, 42

Gagauz, 62–63, 88, 139
Gamsakhurdia, Zviad, 7, 59–60, 135, 138
Gandhi, Indira, 39, 40–41
Gandhi, Rajiv, 39, 40–41
Gellner, Ernest, 7
Geography, 101–2
Georgia: CIS and, 60, 103, 104, 124; ethnic conflict in, 6, 9, 33, 58–60, 76, 97–99; joins CE, 101; Russia and, 103–4
Gorbachev, Mikhail, 32, 33–36, 58, 121

Habsburg empire, 6, 9
Hill, Christopher, plan of, 81–82
Horn, Gyula, 107, 109
Horowitz, Donald, 28
Human rights. *See* Bosnia; Chechnya; Council of Europe (CE); Democracy; Minorities; Organization for Security and Cooperation in Europe (OSCE) and Conference on Security and Cooperation in Europe (CSCE); Self-determination; United Nations
Hungary: acceptance of international borders, 101, 103, 105, 107, 109; Magyar minorities and, 99, 101, 104–10; Treaty with Romania (1996), 13, 23n.56, 24n.58, 75, 109, 110; Treaty with Slovakia (1995), 13, 23n.56, 24n.58, 107

Iliescu, Ion, 99, 108, 109, 139, 143–44
India: center-state relations, 38–41, 46; communal violence in, 38, 40–41, 46; democracy in, 27–28, 36–41, 136; eth-

Index

nic and political nations separate, 15, 39–40, 41, 46; language problem, 38–39; management of ethnic diversity, 37–40, 45, 136; political alliances in, 15, 39–41, 46; secularism in, 38
International community: and minorities, 71–72, 90, 107–9; and territorial integrity, 19–20, 51–53, 55–57, 62, 70–71, 77–79, 80–81, 115, 135, 139, 141, 143, 146n.3
Izetbegović, Islam, on Bosnian independence, 55

"Joining Europe," 53, 71–74, 101–2, 105, 107–8, 109–10, 139–40, 141, 143

Kazakhstan, 34, 48–49n.18, 111, 144; and CIS, 110–12; elections in, 89; and Russian minorities, 110–12
Kedourie, Elie, xvi
Khrushchev, Nikita, 31, 34, 48–49n.18
Klaus, Václav, 106
Kosovo: Albanian irredentism and, 79; democratic principles and, xx, xxi, xxiii, 18, 85, 90–91, 137; ethnic division in, xx-xxi, 6, 70, 79-80, 81–84, 87, 90, 132, 133, 140, 142–43; international community and, xx-xxi, 70, 79–84, 86; Rambouillet conference and, 82, 143
Kosovo Liberation Army (KLA), 76, 80, 81, 82, 83, 87, 90, 132, 143, 146n.3
Kosovo Verification Mission (KVM), 76, 82
Koštunica, Vojislav, 138
Kuchma, Leonid, 113, 115
Kyrgyzstan, 63, 64

Latvia: acceptance of post-1991 international borders, 118–19; CE and, 117–18; elections in, 87, 144; EU and, 117–18; extreme nationalists marginalized, 118; independence of, 57–58; Russian minorities in, 115–19, 140; UN and, 117
League of Nations, and Minorities Treaties, xxii, 4–5, 11
Lebed, Alexandr, 102, 119, 123

Lithuania: elections in, 87; Russian minorities in, 116

Macedonia: minorities in, 81; recognition of, 52–54
Magyar minorities: EU and, 107; in Habsburg empire, 9; Hungary and, 104–5; OSCE and, 107, 143; Romania and, 108–10, 111–43; Slovakia and, 105–8
Mečiar, Vladimir, 75, 99, 106, 107, 139, 143
Mill, John Stuart, 7
Milošević, Slobodan, 54, 71, 80, 81, 83, 90, 103, 138
Minorities: individual and group rights, 13, 104–5, 107, 108, 109, 133–34, 140; in international relations, 1–5, 10–15, 51–53, 70, 97–98, 103–4, 107–9, 135, 141; problem of definition, xx, 11–12; self-determination and, 10–11, 51–53, 69–70. *See also* Council of Europe (CE); Democracy; Organization for Security and Cooperation in Europe (OSCE) and Conference on Security and Cooperation in Europe (CSCE); UN
Moldova: elections, 88; ethnic division in, 62–64, 76, 88, 97, 99, 139, 123, 139. *See also* Trans-Dniestr
Montenegro, 65, 66
Moravčik, Josef, 106

Nagorno-Karabakh, 52, 60–61, 140
Nano, Fatos, 80, 103
Nationalism, xx-xxi; and absence of war, xxiii, 91, 97–98, 99, 122–24, 144; compatible with democracy, xvii-xviii, 20, 145; economic hardship and, 103; not always secessionist, xvi, xvii, 145
Nation-state, xx, 2–3, 131–33, 144–45; seldom achieved, 2, 70. *See also* Democracy
Nazarbaev, Nursultan, 89, 102, 110, 111, 112, 144
Nehru, Jawaharlal, 37
North Atlantic Treaty Organization (NATO), xx-xxii, 18, 33, 70, 81, 82, 83, 109, 133, 138

Organization for Security and Cooperation in Europe (OSCE) and Conference on Security and Cooperation in Europe (CSCE): *Charter of Paris for a New Europe* (1990), xv, xix, 1, 3, 18, 54; *Copenhagen Document* (1990), 3, 12, 18, 54, 107, 109; *Geneva Report* (1991), 1, 19; *Helsinki Document* (1992), 18; *Helsinki Final Act* (1975), 13, 18; High Commissioner on National Minorities, xx, xxii, 1, 19, 69, 74–75, 118, 134, 141–43, 146n.1; Human Dimension Mechanism, 74; Missions, 74, 75–76; Office for Democratic Institutions and Human Rights, 74

Pact on Stability in Europe (Stability Pact), 73–74, 83, 107
Plebiscites, 14–15
Putin, Vladimir, 89, 119, 122, 143

Račan, Ivica, 87
Romania: acceptance of international borders, 109; Magyar minorities in, 97–98, 108–10; *Romania Mare*, 108; Treaty with Hungary (1996), 109; *Vatra Romaneasca*, 108
Romanov empire, 9, 10
Rugova, Ibrahim, 81
Russia: ambiguity of calls for "independence," 119–20; and Chechnya, 72–79, 98, 119, 121–22, 141–43; elections in, 88–89; incongruence of ethnicity and territory, 119–20; nationalism not a major issue in, 122–23; relations between Moscow and regions, 98, 119, 120–22; and Russian minorities in "Near Abroad," 97–99, 110–19; state-building incomplete, 122; and Tatarstan, 121; tradition and democratization, 119

Secession, 2; not inevitable, xx, 6, 69, 106, 107. *See also* Self-determination; Union of Soviet Socialist Republics (USSR); Yugoslavia, collapse of
Self-determination: ambiguity of, xx-xxi, 10–13, 14–15, 52–53, 55, 65–66, 77, 80; and democracy, xxii, 15–19; and human rights, 15–19; and minorities, 10–13; and will of the people, 69, 137
Serbia: elections in, 76, 86, 87, 138–39; nationalism in, 97, 99, 135, 140, 141. *See also* Kosovo; Milošević, Slobodan
Shevardnadze, Eduard, 34, 60, 68n.33, 103
Slovakia: Magyar minorities in, 97–99, 104, 105–8; Treaty with Hungary (1995), 13, 107
Slovenia, independence of, 52
South Ossetia, 59, 60, 68n.32, 103
Sovereignty, xvii, xxii, 17–20, 69–77, 79–84, 90–91, 139–40, 141–44; not always a sticking point, xvii-xviii, 15–19, 72, 73, 74, 75
Spain, 28, 36, 37; Basque separatism in, 36, 44, 46–47; consensus through diversity, 41–44, 45, 136; and constitution of 1978, 42–43; political and ethnic nations separate, 15, 42; regions and center, 42–44, 46
Sri Lanka: alignment of political nations, 44–45, 136; discrimination against Tamils, 44–45
Stalin, 9, 31, 32, 34, 101, 110

Tatarstan, not secessionist, 121. *See also* Russia
Trans-Dniestr. *See* Moldova
Tudjman, Franjo, 7, 54, 101, 138
Tudor, Corneliu Vadim, 99, 139

Ukraine: and Crimea, 76, 114–15, 124–25; elections in, 88, 113; ethnic diversity, 112–13; extreme nationalists marginalized, 114, 139, 144; interpretations of "independence," 114–15; and Russia, 112–15
Union of Soviet Socialist Republics (USSR): ambiguity of "sovereignty" in, 51, 57–58, 110, 114, 115–16; breakup of, xv, 1, 27, 57–64; ethnic diversity in, 29–36; failure of accommodation, 10, 29, 31 35–36, 46; identification of Russia with, 33–35; ideology of, 29–

Index

33, 45-46; and Nagorno-Karabakh, 61–62; non-Russians in, 29, 32–34; not a model for multiethnic countries, 1–2, 27–29, 31–33, 51–53; Russian nationalism and, 29, 34–35; Union Treaty (1991), 34, 58, 77

United Nations, 55, 57; Charter of, 1, 11, 13, 15, 16, 85; Commission on Human Rights resolution (1999), 17; *Convention Against Discrimination in Education* (1960), 12; *Convention on the Prevention and Punishment of the Crime of Genocide* (1948), 12; *Convention on the Rights of the Child* (1989), 12, 109; *Declaration on Race and Racial Prejudice* (1978), 12; *Declaration on the Rights of Persons Belonging to National or Ethnic, Religious and Cultural Minorities* (1992), xix, xx, 3, 13, 18–19, 71, 107, 109, 135, 140, 141; High Commissioner for Human Rights, 71; and human rights, 16–19; *International Covenant on Civil and Political Rights* (1966), 12, 15, 16; *International Covenant on Economic, Social and Cultural Rights* (1966), 12, 16; *International Convention on the Elimination of All Forms of Racial Discrimination* (1965), 12; *Universal Declaration of Human Rights* (1948), 11, 12, 15, 16, 17, 85

Uti posseditis, 55–57, 65–66

Uzbekistan, elections in, 89–90

van der Stoel, Max. *See* Organization for Security and Cooperation in Europe (OSCE) and Conference on Security and Cooperation in Europe (CSCE): High Commissioner on National Minorities

Vienna Declaration and Programme of Action (1993), xviii

War: absence of, xxiii, 97–98, 122–24, 144; democratization and, 122–24, 144; and international society, xvii, 97–98; nationalism and, xvi-xvii, xxiii, 2, 69, 97–98, 99–101, 103–4, 145. *See also* Nationalism

Yeltsin, Boris, 6, 35, 49n.23, 78, 119, 120, 122, 143

Yugoslavia, collapse of, xv, 51–57, 100–101

Zhirinovsky, Vladimir, 15, 89, 98, 102, 103, 110, 121, 123

Zyuganov, Gennadi, 102, 119, 120

About the Author

ANITA INDER SINGH is a Fellow at the Centre for Socio-Legal Studies, Wolfson College, Oxford. Dr. Singh has been a Fellow at the Centre for International Studies, London School of Economics and Political Science and the International Forum for Democratic Studies, National Endowment for Democracy. Among her earlier publications are *The Limits of British Influence: South Asia and the Anglo-American Relationship, 1947–56* and *The Origins of the Partition of India, 1936–1947.*

WITHDRAWN

WITHDRAWN